Remember with Advantages

Remember with Advantages

Chasing The Fugitive *and Other Stories from an Actor's Life*

BY BARRY MORSE

with Anthony Wynn *and* Robert E. Wood

foreword by Martin Landau

McFarland & Company, Inc., Publishers
Jefferson, North Carolina, and London

Frontispiece: Barry Morse circa 1963

All photographs herein are from the Morse Family Collection unless otherwise marked

LIBRARY OF CONGRESS CATALOGUING-IN-PUBLICATION DATA

Morse, Barry, 1918–
   Remember with advantages : chasing the fugitive and other stories from an actor's life / by Barry Morse ; with Anthony Wynn and Robert E. Wood ; foreword by Martin Landau.
      p.   cm.
   Includes index.

   ISBN-13: 978-0-7864-2771-0
   (softcover : 50# alkaline paper) ∞

   1. Morse, Barry, 1918– .   2. Actors—Great Britain— Biography.   I. Wynn, Anthony, 1962– .   II. Wood, Robert E., 1971– .   III. Title.
PN2598.M6995A3   2006
792.02'8'92—dc22
[B]   2006033776

British Library cataloguing data are available

On the cover: Barry Morse, Sundholm Estate, Portland, Oregon (courtesy of Robert E. Wood); background ©2006 PhotoAlto

Manufactured in the United States of America

McFarland & Company, Inc., Publishers
  Box 611, Jefferson, North Carolina 28640
   www.mcfarlandpub.com

For Sydney Sturgess,
the lady whom I lovingly called "The Management."
She was my partner in everything for more than 60 years.
There is no way to express adequately the range and scale of her giving;
but this volume is dedicated to her, gratefully and with love.

Contents

Foreword
by Martin Landau

I FIRST BECAME AWARE OF Barry Morse, and became one of his staunch supporters, long before I had the privilege of working with him on the TV series *Space: 1999*, which we filmed in London's Pinewood Studios in 1973–75. Of course, I watched Barry on the TV show *The Fugitive*, as did countless others worldwide, and saw the many guest-starring appearances he made on other U.S. and Canadian TV shows over the years, as well as his movie roles. But the first time I was overwhelmed by his superior talent was when I went to the theatre, here in Los Angeles, and saw him play the leading role (the Derelict) in Harold Pinter's three man play *The Caretaker*, in which he was superb. That is a lot of years ago, and in the ensuing years I've grown to admire him more and more as an artist. But even more important is having gotten to know Barry as a human being when I had the good fortune to work with him for that year on the series. It was a joy on so many levels! Barry is a unique person, always eager to do his best and then some, no matter the conditions surrounding him, no matter his state of health at the moment. Always prepared with regard to work, always ready with a funny anecdote when things get tense around him, always polite, charming, and ready with a kind word to anybody that needs one.

Barry is also a scholar, an authority on the English language, its history and its countless variations and dialects in England, the USA, and Canada, which is why he is such an excellent dialectician. Although a Canadian citizen, with most Canadians thinking he was born in Canada and most Americans thinking he was born in America, few know that Barry

1

was born in the East End of London and was a Cockney through and through. I met Barry's brother Len, a police officer, while filming *Space*, and was shocked to hear the heaviness of his Cockney accent. That made me even more impressed with Barry's impeccable English accent, which has nary a trace of that difficult-to-lose dialect.

Barry was always there for you when you needed a friend, and I value the time we spent together those many years ago on the sound stages of Pinewood Studios. I was very sad when Barry didn't return to the series in its second, and final, season. Barbara Bain and I fought to get Barry back on the show, to no avail, and I think Barry is aware of that fact, as the series was never as good without his character, Victor Bergman. He lent a large chunk of class to the series, and we missed his presence on the set and on the screen immensely. Whenever I think of London, one of the spots I think of is Pall Mall, where Barry has resided for many years.

Barry's life is a virtual history of the twentieth century, through the peaceful periods and the wars, the very beginnings of television, his vast experiences in film, and his beginnings and enduring love affair with the theatre in England, Canada and the US; and deserves to be read by everyone on the planet, theatre folk and civilian alike. There is no one in the acting profession whom I can think of who deserves more than Barry Morse to have admirers supporting and recognizing what a superb actor and wonderful human being he truly is.

Martin Landau
Los Angeles, California

Preface

I ALWAYS SAY THAT MY favorite role is the next one, not the one just completed! Thus I had always swept aside any notion I might have had from time to time of putting together a book of memoirs such as the one you now hold in your hands. I don't think, aside from the kind of "dreamland" you induce in yourself once in a while, that I ever seriously considered writing a book of reminiscence. But I realize now that mine is a story concerning someone who didn't necessarily achieve world significance in the sense of Clark Gable, Spencer Tracy, or Charlie Chaplin, but who nonetheless—because of the sheer volume and variety of work—has had a career, if not necessarily richer, at least wider and more varied than most people in our profession have ever had.

In that sense, at least, I feel the story I have to tell of my career is quite remarkable. I often think of the many actors who never get, and never really expect, great riches or fame, but who really are the heart's core of our trade—the real blood of it. All of us who have been in this lunatic trade of pulling faces and making noises for a living have encountered great numbers of what we may call the rank and file—and a good old lot they are.

You may not know that my own family had no connection with show business whatsoever. As you'll see in the pages that follow, my parents had been servants, and the occasion which led to their meeting and eventual marriage was when they were working at a hospital just outside London. If you can imagine, my parents had never been to any type of legitimate theatre! They'd been to the music halls a bit, which were popular entertainments among working people of that era. But they'd never seen a professional production of a play or anything like that. So my blundering into

3

the theatrical world was really a rather improbable series of flukes and coincidences. In my own subsequent family, my wife, Sydney, was an actress but also a very devoted mother. We worked together until our children were born and then she put her career on the back burner. When the children were older, she went back to acting again and was wonderfully good in all sorts of different parts. Both of my children became actors and Hayward, my son, has become quite well known both for his work on the stage and as a voice artist for a great many recorded books.

Through my widely varied career I have been what you might call "famous" several times. It comes and goes, like some sort of rash. Occasionally we all require a suitable reminder that obscurity is never very far away and that this week's *Top of the Pops* can so readily become next year's *Whatever Happened To?* It happened to me not very long ago. I was riding on a bus in London and sitting just across the aisle from me was a dear old chap who was looking at me in a very quizzical, puzzled sort of way. After two or three minutes half a penny dropped in the back of his head and he leaned over and prodded me in the ribs and said, "'Ere, half a minute—Didn't you use to be somebody?"

Another time, when I was in Dublin some years ago, I was walking up O'Connell Street quite late at night looking in the shop windows, and I became aware as I went along that there was a little old chap—a tiny little fellow—who was dogging my footsteps and looking in the shop windows in order to get a look at my face, reflected in the glass. So, after we had done this a few times, I stopped and turned round and at that point he said, "Beggin' your pardon, sir, but aren't you that fella—aren't you Barry Morse, of the tele-box—in later life?"

During the creation of this book I have thought about a number of authors, philosophers and thinkers who have spoken, informed, and helped to shape me as an actor. Aside, of course, from the great William Shakespeare, the man who has probably had the most effect on me, both professionally and personally, is George Bernard Shaw. I think he's a wonderful example of someone who quite literally worked his way into becoming the world's greatest living dramatist, having started out with virtually no encouragement or natural instincts towards being a playwright. He realized that the creation of great drama has nothing to do with words on paper. It was he who said (and I always stress this) that 95 percent of the audiences who crammed into the Globe Theatre to see the original productions of Shakespeare's plays were illiterate; they couldn't read or write.

Among other writers, one of my favorites is John Bunyan. His *Pilgrim's Progress*, although not really written as a drama, is really one of the world's great dramas. When you get to the end of the story of "Mr. Valiant for Truth," the leading character, the whole thing winds up with, "...and so he passed over and all the trumpets sounded for him on the other side."

Of course, you are about to read a good deal more about various actors and authors, plays and experiences from my life and career, and I am reminded of how this book has come into being. Although our paths had briefly crossed before, it was not until 1995 that my working relationship, and friendship, with my coauthors, Anthony Wynn and Robert Wood, really began. Anthony was producing a quite touching Broadway play, A.R. Gurney's *Love Letters*, in Portland, Oregon. This production was a fundraiser for Parkinson's disease treatment and research, a cause which you will learn is very deeply close to my heart.

Following the success of our first effort, I soon returned for another fund-raiser and was aided by Anthony and Robert in a short tour of my one-man show, *Merely Players*, in Oregon. A memorable evening became unforgettable when my chums presented me with a proposal for the three of us to work together to write my memoirs. Having returned to London to get my dear wife Sydney's blessing on the project, I began the quite extraordinary process of recording my memories, stories and diaries onto a series of audio cassettes which Robert and Anthony then had the challenge of putting into the shape of a book. By the time we completed that process I had recorded more than sixty audio tapes, each one ninety minutes in length!

The ensuing years have seen the three of us work together on—by my last count—no less than fifteen stage, television and audio productions, as well as many more signing appearances throughout the USA and Canada. We have become a very effective team and it was with pleasure that I took to calling them my "minders."

Recently someone asked me why I wasn't thinking of retiring after surviving more than eight decades on this planet and I said in response, "Well, so long as you can say the lines in the right order and not fall over the furniture, you don't want to retire!" I've also been asked what my greatest achievement in life has been. I have one simple answer: It's not a television show, a film, or a stage production. It's parenting two lovely children, and being a grandparent to all of my grandchildren and great-grandchildren. There's no question, it's the simplest answer in the world! All the stuff that you do professionally doesn't add up to that, does it?

Throughout the process of writing this book, a number of individuals have helped to make it a reality. These include Martin Landau, Charlene Scott, Kit Bevan, Terry S. Bowers, Dr. Susan Doyle, Dan and Camilla Sundholm, Sandra Sprecker, David Ross, my son, Hayward Morse, and all the rest of our friends and families—far too numerous to list individually.

A special thanks also goes to others who have very kindly provided images for inclusion in the book: Robert C. Ragsdale, Lou Hirsch, Stephen Lodge, Michael Lindow, and Melody Thamar Saunders; and of course, my old friends Yuri Rasovsky and Bill Freedman.

It's thrilling to have had the good luck to encounter two such lads as Anthony Wynn and Robert Wood, who have encouraged me to the extent of starting to believe that having such a book as this was both possible and worthwhile. So, above all, I acknowledge my gratitude to both Robert and Anthony for so much help in so many ways.

Quite literally, I couldn't have done it without them.

Barry Morse
London, England

1

"Make Much of Your Horses!"

OVER THE YEARS I'VE THOUGHT of a number of different titles suitable for a book of reminiscence. One I've always been very fond of is from Shakespeare—can't go to a better source, can you? Before the battle, in the speech about Saint Crispin, King Henry V says, "Old men forget; yet all shall be forgot, But he'll remember with advantages what feats he did that day." I've always thought *Remember with Advantages* is a marvelous kind of title. It shows how we—all of us—are encouraged to insulate or to edit our remembrances, whether good or bad, by the infallible benefits of hindsight.

Many of the facts we shall deal with are ascertainable, traceable, verifiable. Many of the impressions are not. It's rather like the perception of anything, really. All of us tend to reflect in our reminiscences something of our own nature. A great deal of what will be expressed here will be my own personal opinion, often tempered, edited sometimes, perhaps recreated, by the benefit of time and hindsight. Time is very merciful in that respect at least. For many of us it serves as an insulation, a cushion, sometimes even as an eraser.

So, to begin at the beginning.

First of all my father's family, whose name I bear: Morse. They originated—if any family can be said to originate anywhere in particular—in the western part of England in the county of Wiltshire. My father's full name was Charles Hayward Morse. We later passed his middle name on to our son. My father's father had married a lady whose maiden name was Hayward. The name goes back to Saxon times, to around the ninth century. Wiltshire has always been, and still is, a great place for raising sheep. In order that the sheep be kept within their pastures, the building of hedges became very important. An alternative name for a hedge in ancient times was "the hay." Therefore a name grew up, given to a man whose responsibility was to build and maintain the hedges—the hays. He became known as the hay ward. That is how the name Hayward came into existence, which gives us a clue that my paternal grandmother must also have come from Wiltshire.

My father's father came up one time from Wiltshire to visit us, as a quite elderly gentleman. He hadn't been to London since he'd worked there as a gardener when my father was born. I was taken by my father to Paddington station, which was where trains from the West Country came in, in order to meet my grandfather. I was no more than five or six, and I don't think I'd seen him before. As he got off the train I remember being struck by the fact that he so obviously was a country man. In those days you could tell more or less at a glance if someone came from the country because they dressed differently. He was wearing a dark brown heavy tweed suit, with brown boots. I don't think I'd ever seen anybody with brown boots before. People tended not to wear brown boots unless they lived in the country. He had a bristling, cavalry style mustache and was also carrying a stick, another characteristic of country people. His stick fascinated me because its handle was a brass molding in the shape of a horse's head.

My father was one of nine brothers and sisters. My paternal grandfather and his wife were married reasonably young and had a large number of children—although not uncommonly large for Victorian times. My father was born in 1882, on December 8, in a northern district of London called Highgate—in a gardener's cottage attached to a big house where his father, George Morse, had taken the job of gardener.

One of my father's sisters was named Minnie, who never married. Minnie had an air of almost terminal gentility about her, the sort of woman who is very scrupulous about her ladylike image. My father was a great laugher—he's the only person I have ever known who actually ruptured himself while laughing—and his sister Minnie gave him great amusement. He used to do an impression of Minnie and said she always spoke as if she had her little finger crooked, the way genteel people do when they lift a cup of tea or coffee. He remembered once taking her into a pub. Such was her inflexible gentility it appeared she'd never been in a pub before. When it came time to order my father asked her what she would like, and was greeted with the response "A small port and a banbury." Well, a small port, she had somehow divined, might be a sufficiently ladylike drink for her to indulge in. She thought she ought to ask also for a banbury, which was a kind of digestive biscuit sold in pubs where there might be ladies going, I suppose as a means of making their actual drinking in some way respectable.

My mother was born on September 9, 1882, and came from a family called Hollis. I remember my mother's mother because she lived to a fairly great age and into my early childhood remembrances. She lived in Kennington, a southeasterly district of London, quite close to a couple of her other daughters, and had eleven children. My mother, as an unmarried girl, was Mary Florence Hollis.

Her father, my grandfather, had died before I was born and I didn't hear much about him, beyond the fact he was something of a ne'er-do-well, and I gather had been a bit of a boozer. There were stories about his having various jobs, one of which my mother and her sisters told with some amusement. At one time he had a job in some rather posh restaurant, perhaps in the West End of London, where in those days—Victorian times, of course—they had carvers. Carvers were chaps who went around dressed in a chef's cap and a white apron, with a trolley with joints of meat on it. It was their job to carve, at the table, whatever the particular customer wanted. If they did well they were likely to get a tip. Apparently Mr. Hollis was considerably independent minded and didn't take very kindly to being ordered about by posh people saying things like, "No, no, no. I want something off the rare side of the beef. No, don't give me too much fat…" and all that stuff. He was also given to having a drink or two, and one night when perhaps he'd had a drink or two, he was pushing his trolley round, and came to some particularly demanding customer who said things like, "No, no, no, I said the lamb! Come on now, pull yourself together. I want the leg of mutton there, and cut it, no, no, *much* more thinly than that! No, *don't* put gravy," and went on and on until the impetuous Mr. Hollis said, "Oh, well, help yourself," and tipped the whole lot over him. Whereupon, of course, he was fired, which I imagine damaged his employment prospects a bit. Nonetheless, he managed to raise—or to sire—a quite large number of children.

My uncle Will was the eldest of the family. He became a police constable in the City of London. Right in the heart of London there is a separate police administration, regarded as something of an elite force. Even as far back as this would have been—the 1890s—in order to join that force, a recruit had to be more than six feet tall, which was uncommon in Victorian times. Well, Uncle Will was over six feet tall, and so he joined this elite force. That was a great source of pride to me, and may have had something to do with influencing my brother Len—much later on—towards the idea of being a policeman.

Then there was my aunt Flo. She was given the first name Florence, which was also my own mother's middle name. I remember Flo quite well. Her husband's name was Tom. They lived in Camberwell, another district to the south of the River Thames. The buildings in which they lived—a block of tenement flats—is still there to this day. Uncle Tom was a brewer's drayman. A brewer's dray was a huge, lumbering cart, drawn by two great horses, the kind of horses that have lovely fur muffs around their hooves. These drays conveyed barrels of beer all over London. Uncle Tom was driving his dray in the days when I was a child, up until I was a student at the Royal Academy. I was walking along the Strand one day with a rather posh girl, a fellow student. She had a double-barreled name like Pamela Simkins-Hodgkinson. We were walking along and this huge cart came past, driven by my uncle Tom. He cracked his whip, and yelled out "Oi, oi! Oi, oi!" This poor girl looked in horrified amazement at this person who had hailed me so enthusiastically, and said, "Who was *that*?" And I said, "Ah, that is my uncle Tom, from Camberwell."

"Camberwell?" she said, "*Where* is Camberwell?" as if I'd said Mars. So I said to her, "Well look, here we are on the Strand. And just down there is the River Thames. And if you go over one of the bridges you will get to the south side of the river. If you go a little further to the south, you'll get to Camberwell. In other words," I said, "it's south of the river." She looked at me in genuine disbelief and said, "Oh, but surely—nobody lives *south* of the river!" She'd never heard of anybody living there before; it was to her not like another country, but like another planet. People of her class in those days might never set foot south of the river in the whole of their lives, except perhaps en route to France.

I realize I don't know half as much as I would like to about my family. One tends to take one's parents for granted, and not be very curious about what their lives and backgrounds and feelings might have been. My father would have left school at the age of 12 in those days, and therefore started to work around 1895. He started to work as errand boy and general help in a baker's shop in that area to the north of London, Hampstead or Highgate. It was a much respected shop run by one Daniel Callard. My father was responsible for keeping an eye on the shop and taking out deliveries of bread or cakes. Also, he helped the baker's wife, Mrs. Callard. She, as a side project, started to make sweets in the back of the shop, which they then sold up front. Whether she was a Scotswoman, I don't know, but her husband was certainly a Scotsman—so she started to make butterscotch. They had a son a little older than my father and he was somewhat spoiled. Because Mr. Callard and his wife were employing my father to do these various errands and deliveries their son became rather jealous. He was their only son and seemed to feel entitled to rather more of his parents' attention than he was getting.

There came a point when money was missing from the till in the shop.

My father had means of knowing, apparently, that it had been filched by their son. However, he, seeking to extricate himself from suspicion, blamed my father. This brought things to a rather unpleasant crisis, and my father was grossly offended that this boy should have thrown suspicion on him.

The extraordinary afterpiece to this story is that Mr. and Mrs. Callard, on the strength of the candies which Mrs. Callard had started to make in the back of their baker's shop, went on to found a very successful company producing candies of all kinds, in particular, the butterscotch. To this day you still see sold, pretty well all over the world, a product known as Callard & Bowser's Butterscotch and now other products such as Altoid breath mints. That company was founded by Mr. and Mrs. Callard—the baker and his wife of Hampstead and Highgate.

My father turned his back on his job and resolved to go off and join the army. Just at that time, the Boer War had begun in South Africa. The Boer War was an attempt by Britain to uphold its Imperial grasp over South Africa. It broke out in 1899, lasted until 1902, and was regarded as one of the high Empire causes. At this point the British Empire was at the peak of its power and influence. Queen Victoria was still alive, and was regarded as the matriarchal leader of the greatest empire the world had ever known. This Boer War was a sacred cause. My father, caught up in all the emotional excitement of that time, decided he would go and join the army, to fight in South Africa. He also resolved—heaven knows how he made this decision—to try to join a famous cavalry regiment. As far as I know he'd had no experience riding horses, although I suppose in the course of making his deliveries for the baker, he probably had driven a horse and cart. But he resolved to join this famous regiment—The 18th Hussars.

My father would tell my brother and me this story completely collapsed with laughter, at the remembrance of how ridiculous it was that he came to be a Hussar. There was a good deal of recruiting going on in those days, and the way in which a recruit was acknowledged as having joined was they were given what was called the Queen's Shilling. That was a token they had actually been admitted to the army and were now under army control and discipline. So my father went down to the recruiting station, and there was this great big, fierce, mustachioed recruiting sergeant, dressed up in the uniform, and looking very terrifying, I'm sure. With the typical Recruiting Sergeant's voice, he said "What do you want, son?"

"I want to join the Hussars, sir."

"Right. How old are ya, son?"

My father said, "Sixteen, sir." The recruiting sergeant looked at him quizzically, dubiously, and then went on to say, "Well, I'll tell you what you do. Go out that door, do a quick about turn, and come back in again—

when you're *eighteen*. All right?" Giving him a broad wink. My father caught on, went outside the door, did a smart about turn, came back in again, and confronted the same recruiting sergeant, who then said "What do you want, son?"

"I want to join the Hussars, sir."

"How old are ya, son?"

"Eighteen, sir."

"Right. Here's your Shilling. You're in!" That was how my father became a private in the 18th Hussars—the Queen's Own. He went off for training, and used to tell me about the sort of orders they were given. They were trained very strictly in all kinds of maneuvers—how to get their horses to move this way and that, to move backwards if necessary, to pull up sharp, canter and gallop—all that stuff. After they'd been on the parade ground for an hour or so, doing all these maneuvers, one of the last orders of the sergeant major was "Make much of your horses!" This meant the troopers were required to bend over their horses' shoulders and pat their necks, and tickle their muzzles, the thinking being you would always get the loyalty and obedience of your horse, if you were prepared to "make much of him" once in a while. And apparently, my father said, the troopers would often have in their pockets a couple of lumps of sugar. When the order came they would smuggle a piece of sugar into the horse's mouth.

My father in the uniform of the 18th Hussars, black with gold trimmings. The photograph was taken in Richmond at the end of his military service (note the spurs on his boots, but no horse in sight!).

It must have been in 1899 that my father succeeded in joining the 18th Hussars, and after he had been under training for a while they were all shipped out. My father's regiment was transported with their horses down to South Africa, where they landed at Port Elizabeth. (When my wife, Sydney, and I were in South Africa in 1991 we made a point of going to Port Elizabeth to see the place where my father landed as a 16- or 17-year-old boy in the Hussars, to enter the struggle of the Boer War.)

They were soon engaged in an action against the Boer troops. Like so many of his companions, my father had his horse shot from under him, and was himself wounded in the shoulder, seriously enough to be out of action. He then spent a number of weeks being shuttled about—here, there and everywhere around South Africa, according to the way the tides of the war went. They were finally able to get him on a hospital ship back to England. My father was discharged from the army at that point.

My father was not immensely communicative about his life. He may have had reasons of his own why he chose not to talk about those years. I only know that about ten years later, by 1910 certainly, he was working in a hospital in Richmond, Surrey. Now, with the passage of time, Richmond has become a suburb of London, but it was in those days a separate semi-rural community on the southwest outskirts of London. There was a hospital there called the Richmond Royal, and some of the buildings still exist.

My father was a porter, which meant he had to do pretty well anything in the way of odd jobs, such things as carting out the bodies when people died in hospital, which they did in fair numbers in those days. There is a photograph of the whole support staff of this hospital, in which you see my father looking very smart in his Sunday best uniform, with his military mustache trim and probably waxed at the ends. Sitting in the group on the other side, among the various maids of the hospital staff, you'll see a very smart looking woman who is my mother. That is where they met.

My mother left school at the tender age of 12 and went to her first job as a maid at a hospital in Southwark, near where she lived when she was a child. This was the Evelina Hospital for Children. This job was a daily one and she continued to live at home with her mother. When she moved to the Richmond Royal Hospital, where she was a maid and met my father, I don't know. She certainly had been there for a couple of years before she married my father in December of 1913.

The war, which they used to call "the war to end all wars," the First World War, began in August of 1914. Inevitably, my father, having been a regular serving soldier in the 18th Hussars, was called up again. By this time he was 32 and not a nipper anymore. He was sent again into the cavalry. Of course, fighting on horseback in the mud of Flanders in 1914 and

Richmond Royal Hospital, circa 1910. My mother is in the front row, third from the right. My father is in the front row, on the far left side.

1915 was not calculated to bring much success. There are endless stories of cavalry regiments becoming completely sunk in the mud, virtually unable to move and being sitting targets for anybody who wished to shoot at them. But they persisted with it. The lunacies of some sections of British military leadership were almost unending.

The net result was that my father was wounded twice more. He was wounded slightly quite early in the war, towards the end of 1914 or the beginning of 1915. He then was wounded again, after his first wound was mended and he was put back into action. The first wound apparently was in the leg, and not too serious. The second wound was in the chest, and he showed me the considerable scarring towards the right side of his chest. One always had the feeling with my father that, alongside his natural reserve, there were some things he chose *not* to talk about. One was his service in the First World War, which was obviously a hideous experience for him as it was for so many hundreds of thousands of other people. It had been deeply psychologically wounding in every kind of way. To a very large extent, his future had been virtually destroyed by those experiences in war. I vividly remember all through our childhood, around the time of November 11, celebrated as so-called Armistice Day, my father would say with considerable emotion, "Armistice Day. Yes. It's not over. Armistice doesn't mean it's *over*. It's just been *postponed*. It's just been *suspended*. They'll get it going again." And how right, in the event, he turned out to be.

Being a semi-invalid due to his injuries, there was a limit to the number of jobs he might have been able to do. But his brother Frank previously had a little shop. It was a rather unusual shop which in those days was simply called an "Off-license." It was so called because it had a government license which allowed it to sell beer—only beer—to be consumed *off* the premises, hence the expression off-license. My father (as a discharged wounded soldier) was given some degree of preference in taking on, as a tenant, a little shop like this in Shoreditch.

And that was how my brother, Len, and I came to be born there.

2

"Troublesome and Truculent"

MY FATHER WAS NEVER ENTIRELY well in my knowledge and observation. He should have spent less time working, but because the shop was open from 10:00 a.m. to 3:00 p.m., and 5:00 p.m. to 10:00 p.m.—seven days a week—it was impossible for either of my parents to ever have any time off. In the whole of my childhood they never went on holiday. There was no one else to run the business. My mother would take us, Len and myself (and then me alone after Len grew up), to visit her and my Dad's various relations in other parts of London, but neither of them ever had a holiday together out of London.

I now realize my father's was a very sad life. He never stopped agonizing about the likelihood of another world war. When it came to the point the Second World War began, he had been faintly ill off and on—in various ways—all through my childhood and youth. By the time the war began I was married and working in the provinces. Sydney and I were playing in repertory theatres all over the country. I wasn't around with my parents, who were back in London. I was able to get to see them every once in a while, but not very often. The Second World War began on the third of September 1939. A couple of weeks later, my father suffered a very severe stroke.

I think the emotional build-up of those 21 years between the wars was more than he could handle. Two wars having already virtually destroyed his prospects in life and his health, the possibility—no, the *likelihood*, as he saw it—of the Second World War coming was something more than his psychological structure could stand, and he had this huge stroke. My mother, helped very greatly by my brother, Len, who lived nearby, was able to give up the shop and move into a small flat where she continued to

16

live with my brother and subsequently with Maisie, his wife, after their marriage.

My parents therefore went on living in Shoreditch and my dad was now severely handicapped. My poor mother tended him as best she could. Then he started to complain of having severe stomach pain. The conclusion was that his pain was an illusion—a hallucination—suffered by my dad as a result of this stroke. Well, time went by and the blitz began, and there were terrible bombings all over London's East End, all around where they lived. Buildings were destroyed and people spent their nights either in the air raid shelters or crouching underneath their beds. My parents chose not to go to air raid shelters, feeling they'd sooner stay in their own home and take their chances, a choice a great many older people made. They couldn't face the prospect of trudging off every night with their bedding and going down into the underground tube stations.

My father continued for months to complain of intense stomach pain. Several attempts to get medical opinions were made and always we were told this was nothing we need pay any attention to. It was due to his confused state and it was hallucinatory. One day (I've chosen not to remember the date) my brother was out of the flat on night duty. Late at night, or very early in the morning, my poor father got up out of bed, leaving my mother there asleep, and went into the kitchen. He put his head in the gas oven, turned it on, and killed himself.

I was out of London at the time, and heard of this via Len. Because Len was in the police force and very highly respected, he was able with the connivance of the Metropolitan Police to avoid having an inquest bring in a verdict of suicide. If a suicide verdict had been brought in, my mother would not have been able to collect anything of the small insurance policy she had on my father. None of us had anything in the way of money at this time, of course. So the police somehow contrived to arrange for a verdict of accidental death. However, a postmortem examination had to be carried out, and it disclosed my father's stomach was *blazing* with ulcers! They had not been found by the various medical people who had supposedly examined him in the preceding months. This was one of the many contributory factors to my deep skepticism about the greatly cherished "omniscience" of the medical profession.

This was a terrible blow to my dear mother, who had spent her whole married lifetime taking care of her family. I didn't realize the immense burdens falling upon my mother, and the saintly—*superhuman*—dedication she brought to the care, not only of us her sons, but in a much more intense way, of my dad—her poor husband. What might have become of him, what he might have achieved, one can only speculate. I see now, looking back at the course of my own life, how much has been brought about by the coincidental flukes which either open up or shut down avenues of opportunity. My father had all avenues of opportunity slammed shut for him, almost everywhere he turned, and almost throughout the whole of his life. I must say he contrived to sustain a marvelously wild sense of humor, in the face of such misfortunes as might have made him a melancholic and embittered man. There were certain kinds of incidents and quirks of human behavior which would tickle him uproariously. There were certain kinds of human beings whom he found to be hilarious, and I remember he would tell us when we were children of some of the freakish characters he'd observed, in many instances people who'd come into the shop or who lived in the neighborhood.

One character he particularly enjoyed was a street vagrant known as "Engine Bill." We saw Bill as children, going about the streets of the East End. This poor chap had developed the delusion that he *was* a railway locomotive. He would trot along the gutters—not walking on the sidewalk nor on the road—just along the gutters wherever he was, making a choo-choo noise. "Choo-choo-choo-choo-choo…." Then, every once in a while, he would let off a sort of whistle, in imitation of that used by railway steam locomotives, "Whoo-woo! Whooo!" He would carry with him a penny— in the old British currency—a bronze coin about the size of a silver dollar, which he would hold in his hands in the manner of a steering wheel. The children of the district were—as I'm afraid children so often are— quite merciless in making mock of him. I hope I wasn't one of the participants, though I might well have been. Children would say to him as he went chugging along the gutter, "'Ere, Bill, if you're a railway engine, what ya got a steerin' wheel for?" And he would say with great dignity and unanswerable logic, "Well, there's no *rails* here." This amused my father, and he used to love to do that turn of Engine Bill. There were all sorts of extraordinary characters in those days who inhabited the streets of the East End of London. My father seemed to know them all, and cherish them all, and have great enjoyment in all their eccentricities.

My mother was an immense helpmate to my father. She was incredibly loyal, marvelously brave and good-humored in the face of his sometimes uncertain temper. He was excitable, whereas my mother was—or at least appeared to be on the surface—tranquil and stoical. I'm sure it was achieved at the cost of a good deal of anxiety on her part—but she had a calm and heroic fortitude, which saw her through the various ups and downs. I grew up with a good deal of compassion for my father, and an immense admiration for my mother.

I must relate, apropos of my mother, that her stoicism was never better exhibited than after my poor father's death. She went on living at home and looking after Len, and then Maisie when Len got married in 1940. By 1943, Len was allowed to leave the Metropolitan Police force in order to join the navy. Again, I was away, out of London. In 1946 my mother gave the supreme example of her stoicism. Maisie remembered this, because she was living in the flat and recalled my mum having more than a bit of a cold or the flu. However, such was her fortitude that she eventually collapsed in her kitchen doing the washing up. By the time they got the doctor to her she was at the point of death, having developed what turned out to be double pneumonia, which she hadn't thought serious or important enough to mention to anybody, or to call a doctor for. That sounds incredible, doesn't it? But,

My mother, photographed while on holiday in Margate, before she married my father.

people of my parents' generation—of their class—would never dream of calling a doctor. If you wanted a doctor, you had to pay for one. Nobody ever thought, among working class people, to call a doctor unless they genuinely considered themselves to be seriously ill.

Now we come to my brother, Len. Born Lenard Frank Morse, it's not an affectation to say Len was really the hero of the family in my eyes. He was born on the fifteenth of March, 1915, and was always an outstanding athlete. In today's world he probably would have been encouraged to become some kind of professional athlete. Well, he didn't. But he went through a more thorough education than I did. He went to school until he was 16 because he won a scholarship which allowed him to go to technical school to train as a civil engineer. When it came time to leave school, it was slap in the middle of the great depression which followed the stock market crash of 1929. There were something like two million unemployed in the UK. Len managed to get himself accepted—it wasn't difficult because of his athletic abilities—by the Metropolitan Police of London, as a bobby. In no time at all they recognized his great athletic prowess, and he became the boxing champion of the police force. This was before the war, and Len would box in all different parts of Europe when a team would go to France, Denmark or wherever. He also began to run in a lot of racing events, and became very successful and popular as a police officer. He managed to get himself appointed to a police station at Commercial Street in the East End of London, close to where we lived, which was a great advantage.

I remember walking around on the beat with him when he was first working in the East End. Near where we lived there is a district called Bethnal Green, where there were a great many Jewish families. We came to a row of the usual Victorian terraced slum-type houses. He stopped and said, "Hang on here a minute," and left me standing on the sidewalk outside. He went up to the front door and pulled out the front door key, which was on a piece of string, through the letter box. (There's a sign of the times. It was quite customary for people in those days to leave their front door key on the end of a piece of string which could be pulled out through the letter box. This way their children or anybody else who came to visit would be able to get in when they wanted to. That's how secure such districts were.) Anyway, Len let himself in and was gone for 10 or 15 minutes. When he came back out, I said, "What was that? What were you doing in there?" He said, "This is where the Rosofsky family live," or whatever name it was. "They are a very devout and orthodox Jewish family, and this is one of their high holy days, when they're not allowed to do anything in the way of domestic work. They're all down at the synagogue. So, I go in and light the fire, put out the rubbish, feed the cat, light the gas—so it's all ready for when they come home." *That* he regarded as being all in a day's work. I tell people nowadays and they can hardly believe this was what an ordinary local bobby took to be part of his job, circa 1935.

There's a lovely story of Len's about the blitz. He was out one night while a terrible air raid was going on. He came across a little group of slum houses which were almost totally destroyed. He was on his own and had to scramble down in the ruins to see if anybody was alive. Most of the people were not. When he got to the end of this little row of houses he saw that there was an elderly lady buried deep beneath all this rubble which had tumbled down on her, but she was not seriously injured. In fact, all that was troubling her was that she was pinned down by all this lumber. Len made his way down among the wreckage, got alongside her, and realized that he was not going to be able to take her out by himself. He took hold of her hands and said, "Now you'll be all right, Ma. I'll get the boys with the rescue equipment to come round a little bit later on and we'll be able to get you out." Then he noticed that behind her head there were the remains of one of her kitchen cupboards. On the shelf of this little cupboard there was a tiny bottle of brandy which working people always used to keep in their kitchens in case somebody was—as the phrase used to go—"taken queer." He saw that this little bottle was undamaged, so he reached past her head and took it out, blew the dust off it, and said, "Now look, the boys will be here soon, but it's raining and it's very cold. So to keep you warm I'm just going to give you a little swig of this." She reached out, slapped his hand, and said, "Don't you go touching that. I'm keeping that for an emergency!"

With my brother, Len, in his police uniform as a bobby (note his war medals). Just on the right side of the image you can see part of his Metropolitan Police Officer identification number, G119.

Len came—partly as a result of his extraordinary dedication to the humanities of his job—to know virtually every man, woman, child and dog on what he used to call "Our Ground." In fact, he used to call the people "The Customers on Our Ground." Len served the whole of his police career, aside from the spell he went and served voluntarily in the navy, at this one station, which was then Commercial Street, G Division. His was the longest record of service at one station by any bobby in the history of the Metropolitan Police. He turned down any attempt to promote him, and there were many. To accept promotion would have meant he would have to move to another district, and he didn't want to leave his "Customers." In his later years in the police Len became known (only partly as a joke) as "the Rev" because people felt he behaved more like a priest than a bobby.

Len volunteered for the Royal Navy and became a master at arms, which is the senior rank for a noncommissioned officer. He wrote me wonderful letters describing some of the events he was mixed up in. For example, he served on a destroyer which took part in the invasion of France in 1944, and wrote me a marvelous letter in the middle of the night when all the sailors were asleep the night before they went ashore and faced the fire on the beaches of Normandy. After the war, Len went back to the same police station. As a mark of how respected Len was, when it came time for his retirement, he was offered a job as one of the court ushers at the Old Bailey, the famous courthouse in the center of London. I never knew my brother Len, who was so shy, self-effacing and modest, had such histrionic talents! As the court usher, he was the one who would come in at the beginning of the day's trials and say in a loud voice, "Crave silence for my Lords, the Queen's Justices. All persons having anything to do before my Lords, the Queen's Justices, draw near and give your attention!" or something to that effect, which he would emote in a marvelously theatrical way.

My mother was a woman of considerable common sense, capable of wry wisdom. I always remember one thing she said to me. She was pointing out that knowing this or doing that was very much a matter of common sense. Then she added, "But you will find common sense is far from common," and how right she was. So often one comes across people with the most elaborate and expensive educations who haven't got the remotest common sense. I must have been a great trial to my mother. I was relentlessly inquisitive. All children drive their parents mad by saying "Why this" and "What's that" but I recall—before I started the pretenses of going to school—plaguing my mother, particularly one washing day. I pursued her around asking her things like, "Well, if that is that, why is this, this?" and all sorts of impossible questions. Eventually, more in sorrow than in anger—she never seemed to get angry—she said, "Oh, son, son—Why don't you leave your mind alone?" I thought that was a marvelous recommendation for an inquisitive child.

One of my memories of childhood was how the smell of beer was fairly prevalent in our off-license. The cellar was right underneath the shop, and contained the beer barrels. The spillage from the pump machine led to an aroma which I found quite distasteful. On my way to school I had to pass three very run-down grubby pubs. At that time of the morning they would have their cellar flaps and their bar doors open, trying to rid themselves of the stench of a hundred years of stale beer. I can remember crossing to the other side of the street in order not to get too close to these pubs. That has led to my never having so much as tasted beer. When I got to my teens, people would say to me, "Well, try it. Have a taste of beer. It's a bit of an acquired taste, but you will like it." Well, I have never been able to bring myself to have even a sip. I enjoy a glass of wine, and have been known to drink other sorts of drinks from time to time, but never, ever, beer.

London in the '20s and '30s was a very different city than it is now, in so many ways. Among other things, people who lived in London in a particular area very seldom would move from that area to another. You came to think of your particular part of London almost as a kind of village. My father once said to my mother, with considerable alarm, "Mary, you know them so-and-so's down the road?" "Yes, yes—what?" "They're *moving*!"

That note of alarm was brought about by the understanding between them that people very rarely moved, and only, as a rule, for unhappy reasons. People moved for only two main reasons in the poorer quarters of London. One, they were not able to come up with their rent anymore and had to do what was called a "Moonlight Flit," in other words, decamp with all their belongings, owing X weeks or months rent, before the landlord caught up with them. The other was simply that the Old Man, the father, the breadwinner of the family, had been drawn into some kind of criminal activity, and had been arrested and had gone in the Nick—"in the Nick" meaning the police station, or in prison. Therefore, the family was going to be turned out. It was even rare for people to venture far from their own district. As an example, my mother had never set foot in the central fashionable part of London until I was playing in the West End, on Shaftesbury Avenue, as it happened. By this time I was married, and we were in touch with my mother all the time and wanted her to come and see this play in which I was starring with my name above the title. We arranged one matinee day to bring my mother up to the West End. Sydney went and picked her up and we got seats for them right in the front stalls. She sat through this play, and we took her out for tea afterwards, then back down to Shoreditch, and afterwards I said to Sydney, "Well, what was it like? What did she make of it?" And Sydney said, "Oh, it was extraordinary. She was so excited and thrilled—just trembling with excitement. Sitting in this theatre where she'd seen your name on the posters over the title. She sat there and lapped it all up with great excitement, but you could tell all the time she was half afraid a hand might fall on her shoulder, and someone would say to her 'Here! What are you doing here? *Piss off out of it!'* She didn't feel entitled to *be* in the West End." There was the feeling among working class people that they weren't entitled to be in this other part of London, that they needed some sort of permit or passport to be there.

Much of my education, as far as I had any, was derived from the Boy Scouts, and from singing in the church choir. I owe my introduction to the

Scouts to my brother, who had joined before I did, and remained in the same troop pretty much the whole time I did, as well. Our troop was run by a remarkable man called Alec C. Kearley, a bachelor and junior civil servant, I think in the Ministry of Education. Initially we had our headquarters in a disused railway lineman's hut. Mr. Kearley, whom we always addressed as "Skipper" because he was our captain, then persuaded a local church to allow us to use a patch of land beside their church as a place to build our own hut. It was built from steel framework, filled with a form of asbestos sheeting available in those days, which forestalled the possibility of fire. Our troop was highly unconventional and brilliantly conceived. We never wore the official Scout hat—that rather unsuitable South African type of hat which had been imposed upon the Scout movement by its founder, Robert Baden Powell. We wore in the wintertime a seaman's woolen jersey, navy blue, and shorts of a quite heavy serge in navy blue. Our scarf was a bright royal blue, making for a rather smart looking outfit. We were recognizably—or rather *un*recognizably—not typical.

An early shot of Len (left) and me, taken at a trade fair called "The Ideal Home Show," posed in front of one of the ideal home sets. It's interesting to note I appear to be nearly the same size as Len despite the fact he is three and a quarter years older than me.

I think the reason I've lasted so well is the grounding in physical fitness I got as a Boy Scout. One year all of the senior events—100 yards, 220 yards, 440 yards, 880 yards, high jump and long jump—were won by Len, and all the junior events—the same as the senior events but without the 880 yards—were won by me. In other words, Len and I between us won all the athletic events there were!

Among Skipper's other talents, he was immensely gifted as a musician. He arranged—no I shouldn't say *arranged* because he never seemed to be arranging anything—he encouraged *us* to arrange the presentation of a Christmas pantomime every year. The conventional British pantomime is not so widespread and popular as it once was, but in those days everybody went to see a pantomime at Christmas. We wrote ours more or less ourselves, and they were usually based on some well known story. The first one we did was *The Babes in the Wood*. Other years we did *Aladdin* and *Sinbad the Sailor*. We would write all the comedy effects, and use various popular songs with specially adapted lyrics. Skipper was a beautiful pianist, and he had trained a couple of the other boys to play musical instruments, and they would form a little orchestra to accompany our performance.

This was where I first learned that to be up in front of a bunch of other people was a friendly experience, and not terrifying at all. To be onstage was not an occasion for crippling terror, but for ecstatic excitement. As I always say, it was rather like Christmas Eve every day. All our performances were on the little stage in our local church hall. We sold tickets to our friends and families and all the neighbors, and the shows were really rather good.

In this pantomime, *The Babes in the Wood*, I played Baron Hardup—the villain, as it were. I had a lot of white shoe polish on my hair to make it look gray, and shaggy eyebrows made with cotton wool. Part of the legend, the fairytale of *The Babes in the Wood* is that the Babes are kidnapped by some robbers who are the employees of the rascally Baron Hardup. One of our big sight gags took place in a scene where the dialogue went something along these lines: The Baron says, "Now then, you say you're proper robbers and villains, and you can steal anything. You reckon you can kidnap these Babes?" "Yes. Yes, of course we can. We can do anything like that."

These two robbers had this scene with me as Baron Hardup, in which they were trying to prove they could steal anything. We rigged up the set so I sat behind a table and you couldn't see my legs. The robbers were over the other side of the stage haranguing over whether they could successfully steal things. The tag to the scene was as they said, "Well, we can steal anything we like. You'll see. You'll see…." As they went off I got up from behind the table. Concealed under the tablecloth was one of our smallest boys, whose job it was to pull off my trousers during the course of this scene. So the audience, having seen me sit down behind this table with my trousers on, at the end of the scene saw me get up saying, "Well, I'm not sure whether they—Oh my! Oh look!" And I'd lost my trousers! That was the kind of gag we used to work.

I had a good, strong, pure boy's treble voice, and on the occasions when I was at school, when we were required to sing the national anthem or a hymn in the mornings, people would say, as I recall my schoolmaster, F.J. Fuest, saying, "You know, you've got quite a useful voice. You ought to sing in some sort of choir." I thought, "That doesn't sound like much."

But I eventually learned—again through some gutter telegraph that operates among Cockney youths—there was a church in a remote part of London called Belgravia, traditionally one of the poshest areas, where they paid their choirboys better than any other church. In fact, many church choirs didn't pay their choristers at all—but this one, called Saint Columba's, did. The music director was T. Arnold Fulton. (I never learned what the T stood for.) He was fierce and very strict. He called singing "melodious breath." When I first went to see him he said to me, "Can you read music?" Well, of course I couldn't at all, but, not outfaced, I said, "Yes, of course." So he gave me a hymnbook, open as good luck would have it—the flukes that govern one's life!—at a hymn which I already knew! So when he struck up and gave me a note, I sang it perfectly, after which he said, "Oh well, that's quite good. Yes, yes." And so I started off as a chorister. I went on singing there three services most Sundays. Because the program of music was so ambitious and so high in quality, we quite often got to broadcast! I actually did broadcast on the BBC Radio—no such thing as television in those days—sometime around 1928—my first broadcast ever. Sometimes I sang as part of the choir, but sometimes I sang solos in things like Handel's *Messiah*. I can remember singing the great soprano aria, "I know that my redeemer liveth...." We would broadcast from either the church or the BBC headquarters, which were then on Savoy Hill, just off the Strand. After a while I became "Head Boy," responsible for all the treble solos. And I did, more or less by trial and error, learn how to read music. So I can cheerfully say I have been "making noises" now for 80 years!

The following year I played the Emperor of China in *Aladdin*—a strong character part—at the ripe old age of thirteen. I was always interested in getting myself up in heavy disguises, and as the Emperor of China, I had a long mustache, made out of boot laces, gummed onto my upper lip. To show his general preeminence it reached clear to the floor. In a later pantomime, *Sinbad the Sailor*, I played Ben Boloney, captain of the ship on which Sinbad sailed. I conceived the idea he ought to have one leg, a peg leg, rather like Long John Silver in *Treasure Island*. I discussed this with my mother, who was marvelously patient and cooperative about all these lunacies I got up to, and I fixed on the idea to use a kitchen sink plunger, which I turned upside down and fitted my knee into. I had it attached around my knee in some way, and then wore a voluminous pair of breeches which concealed the fact the lower part of my leg was doubled up behind. It would look as if I had just a peg leg. My mother, bless her heart, constructed the whole thing. It created quite a sensation when I came on.

When I elected not to go to school it wasn't always easy to find something else to do. One had to consider the weather conditions, and the weather in London can be, almost any time of the year, less than friendly, so I sometimes had to find my way out of the worst of it. It's wonderful how these flukes can sometimes act to your advantage! Inevitably I found my way to such places as the public libraries, museums, and art galleries, where I gathered an education of my own—so that much was good.

I suppose everybody's upbringing does influence their religious and political views, and my religious and political views were probably a bit wider—or were made a bit wider—by the pattern of life I lived. Through my years as a chorister at Saint Columba's I was exposed to the best of Christian teaching. I listened carefully, when the lessons were read and when the sermon was preached, to all the precepts of Christianity. I believe I thought of myself as a reasonably convinced Christian.

But, living where I did, and moving about among the wide variety of people I did, it wasn't long before I came to realize there were other religious faiths in the world. This Christian faith I was exposed to seemed to regard itself as being exclusive. In the part of London where we lived there were a great many Jewish people, but not so many people from overseas as there are now. There weren't the Caribbean and African people, or people from India and Pakistan, but nonetheless there were enough people of other faiths—most particularly Jewish people—to make me realize there was something a bit dubious about this Christian exclusivity. As I gradually learned more of what went on in the rest of the world, I came to understand that a great deal of the misery, murder and mayhem that went on was carried out in the name of what was called Religion. I came to learn a lot more about the terrible activities of anti–Semitism, for example, under the Nazis. That troubled me a good deal as a young man.

The other half of it, about politics, has to do with my observations as a child, and even more as an adolescent, that there were in England obnoxious class divisions. Almost by definition they sealed off certain kinds of people into certain kinds of lives. Based mostly on the accidents of what their parentage and place of birth were, and consequently on their way of life or of speaking; all those class divisions I found revolting and obscene.

So my political views, like my religious views, came to take shape. I wasn't able to express them then as I try to now, but my political views began to become more and more radical. I always say, when people ask me about my political views, "I'm way to the left of the Anarchists!" because it does seem to me that our planet—and I persistently think of our society, our species, as being a planetary organization—is a very small place. To have such political divisions as we've had historically, and still do, seems to me quite preposterous.

I like to dream of a day when a green globular spacecraft lands on the White House lawn and a green globular man gets out and says in the usual cliché, "Take me to your leader." He's taken to whoever is the president of the United States, and says—obviously speaking every language known to the universe—"We come from the planet XYZ, and forgive us intruding on you, but we have observed in recent eons—for the last several thousand years—that you ... what is it you call yourselves? ... humans, yes, have been increasingly polluting the atmosphere of the universe, and making a lot of unnecessary noise and dirt everywhere, and with great respect, sir..." says the little green globular man, "unless you can, as I think you put it, 'clean up your act' by tomorrow morning, we shall—regretfully, of course—have to dust your little planet off the face of the universe." It would be interesting to see, wouldn't it, what the powers of this planet would do to clean up their act before tomorrow morning. It was your friend and mine, George Bernard Shaw, who said the human species only makes any real progress when motivated by extreme anger or by extreme fear.

Due to the views I had, and have gone on having, even to a much wider degree than I did in those days, I must have become regarded as being troublesome and truculent. There were all sorts of ways I tried to resist or overturn received opinion. There were all sorts of ways I ran up against what was being accepted as the way the world was. I didn't always accept that the way the world was, was the way it *ought* to be. Inevitably I encountered a lot of conflict, which I'm not altogether ashamed of. It's always interesting to look back at the world as it seemed to me when I was coming into my supposed adulthood. I could scarcely have avoided being regarded as troublesome and truculent.

Having not been at school all that much, I wasn't very optimistic about being able to get a job. We were in the Depression and there was very severe unemployment. But I was lucky and got hired as an errand boy through some government-run job center, where you were sent off to be interviewed for possible work. When I went to see these people I found they were a company which manufactured glass bottles and jars, a German firm. So I saw the manager of the distribution place where they sent out all these samples. He particularly wanted to know, before he hired this errand boy, how well they knew their way about the city. Well, my knowledge was considerable, because I had spent so much time wandering all over London on my truancies from school. So, partly to my surprise, but I see now the logic of it, he hired me.

For more than a year I was in that job, which just by sheer fluke led me to get into this business of pulling faces and making noises for a living.

3

"Curiously Touching"

IN THE SPRING OF 1935 I was going through Bloomsbury, where London University and various other academic institutions are, on my delivery round one day. I saw a hoarding alongside the street, which said:

Thursday, April 11—2:00 P.M.
Public Performances by Graduating Students
of the Royal Academy of Dramatic Art.
Admission Free.

I always say that was the grabber—*Admission Free.* As I was able to make my deliveries more quickly than my employer thought was possible, I could dodge off and go to the pictures once in a while or go and see a football game. So, I thought, "Well, that'll be a good place to go," because I had learned around that time a bit about the Royal Academy of Dramatic Art. There was a prominent and successful actor of the mid-thirties named Charles Laughton, who had just won an Academy Award. I had learned, somehow or other, that he had been trained at the Royal Academy on a scholarship, and so I thought I'd go along and see this performance by these graduating students, because they must all be, I supposed, budding Charles Laughtons! So, along I went on the appointed day, to the theatre at the Royal Academy, expecting, of course, that they were all going to be blazingly effective actors, and—with all the shy, bashful modesty which characterizes Cockney youths of sixteen—I thought they were terrible!

You must understand that I had never seen a play performed by professionals in a proper theatre. I had sung for some years in church, and on the radio as part of my church choir. I also had performed in my Boy Scout pantomimes for several years, and I'd been to the movies, but somehow I

29

didn't associate that with the Royal Academy. I knew nothing, nothing at all, about this profession which I eventually took up. But I did feel that these graduating students at the Royal Academy were not really very good. Something clicked in my head, and I said to myself, "This acting business is something I might be able to do. At least it'll beat riding this bicycle for a living." So I wrote off to the Royal Academy. I wish I had a copy of the letter I wrote, because it couldn't have been very grammatical or eloquent. I said something like, "Look 'ere. What about this 'ere scholarship the which of what you give out. I would like to 'ave it!" There were no dropped aitches of course, but it was phrased something like that.

They were very gracious and wrote back in due time and said, "Yes, there is a scholarship which is awarded annually to a deserving student. But you must understand that there are a couple of hundred other young people who would also like to have it. However, if you would like to compete, here is a list of speeches from which you must choose two."

Well, there was a list of classical things like Shakespeare and Greek drama and all that kind of stuff. I scarcely knew any of them. So, eeny, meeny, miny, mo—I picked a couple of them. But then it said "you must also present two pieces of your own choice." Well, that was a bit of a challenge, of course, because I'd never seen a play. So I thought, "I know what I'll do—I'll do something in my own native tongue," as it were. "That'll be a bit of a novelty to them." I had heard and learned a good deal of the "sales patter" that some of the Cockney street-market characters used to use. So I put together a sort of montage (I didn't know the word then, but that's what it was), a montage of market cries of old London, one of which was this piece—which I use in my one-man show—about "The Unguent."

The Unguent was a green oleaginous substance which came in little round tins, sold by an old guy who led you to believe no matter whether you rubbed it on you, or shoved it in you, would cure whatever was up with you! It was a sort of cure-all. And of course, like so many people who sell cure-alls, he was of desperately sickly appearance. He used to wear a battered cap and a decaying raincoat and he would stand at the curb with these tins of The Unguent ranged in front of him, and address the passersby somewhat like this:

> [*Wheezing cough*] Do you have them horrible shootin' pains from hip to thigh? A coating on your tongue which cannot be removed by knife, fork or spoon? An offensive sediment in your chamber utensil? A fluttering sensation in your stomach as of two birds mating in a paper bag? Well then, what you want is the Unguent! Rub it on ya, shove it in ya, it'll cure whatever's up with ya!

Believe it or not, on the stage of the Royal Academy as one of my audition pieces, I actually performed that! Heaven knows what they made of it. The other thing I realized I ought to do was something where I could speak posh—standard, proper English. So I thought, "Where am I going to find something posh, where I can speak like a gent?" I went down to the public library. I knew the lady there, or rather she knew me, because I'd been there a bit before. And I said, cocky and pushy, "'Ere, where's the plays?" and she said, "In there!" pointing behind her.

I went into this great big room of floor to ceiling shelves crammed with plays. I thought to myself, "I'll never find anything here—I'll die of exposure here!" But then, as they say, providence takes care of idiots, and my hand fell on a book, which I took down and opened up. It had in the front of it a list of characters in a play, the very first of whom was named Algernon. Well, you can't get posher than that, can you? I'd never even heard of anybody called Algernon! It was *The Importance of Being Earnest*, and I did a couple of speeches from the first act to go with my Cockney piece, "The Unguent."

Those were the two pieces of my own choice, but now about the two pieces I selected from the set list. The first was a speech from one of the Greek dramas by Euripides. It was in a sort of measured verse, in an English translation. The other piece I chose was an intensely dramatic speech— was it prophetic I should have selected a play by George Bernard Shaw? Well, I did. It's a speech from the concluding stages of his play *Saint Joan*, and spoken by the chaplain who's been partly responsible for Joan being burned at the stake. He comes back onto the stage, having witnessed her execution, in a state of almost hysterical distress and remorse. It gave me a chance to be intensely dramatic. I thought that would make a good contrast with my other material.

There was a kind of elimination process, where the original number of people competing for this scholarship—a hundred and fifty or so—was reduced to about twenty. These twenty would have to come back again on another day. Remember, I was stealing this time from my employers. I went to the Royal Academy for the first competition. I did my bit and was only there for about a half hour. Then they wrote and said, "Yes, you've been included in the last twenty. You are required to come and do your pieces again." I wish I could say I was trembling with apprehension and anxiety about who was going to get this scholarship, but I felt, curiously enough, that I was going to get it. The only trouble was that they had told us we all must wait until the end of the afternoon when the result would be announced. I was aware that I was supposed to get back to the factory in order to do up my parcels for the following day's deliveries. When I'd done my bit, I went to sit in the hall to wait for the judge's decisions.

I didn't have much fear that I wouldn't win, because I had been able to sneak a bit of a look, by lurking about in the wings of the theatre, at one or two of the other competitors. Although they were obviously posh people—gently bred and expensively educated—I could tell that they weren't greatly gifted. So that gave me a certain amount of encouragement.

One of the judges was the great actress Dame Sybil Thorndyke, and there were various other leading theatrical figures of the day who were judges on that occasion. I'm sitting there looking at the clock, thinking "I'll never get back to the factory on time, and there's going to be all hell raised if I don't. But I can't leave. They've told me I must stay until the result is announced." I hung on and hung on until about five o'clock. In due course the judges appeared, accompanied by the principal. Our principal was the son of a bishop and the brother of two distinguished actresses—Irene Vanburgh and Violet Vanburgh. But he maintained his family name, which was Barnes; his name was Kenneth Barnes. He was a very pompous, snobbish chap, always terribly impressed by any of the students who happened to come from a noble family. If their father was Lord This or the Duke of Ditchwater, he was always very friendly disposed towards them. I didn't like him very much, and he didn't like me at all. He thought I was common beyond bearing—which, of course, I was. So the judges finally came out and announced the winner—and lo and behold it was me! I was awarded the Leverhulme Scholarship.

Well, I could scarcely get further than saying, "Thank you very much," before I was down the stairs and on my bicycle, pedaling like mad to get back to the factory, all the time thinking, "This is going to change my whole life." The thing I haven't told about the scholarship was that, as well as paying my fees, it paid a maintenance grant. It was assumed whoever might win this scholarship might not live in London and therefore would need to support themselves. So the scholarship carried as well as all the fees for the two-year course, a maintenance grant of two pounds ten shillings a week! That was probably as much as my father ever made out of his shop. I was thinking about all this as I was pedaling madly back to the factory. When I got there it was quarter to six, long after I was supposed to be back. Sure enough, as I arrived the factory manager was standing at the door. This bloke had been my boss all this time I'd been working as an errand boy. He had his watch in his hand and was obviously about to raise all kinds of hell. So I skidded my bike to a theatrical halt right up against him and before he could even speak, I said, "You can't sack me—I'm packin' it in! I'm leavin' right now! You don't have to pay me nuthin! I've got a scholarship at the Royal Academy of Dramatic Art up west—where they make actors!" I actually said that—"Where they make actors." This poor chap was absolutely dumbfounded.

My next target was to go home and tell my parents, because I hadn't told them anything about going up for these auditions. So I thought, "I know—I'll get Mum some flowers." I felt this was an occasion for a celebration. I went to some nearby street market for the flowers and tore into the house to the alarm of my mother, who'd never seen that before—the flowers I mean. She knew something was up. I said, "Look, Mum, I've won this scholarship thing at this posh place up west. It's called the Royal Academy of Dramatic Art— where they make actors. And they're going to let me go there for nothing. And not only that, they're going to pay me two pounds ten a week for going there!" Well, she looked deeply alarmed at that, because it seemed an extraordinary amount of money. Up west? The Royal Academy? She obviously thought there was something

At home in my parents' house, looking rather sulky, prior to RADA. Above, a childhood portrait of me at the age of four (desperately wanting to kick the football!).

a bit morally dubious about this. She and my father had never been to an ordinary theatre. They'd been, in their courting days, to the old music halls occasionally, but they'd never been to see anything like a proper legitimate play. So it was all a completely foreign world to her. But she collected herself with considerable courage and resolution, and said a very wise thing. First of all she said, "When do you start?" and I said, "Next Monday." "Well, all right," she replied. "Now listen. You'd better have a clean shirt." Isn't that wonderful wisdom? If you are going to change the whole course of your life, which indeed I was, you should always have a clean shirt.

So that was the big turning point. How it really came about I shall never know. Years later, when I was working with Dame Sybil Thorndyke, she remembered she had been one of the judges on that occasion when the competition was taking place. I asked her how it was that they came to award me the scholarship, and she answered that they had found my offerings "curiously touching."

I was apparently the youngest student, at that time, ever to have been admitted to the Royal Academy. Of course, it was a complete cultural turn-around. It was almost unbelievable as I look back at it now. It must have seemed very alarming and bewildering to my parents that I was going to go and mingle with groups of people with whom they had no dealings at all, and no understanding or knowledge of. It must have been for them as much of a culture shock as it was for me.

The whole process of being introduced to the Royal Academy life was extraordinary. To begin with I realized right away that I spoke totally unlike any of the others. Most of the others had the sort of manner of speech that I now have, whereas in those days I had a Cockney accent you couldn't cut with a knife! So I became alternately an object of either scorn or derision, or in some cases of a sense of amazement, as if I were from some other planet. But, by a process of osmosis, I fairly swiftly adjusted my manner of speech to the style which they all pursued. It's part of the benefit of having that sort of an ear. It's no great talent in itself, it's rather like having an ear for music. To this day, indeed, I can do any kind of accent. I've played in many, many American shows and portrayed countless American characters. I mustn't be boastful about this; it just happens to be a knack I have, like some musicians have a sense of pitch, and are able to pull a particular note out of the air. In that same way, I can pick up any accent I am required to.

The Royal Academy was not a very good training school for young actors, because it was run along rather commercial lines. Aside from myself, and my fellow scholarship holder, everybody paid fees. If people didn't have a certain amount of money, they couldn't go there. The Royal Academy had to maintain a much larger number of students than they could ever expect to have consistent work as actors. A high percentage of those people who went through the Royal Academy in my time never worked professionally at all. Only a small minority of them ever had consistent employment. That meant a lot of time was wasted. For example, a great number of the young ladies who were sent there were not sent with any serious intention that they would become professional actresses. They came from families of independent means and were going to be presented at court and marry junior noblemen, and things of that kind. They were using the Royal

Academy as a finishing school. As well, there was a great disproportion between the sexes. In the time I was there, there were about four girls to every boy. This was at a time when the large majority of characters in plays, films, and radio dramas were male. It was paradise for me. But the Royal Academy was not a very helpful training ground; many of the teachers were just hard-up older actors who couldn't think of anything else to do. But there were one or two who were very good.

In particular, I was attracted to the classes given by Alice Gachet, a French lady who had been with the company of the Comédie-Française in Paris. It was she who had trained the great actor Charles Laughton, who had first drawn my attention to the Royal Academy. He, when he had been at the Academy, had been in her French class and had blossomed to such an extent that at the height of his fame—not long after he won the Oscar— he went to France and played in French with the company at the Comédie- Française, and slew them! So I thought, "I must get into Alice Gachet's class and work in French." But of course, I didn't know any French! So I started to go, in whatever time I could steal—I always seemed to have had a kind of 23-hour-a-day schedule—to evening classes in order to learn enough French to get me through the rehearsals with Madame Gachet the follow- ing day. These evening classes were given by the LCC—the London County Council—and were elementary lessons in French meant for so-called deserv- ing students. I represented myself as deserving, and I still can remember some of the lines from a character I played called Albert, in a French play, the title of which loosely translates into *Love's Lunacies*. I recall precisely the entire final speech from that play, which I learned way back in 1935 as a student. I felt that was all very beneficial. It certainly was when I got to Canada many years later and started to actually work in French.

Another lady I enjoyed working with a great deal was an older actress who had kept working with some distinction. She was a Shakespearean actress and had been with the famous Benson Shakespeare Company. She did various Shakespeare productions, and the first time I played in one of Shakespeare's plays was in a class of hers, in which I played the pompous and self-satisfied Malvolio in *Twelfth Night*. It was my first part at the Academy. I, of course, had very much admired Charles Laughton, and so I modeled my performance rather too much on how Charles Laughton might have played Malvolio. That was, I should think, not a very impres- sive performance, but it was a memorable occasion. And she—Dorothy Green her name was, though we all called her Greeny—was a marvelously friendly and motherly teacher, and a very fine actress, too. I did work with her in a play in London some years after I had graduated.

However, many of the other teachers were rather pedestrian. One was an older lady who wasn't any kind of a teacher at all. All she did was sit at the back of the theatre and periodically just shout out, "Can't hear, dear! Can't hear, dear!" So to wind her up, I one day said, in a very low tone of voice, "Of course you can hear, you silly old cow." Well, she heard that all right!

While I was a student, I did play Romeo in *Romeo and Juliet*, and Angelo, the leading character of Shakespeare's *Measure for Measure*. We had a fair ration of Shakespeare, I will say that in favor of the Royal Academy. One of the few scripts I have kept to this day is the First World War play *Journey's End*, which we did as students. It's an all male play about a bunch of fellows who are in the front line of one of the battlefields of the war, and it was regarded as being one of the most properly fulfilled dramatic reconstructions of what life was like in the trenches.

My last part as a student was my best. I was chosen by Dorothy Green to play the king in her full-length production of Shakespeare's *Henry V*, which was presented to honor the Coronation of King George VI and Queen Elizabeth, who attended as Patrons of the Royal Academy.

My very first paid job as an actor was while I was still a student, in my last year. One of our teachers was directing a play at a theatre, which unfortunately no longer exists, called the People's Palace which was in the Mile End Road in the East End. The play was called *If I Were King*, and it was a romantic historical melodrama about the life of François Villon, the medieval French poet. It was very old-fashioned, even by the standards of 1936, but it was thought to be a suitable offering for this theatre which was intended to attract audiences from the working classes, as it were. This was a sizeable theatre and could therefore sell its seats fairly cheaply. This chap who was directing the piece thought that I had some promise, and so he offered me a tiny part as the French Herald, with the additional responsibility of understudying the leading part of François Villon, the sizeable romantic hero. I was paid some pittance of about £2 a week for this dual job of playing the small part of Mountjoy and understudying the lead. With the kind of good luck which so often seems to have attended me, I got to play the leading part. Thankfully, I had learned it very conscientiously. The leading man got the flu and missed a couple of performances towards the end of our run, and so I was on, playing this leading role. I managed to rustle up several of my fellow students to come and see me because I wanted to show off my first professional job. I'll always remember I had to make an entrance in the last act on a white horse. I'd never even sat on a horse before. Mercifully the horse was fairly well behaved and reasonably well trained, so I managed to do it without too much embarrassment.

The great Bernard Shaw was one of the persons most stimulating to us while we were students. Shaw was on our governing council, and would come (unlike so many others of our council whom we never saw) to see performances we gave, and in some cases see our rehearsals. One time we were doing a production of his play *Androcles and the Lion*. I was lucky enough to be playing the lion. He came to one of our rehearsals, and this was the first time I had actually been in contact with him. In his exquisitely cut tweed suit, he lay on his back on the floor and waved his arms and legs back and forth in the air to show me how I was to behave as the lion, when—as he said—"he wants his tummy tickled." He was just so wonderfully friendly to us, and encouraging, and treated us all with exquisite courtesy. He called us all Mr. This and Miss That—me, a snotty-nosed kid, being called Mr. Morse by Bernard Shaw. The result was that we didn't for a moment regard him as one of the most influential and famous people in the world, which he was, of course. We regarded him as this cheerful and extremely polite old chap who was, as it were, on our side. When I had been at the Royal Academy for a couple of terms, and there were just a few of us who were desperately dedicated to the idea of being professional actors, there was an atmosphere of considerable disquiet as to the quality of the training we were getting. So we formed a student council and I was elected one of the chairpersons.

We decided, as the student council, that we had to inform the governing council about how we felt the standard of tuition at the Royal Academy could be improved. We came up with various single sentence ideas, like "Reduce the number of students," which was very important—there were far too many students. When I joined RADA there were a total of nearly a hundred students joining at the same time, which brought the total of students to over three hundred. It was far, far too many for any intensity of tuition to be applied. We thought, "We must get an ally on the council to help us and support us." The logical choice was Bernard Shaw. We got in touch with his secretary, and arranged an appointment to go and see him at Whitehall Court. On the appointed day and at the appointed time, my fellow chairperson and I were ushered in, sat down with the great man and babbled on about our concerns. The Royal Academy's shortcomings were mostly caused, we felt, by finance. In order to keep going they had to keep fees at a certain level, and also take in more students than they ought to have done, simply to balance the books. We realized that, and I think Shaw realized that. He knew a great deal about the place and its workings, probably more than our principal.

Having listened patiently to our burbling, Shaw then said, "Well, now, what you need is a manifesto." We looked as comprehending as we could—I had no idea what he meant—a *manifesto*? Seeing that we didn't know what he was saying, he said, "You need to list in a very simple way, sentence by sentence, the various reforms that you think necessary." He got out one of his pads of green paper. (Shaw suffered from a form of intense headache, almost like a migraine, periodically throughout his life, and in order to minimize the pain from this headache he'd been advised that it would make eye strain less intense if he used green scribble paper.) He took one of these pads and wrote briefly on a couple of sheets the subject headings that we had mentioned as needing improvement. He said, "Now put that all together and present it to your principal, who will no doubt present it to us, the council, at our next meeting, and you may perhaps be required to be present to explain yourselves." So we said, "Yes, sir. Yes, thank you very much." And we went back to the Royal Academy with our bits of green scribble paper, and had one of our chums who was able to work a typewriter type it all up for us to present it to the principal. And then, having got it all copied, we threw the bits of green scribble paper away! "What?" I hear you cry. "Throwing away handwritten notes made by the man then probably regarded as the greatest writer on Earth?" Yes, because we didn't think of him in terms of being an international celebrity. He was this kindly, exquisitely courteous old gentleman, who had chosen to give us his advice and his help. It was the greatest possible compliment. And so—what would and should have been—greatly treasured pieces of memorabilia were lost. However, we did present our manifesto to the principal, and indeed it was presented to the council at their next meeting, and we were instructed to be present.

Our petition was read out and circulated among the council, who all hummed and hawed and tutted and said various more or less unhelpful kinds of things. Discussion went around the table until it got to Shaw, sitting at the far end. He'd given no hint at all that he'd had a hand in the preparation of this petition. Talk about a Shavian situation! When it got to his turn, looking at our manifesto, which he himself had more or less written, he said, "I think these young people have shown quite admirable common sense and constructive interest in the Royal Academy by the manifesto they have presented here. Many of their suggestions on a number of subjects will bear investigation and require urgent attention." He went on like this, supporting the various things that we proposed. Indeed, it did have some effect.

There was a beautiful girl whom I was very fond of named Kathleen Laurie, and she was probably the most gifted of the girl students of my time. She was half Scottish and half Spanish, and the combination of those two strains in her blood made her not only extraordinarily beautiful, but also very interesting temperamentally. In our final performance, the graduating performance—the equivalent of what I had first seen at the Academy—I was lucky enough to be playing opposite her in a scene from a very well known play of the thirties called *The Barretts of Wimpole Street*. It was all about the courtship of Robert Browning, the poet, and Elizabeth Barrett, who became his wife—Elizabeth Barrett Browning. I knew that this was a very crucial performance, because the medals for the Royal Academy were always awarded for that public final show.

I was very sure that the gold medal was not going to come to me, because Kenneth Barnes, our principal, as well as being a rampant snob, was violently disapproving of me because I had been the ringleader of the activities of the student council, which had been more than a little embarrassing to him, as they rightly should have been. So I knew I was not going to get that award. But I was equally determined that my loved one, Kathleen, was. So, in defiance of the person who was supposed to be directing this courtship scene, I arranged the furniture in such a way that I played a great deal of it with my back to the audience, while Kathleen got to play most of the scene facing them. We had a public performance at the Aldwych Theatre that year and I was right—Kathleen got the Gold medal, which is the top award for any student graduating from the Royal Academy.

I got the honors diploma, a secondary award. But I also did get another prize—the BBC's Radio Prize. It came out of a part of our course which was devoted to studying microphone technique in order to be able to perform on the radio. We used to go one afternoon a week for our last term to the BBC headquarters, to be given classes by various BBC producers— among them Val Gielgud (the elder brother of the great actor John Gielgud), who was the BBC's director of drama. I was given the award by the BBC as being the most promising student in radio drama, which was very useful because it led to my starting to do paid professional jobs for the BBC on radio. Indeed, I ended up working a great deal for Val. But Kathleen, who won the gold medal, never worked professionally at all. Not long after she left the Royal Academy and went back to her home in Scotland, she met and subsequently married a wealthy ship owner. I remember her coming to see me in a tour which led me to play in Edinburgh, a few years later. She was now a happily married lady, and not really regretting having given up our trade. I thought it was a great waste.

Also at RADA I fell in love with another student named Patricia Hicks, a beautiful girl who lived in Epping, to the east of London. I was so attached to her that I used to ride my bicycle out there, a distance of some eighteen miles, in order to be able to spend time with her. Very often we would walk her dog, a lovely big Alsatian called Tigger, in Epping Forest. I've kept in touch with her. She married a delightful actor called Jack Watling, who became the chairman of the Royal Theatrical Fund, one of our principal theatrical charities. In October 1998, I went to a function of the Royal Theatrical Fund. Patricia was there with her husband. She was looking as beautiful as ever, and they brought with them two of their granddaughters, to whom Pat introduced me as her first boyfriend! We told the two young girls about how we used to walk Tigger in Epping Forest sixty-two years before.

There is another lady named Doreen Oscar who was a fellow student of mine at the Royal Academy. She now lives in the country, in the Cotswolds, to the northwest of London. We kept in touch on the telephone and by letters and cards, and whenever she got down to London. We have been friends for more than 70 years. She came to the Royal Academy at the same time I did, and we've remained friends all that time. She was never a girlfriend, in that sense, but she's been a marvelously loyal and loving girl-*friend* all that time. I'm godfather to one of her daughters, named Juliet, who is a writer of children's books. When I was a student at the Royal Academy, and falling in love with a new girl every five minutes, she was the one who listened patiently to my enthusing about whoever the latest passion of my life was. She loves to remind me of how I was talking to her once on one of the landings of the staircase at the Royal Academy, about this latest girl whom I was crazy about, and I was saying, "Oh yes, this girl, she's part Egyptian you know, and she has these beautiful green eyes, and the most wonderful bronze hair, and the most gorgeous.... Oh! Who's *that*?" And in the same breath I'd caught sight of another girl whom I was going to fall in love with five minutes later. She loves to remind me of that, and does a wonderful impression of it. She is still a very valued girl*friend.* We are the closest and most loving of friends.

There were umpteen other girlfriends—in the other sense—whom I was crazy about for ten minutes or two weeks or whatever. It was a great novelty to me to be thrown in at the Royal Academy with these beautiful, gently bred and expensively educated, and above all sweet-smelling girls. So many of the girls I knew in our part of the world, because they weren't able to bathe any more often than I was, didn't smell that sweet. Well, here at the Royal Academy, suddenly I was introduced to a whole new species of females.

Here I have to make a confession to you. My first name was not Barry. That was not the name my mother and dad gave me. I came by my first name because one of the greatest popular heroes during the First World War in England was the military field marshal Lord Kitchener. He's the fellow who used to appear in those old posters saying, "Your country needs You!" Well, Lord Kitchener was lost in the sinking of a cruiser during the war. A great many working class mothers, out of patriotic sentimentality, gave their babies one of Kitchener's names. Kitchener's two names happened to be Herbert Horatio. We couldn't afford a second name, so thank God my mother selected Herbert. I was known, in fact, for the early part of my life, as Herbert Morse. It was a group of girls at the Royal Academy who decided I needed a name which would look more impressive on "the bill," and Barry Morse was born.

Although my time at the Royal Academy occupied two years, our course seemed to be over far too quickly. Groups of us became firm friends, and they were memorably happy times. And when the time came to leave the Royal Academy it was a great wrench to be suddenly thrown out into the real world.

4

"A Sharp Twist"

IN THE 1930S, GRADUATING STUDENTS from the Royal Academy of Dramatic Art would often have the good luck of having various theatre managements come and see their performances. This was because the people who ran the various repertory theatres all over the country needed to recruit gifted young students, partly because they came cheap.

By this time the movies had started to make inroads into the habits of theatregoers (television had not yet come into existence). The word repertory is a misnomer; because a true repertory theatre is an organization like the Royal Shakespeare Company, or the National Theatre in London, which has a repertory of plays—a half-dozen perhaps—which are played on an occasional basis. But these other so-called repertory theatres existed on the basis of being able to play a new play every week, in most instances, or a new play every two weeks where there was a larger audience, and in some rare cases there would be a new play every three weeks.

There were scores of such theatres all over the country, ranging from the major ones in the bigger cities like Glasgow, Liverpool, Manchester, and Birmingham to smaller cities like Bradford and Leeds. They would have a weekly rep, that is to say, a new play each week, with another play being rehearsed during the daytime. Even smaller companies existed where two new plays were presented every week, one on Monday-Tuesday-Wednesday, and a second play Thursday-Friday-Saturday, while yet another play would be rehearsed during the day. So the range of the repertory theatres was considerable. In all but the largest cities the repertory companies would present two performances every evening—usually at 6:30 p.m. and 9:00 p.m. Matinees were relatively rare, since potential audiences were mostly working people with no free time during the day.

When we were in our finals term at RADA we had several of the managements who ran these small repertory theatres come and see us. I realize now that we took those sorts of things for granted in those days, but I really was very lucky to have the offer of a job to go to even before I actually left the Royal Academy. My friend and fellow student, Don Manning Wilson, and I both were engaged by a chap called Arthur Brough. He was an actor/manager and ran companies in the seaside town of Folkestone in Kent, Leeds, and one in Bradford. Don went first to play briefly in Arthur Brough's theatre in Folkestone. Meanwhile, I was engaged to play in the company up in Bradford in the county of Yorkshire. I was joining an established company with a loyal audience. That was always a feature of the success of the repertory theatres.

As a result of attracting audiences on a regular weekly basis, repertory companies built-up a sort of fan loyalty for their local theatres. It was an extraordinary phenomenon which didn't last very long, a matter of 20 years or so between the wars. By the time the Second World War was over and the onrush of television had begun, the day of the weekly repertory theatre was virtually over. I fell pretty well into the middle of this and I was engaged to play "as cast." There was no question of being guaranteed this or that kind of part; it was entirely up to the director of the particular company that you played in. You would, if you were halfway good, get a great deal of loyalty from an audience who saw you playing different sorts of parts week after week. This repertory system—and I'd like to stress this because it isn't sufficiently understood or appreciated—was an invaluable and irreplaceable experience for actors serving their apprenticeship. It exposed you to that best of all professors of acting—the cash customer. I've always had the conviction—and still have it—that the best teacher of acting is the Warm Bum on the Cold Seat. He'll teach you more than any professor who ever lived.

No matter what highbrows and academics may say, the best means of an actor learning his job is to be in front of an audience. It's a similar kind of process to testing the acid or alkaline content of a liquid by dipping a litmus paper in it. You can very readily tell when you're on the stage whether or not the audience is understanding and appreciating what it is you're seeking to do. Are they still? Are they holding their breath at a moment of high tension in a play? Are they fidgeting, perhaps? Are they even, God forbid, giggling? Or if you're playing a comedy, are the laughs coming in the right places and at the right volume? All of those things can only be learned by being on a stage in front of the customers. Like any other form of public presentation, if you've got any sensitivity at all, you can assess the degree of effectiveness with which your offering is being greeted.

I've never forgotten the bliss of triumph that I experienced when I came on looking my best in my blazer and gray flannels, and was greeted by a round of applause because they recognized me and remembered me from last week and the week before. There were instances in some repertory theatres where an actor or actress had been in the company for as much as two years; therefore the audience had seen them playing as many as a hundred different parts. Those actors who had been there for that length of time were more popular than almost anybody on the screen because they were great local favorites and recognized in the streets and greeted wherever they went. So it was an extraordinary world, the repertory world.

Alas, there is no such system today. Most young people in the situation I was in some 70 years ago have no opportunity for serving their apprenticeship in that way. They may graduate from the Royal Academy of Dramatic Art having been carefully nurtured and painstakingly trained for two or three years, but they have no means of measuring the strengths they have as actors. There is no way in which they can consistently and repeatedly get themselves in front of a bunch of cash customers. All they can do is to hope that they get a small part in some touring company or one of the few repertory theatres that still exist. But the numbers of those have shrunken down to the extent that there are only six or seven repertory theatres in the whole of the UK. The changes have not been for the better.

The first thing I had to do in Bradford was to get myself somewhere to live. I'd never lived away from home before and so I did what most young actors did in those days, I sent off to an organization called the Actor's Church Union which was a Christian organization founded to serve the actor. One of the services they provided was a series of Digs Lists — lists of addresses where there were to be found that valuable and extinct species known as "the theatrical landlady." Having checked through the list and making a few possible choices as to where I might stay, I checked those addresses with the Stage Door man. The Stage Door man at any given theatre was always a very valuable source of information with regard to theatrical boardinghouses. One of the things to consider was that if you were working in repertory theatre you were going to have to spend a majority of your waking hours, and a good many of what ought to have been your sleeping hours, in the theatre. So accessibility and proximity was very important. You didn't want to have any kind of a journey to get back to your digs.

So, by fluke, really, more than anything else, I fetched up with some digs in a theatrical boardinghouse on Neal Street, a gloomy Victorian terraced house, blackened by decades of soot from the nearby factories. I managed to get these digs "full board"; that meant all the meals, for 25 shillings a week—less than half my salary—which was very good for that time. But, of course, it wasn't without its shortcomings. The boarding-house was run by Mrs. Chatburn, a fierce Yorkshire woman with a tribe of rather undisciplined children whom she kept in and around the kitchen. I had a room upstairs at the front. There was no loo indoors, but there was a washroom with a washbasin in it. The loo, as in most working class houses, was "out the back." This required a journey out through the kitchen and into the backyard, running the gamut of these riotous children who were almost always in the kitchen. They loved the idea of me going through the kitchen in order to get to the loo. They would all sing out, "Eh, we know where you're goin'" or, "'Es goin' ta 'ave a pee, isn't he!" in their impeccable Yorkshire accents. Mrs. Chatburn was a tough, resilient lady and she needed to be, in her situation.

I didn't see much of Mrs. Chatburn's husband because he was on the night shift at the nearby coal mine and would come back in the mornings. I always remember hearing one marvelous bit of dialogue between the couple. Mr. and Mrs. Chatburn would occasionally commune in their bedroom when he got off night duty before he went to bed, and I expected this was the nearest approach they had to a sex life. One morning when Mr. Chatburn came home from the night shift I was getting ready to go to the theatre. I heard Mrs. Chatburn shout up the stairs to her husband, "Eh 'oney, do ya want me body or should I put me corsets on?"

She was not, I have to say, a Cordon Bleu cook. Her food was pretty miserable and she served up what used to be called good plain cooking; well, it wasn't particularly good but was most certainly plain. There was one offering of which she was particularly proud—it was her specialty. With great relish, she said, "Now you come straight-on back Thursday night, 'cause Thursday night I'll be givin' me best dish, that's 'The Gratin.'" Well, I ought to have known that she had picked up this word somewhere, perhaps in a restaurant menu, and the dish was in fact cauliflower au gratin, which she pronounced "The Gray-tin."

The Gratin consisted of a few bits of chopped up cauliflower floating in a green mucous. The dish was an oleaginous *mess,* which I suppose she thought was some kind or other of a cheese sauce. It was altogether quite revolting. We actors were tyrannized in those days by our landladies, and this one was a rather fearsome character, so I managed to get it down the best I could. I thought, "Oh gosh, is that going to be the diet every Thursday? I must somehow find a way around this."

As this was in my early days with the company, I was just beginning to know my colleagues, and in this company there was a wonderful old character actor, who must have been well into his 70s, by the name of Walter Dibb. He had a kind of solemn magisterial air that made you think that he'd lived through and experienced everything life might have to offer. He had a very ponderous manner of address in the way of old actors of those days. I thought to myself, *That's a fellow who's been around a long time— not only in the world, but in our profession and he might be able to give me some advice about this.* Chatting away at rehearsal one day, he asked in his deep voice, "How're you getting along, laddie?" I said, "Well, I've got these digs up the road there, sir" (you always called senior actors "sir" in those days) "and it's convenient and quite cheap, but I've got great trouble with this dish that she serves up called 'The Gratin.'" He laughed and thought that was very funny. I said, "Do you think there's any way I can get out of eating it, because I can always buy some fish and chips or something if I'm hungry on a Thursday night." He replied, "Tell me this, laddie, do you have a fire in your room?" "Yes," I replied, "it's not exactly roaring, but it's the only kind of heating there is and it's usually kept on until I get back at the end of the evening." "Ah, good," he said. "There is a local publication, a so-called newspaper, bearing the name of *Telegraph and Argus.*" And indeed it was the principal local Bradford newspaper. He said, "Journalistically it is of no great quality, but the paper is of a very stout and absorbent nature. Buy yourself a copy of the *Telegraph and Argus*— it costs only a penny—prepare yourself with it and when the offending dish is presented, empty it swiftly into the *Telegraph and Argus*, wrap it carefully and thrust it quickly into the fire. It will then be consumed before the wretched woman comes to collect the dish."

The following Thursday I prepared myself by buying the newspaper and returned to my digs after the evening performance. Mrs. Chatburn came in with the mucilaginous mess, put it on the table and departed. Quick as a flash I was up with my fork and spoon and scraped it all into the *Telegraph and Argus*, nipped across the room and thrust it into the fire. But alas, like so many beginners, I was over-trained. I had moved just before she quite closed the door. As I was crouching there by the fire with this sizzling, steaming mess gurgling away on top of this not very ample fire, I looked up to see her standing at the half open door looking like an avenging angel. I thought, "*Oh, God!* This is it, she's going to throw me out on the street in the middle of the night!" But a most extraordinary thing happened. She looked down at me and then she looked back towards the kitchen where these unruly children of hers hung out. She shook her head regretfully and with a shrug and a sigh said, "Ey, I know—mine don't like it either."

Later on in my time at the Prince's Theatre, my good friend Don Manning Wilson came to join the same company in Bradford, so we ended up actually sharing digs together. We also shared an old wind-up portable gramophone on which we would play jazz records far into the night, much to the irritation of Mrs. Chatburn. Don also played the piano and had a particular fondness for playing the music of Fats Waller.

The pattern of work in the theatre was something like this: we would start to rehearse usually at 10:00 in the morning and we would rehearse until about 2:00, then break to have lunch and take care of what remained of our lives until 6:00. This time was also supposed to be devoted to learning our lines, because playing a different role each week involved a good deal of time in studying. I was very lucky, as I've been told, that I have blotting paper instead of brains in my head. I didn't have to toil away very much learning the lines. It seemed that out of the process of rehearsing I would reasonably quickly be able to pick up whatever my lines were. But not everybody did. Some actors had to battle their brains out, sit up half the night every night learning anything that was a substantially sized part.

Then would come the evening when we were presenting the performances. Let's say we're doing *Charley's Aunt*. We rehearsed the piece last week and are now playing it and we've been rehearsing another play, say *Getting Gertie's Garter*, during the day. We're coming into the theatre usually at about 6:00 or a little before for the evening performances—twice nightly, do you mind! The plays, if they were a bit more than two hours in length, weren't too worrisome, but if they were much more, then cuts would have to be made. Obviously, if you were doing one performance at 6:30 and another at 9:00 p.m. (which was the usual time for the second house), you couldn't have a play that played two and a half or three hours, otherwise the second audience waiting outside—perhaps in the pouring rain— would very quickly go away. So you had to keep an eye on the clock. That was very much the province of the director. Sometimes when the first performances began on a Monday, if he hadn't timed the play very carefully, we might discover after we played the first act and a bit of the second act, that we were in peril of overrunning and keeping our second house audience standing out in the street. The director would then have to put into place some first aid cuts on the run, as it were. Sometimes, you would see him crouched in the fireplace or just outside the set in the wings miming instructions to cut this, or go straight to that, as a means of making these cuts.

As a beginner in Bradford, I remember being greeted like this by the director, Oswald Dale Roberts. I went off after one scene and was looking forward to a later scene where I had a rather touching speech about my mother, and he was just outside the door of the set as I came off. He said,

"Look, when you go back on, cut all that about your mother and go straight to the point where you attack the other fellow." I thought, "Oh, God, how do I do that?" And in no time at all I was on again and had to make this cut on the run, much to the bafflement of my colleagues, who were waiting for me to talk about my mother. That sort of thing went on pretty much as a matter of course.

This director was an old hand. He had been an actor in Henry Irving's company, so he'd been in our profession at that point for well over 30 years. A very sweet and cultured old chap he was, and I suspect he didn't altogether enjoy this run-of-the-mill job as a so-called director of a twice nightly repertory theatre. But he did it sensitively and gently and didn't bully us kids too much or become too impatient.

There were other kinds of directors who were much more slick and swift-moving. The other Arthur Brough company which I played in on occasion was over in Leeds and we would be switched back and forth between the companies if the size of the cast of a particular play required more young men in one than in the other. We would travel there on the bus, and in this other company there was a director who was an extraordinary character. His name was Freddie Tripp and he had become the "wizard" of the twice nightly repertory directors. He could stage a play not by long disquisitions about subtleties of character or situation, but purely by moving people about on the stage. He had an extraordinary instinct for knowing who ought to be stage center at a given moment because they were about to have an important speech or piece of action to carry out, and who should be downstage, or who should be standing up or sitting down. He managed this, the movement part of the play, almost entirely without speaking. Freddie was able to move people about purely by gesture. You had to keep half an eye on him, like an orchestra player does on a conductor, because he'd be standing in the orchestra pit with his script in his hand, and he'd be waving and pointing to us. His movements had the meaning of, "You move over there, yes, now you sit down." You can imagine the gestures he was making. "Now you get up, cross over to her there…." But he wouldn't say *any* of that! He would be semaphoring it, signaling it to us.

I'll always remember the first time I worked with him in Leeds, in a play in which I had the relatively small part of a police detective (perhaps a foreshadowing of things to come!). He was supposed to be a plainclothes London policeman who went to a dockside café to arrest somebody. The character's name, I think, was Soapy Marx. I was a beginner, of course, very earnest about everything I had to do and determined that I was going to make the most of this small part. Virtually all I had to do was cross over to this guy in this café, the villain, and say "Are you Soapy Marx?" And he said, "Yeah, what about it?" Then I would come back with something like "Were you at the dock gates at Deptford at 3:30 in the afternoon on Wednesday, September the twenty-eighth?" To which he replied, "Well, I don't know," and I growled, "Yes you do.... All right, come on, I'm taking you down to the station."

I was looking forward to making the most of this part, and so, when it came time for my entrance, I opened the door and looked around at the various characters seated in this establishment. But not a second had gone by when Freddie Tripp shouted, "Where's that boy?" To which I replied, "Oh, here, sir, here, here." He said, "Well, come on, son, you're off!" "You're off" meant that you had failed to make your entrance at the appropriate moment, in other words, you weren't on. So I felt, "Oh, gosh, he's spoken! He usually doesn't speak." I thought I should explain why I was looking around. So I said, "Excuse me sir, good morning, I know I haven't worked for you before but I'm playing this character, the police detective, and he's coming into this café, isn't he, to look for and arrest this character called Soapy Marx." He looked at me, "Well, yes-yes, what-what," he said. So I said, "Well he's never been in this place before, has he, so it does seem to me to be sort of logical if, when he first enters, he takes a second or two to look around and see if the chap whom he's looking for is actually here, so I thought there might be—if you'll excuse me, sir—I thought there might be just a bit of a pause...." He just roared, "*A pause?* Christ almighty, son, we *can't* have pauses, this is twice nightly!"

In all, I spent about four years in ten different repertory companies, and by the end of that time—because some of the companies I had been in had presented two new plays a week—I had played well over 200 different characters. These were an extraordinary range of parts, from the manservant Brasset in *Charley's Aunt*, to parts in *Jane Eyre*, to the lead in *Wuthering Heights*; classics, farce, high tragedy. And I wasn't yet 21 years old! Well, there are many actors in today's world who don't play that many parts in the whole of their lives. That's how lucky I was to have had my grounding in that way.

One of my first notices was at the Prince's Theatre in Bradford, after my friend Don Manning Wilson had come to join the company. We were playing in some pop piece of the day in relatively small parts. The productions would get reviews in the local newspaper, but they were of no real quality; we grew used to this and didn't really take much notice of them. In the reviews they would say that those who were playing the leading parts were "outstanding" or "brilliant," those who were playing the medium size parts were "adequate," and then the people who were playing the small parts were just "others in the cast were."

Evidently the person who wrote the notice for this particular production thought he would expand himself a bit. So, after having praised the people who played the leading parts, then mentioning the people who were playing the medium size parts, he finished up his review by saying, "Mr. Barry Morse and Mr. Donald Manning Wilson took their author's small parts and gave them a sharp twist."

Visiting our theatre in Bradford one day was another manager of repertory companies, Harry Hanson, who was a considerable character and rather more prominent in the repertory theatre world than our manager, Arthur Brough, was. Harry Hanson ran a number of different companies all over the country. We all hoped and imagined that he might be on the lookout for promising talent. Somehow or other I got in touch with his office and arranged that after he'd been to see a performance at our theatre I should have an appointment to meet with him. That was the pattern among repertory actors to avoid getting stuck in one place for too long. Actors would tend to move on after a few months, hopefully to a better company, but particularly, of course, to one with a better salary. I should mention at this point that actors working in the provinces never had agents, so you had to do all your business transactions yourself.

Harry Hanson had been a dancer, but now was pink and plump and amiable; a quite overt homosexual who wore a succession of improbable silver-haired toupees, which he imagined were distinguished looking. He would change them, I came to learn, over the weeks, to indicate that his hair was growing. It was quite ridiculous and not at all convincing.

Mr. Hanson frankly said that he thought I was very promising and would I like to go and work for him. First of all, I asked, "Where?" He replied, "I'd like you to come first to the Court Players at Peterborough, but after a short season there, I'd like you to go on to my principal company at Nottingham at the Theatre Royal." I asked, "How much would I be paid?" He replied, "What would you say to five?" So I said, "Oh, well...." Quickly, he interjected, "That's for Peterborough, because that's a smaller theatre, but when you go to Nottingham you will be the juvenile lead and we will pay you eight." Well! My word, that *was* a big jump from three pounds, ten. I hope with not too much undue haste, I said, "Sure!"

As we were then coming up to the Christmas holidays, I arranged with him that I would start work in Peterborough on January 3, 1939. This date would prove to be very crucial, as I would meet that day the person who was to have a larger influence on my life than anyone else.

5

"There's No Shame in It"

PETERBOROUGH IS NOT FAR FROM Cambridge and about 80 miles from London. At that time, I knew nothing about the city; I'd never set foot there, and I didn't know anyone in the company there. In those days you could always keep track of where people were working through the pages of our trade newspaper called *The Stage*. They would print lists in this paper of who was working at what theatre all across the UK. So one would peruse these lists to see if perhaps you knew someone who was working in another theatre, or whether one of your former fellow students from the Royal Academy was playing in this place or that, or even what people were working at the same theatre after many months or sometimes years.

My eye had fallen on a name that I immediately assumed, without any question, was that of a male. No distinction as to gender was made in these lists of actors and actresses, so when my eye came to the name Sydney Sturgess I immediately and automatically assumed that this was a fellow. You know how you start to form a visual image when you see a name more than once—and I had formed a mental image that this Sydney Sturgess fellow was rather my type; someone who would seek to play, and did perhaps play, many of the same sort of parts. I used to say that the sort of parts that were right up my alley were the parts where you wore an open necked shirt, well-cut riding breeches and riding boots, and stood on a balcony, wearing a pith helmet, defying the natives. So, when I knew I was going to Peterborough, in the intervening couple of weeks I looked at a copy of *The Stage* to see who was already in the company there. I thought, *"Oh, there's going to be a bit of competition between me and that Sydney Sturgess fellow as to who will play the pith helmet parts."*

On January 3, 1939, I traveled to Peterborough, when there was a quite

51

heavy fall of snow. There wasn't often much snow in England, but this particular year there was quite a lot. I managed to get myself digs not far from the theatre and went through the snow to arrive there in good time for the first rehearsal at 10:00 in the morning. The stage manager had given me a script and the youngish director, a fellow by the name of Richard Burnett, started by introducing me to Malcolm Russell, the company's leading man, and Keith Lorraine, a wonderful character actor/comedian. Then he announced, "This is *Miss* Sydney Sturgess." And there stood this beautiful flower-like girl wearing Wellington boots, I recall, because of the snow. In my confusion and complete surprise, I dropped my script, my pencil, and my raincoat!

Although we rehearsed every day and had two performances every night, I often would go to see movies in the afternoon. So, a few days later I said to Sydney, "Look, I'm thinking of going to see a film at the cinema today, do you think you'd like to see that?" And she said, "Oh, well, yes, I suppose—yes, thank you." So I said, "Well, I'll see you there then." I guess I didn't want to ask where she was living. In any event, we met at the cinema and saw the film. I realized that I was falling very much in love with this beautiful girl. Unfortunately, I learned very soon that she was in fact engaged to a young doctor named Harold Vyse, whom she had known for a couple of years. Sydney was honest enough to tell me the truth straightaway.

At this point I was just 20 years old and I didn't at first tell Sydney this because I sensed somehow that she might be a bit older, as indeed she turned out to be. She was some three and a quarter years older than me. Sydney and I would go to dances after the second performance, but she obviously had some conflicts in her heart and mind. Nevertheless, I could tell that things weren't going too badly by the fact that she didn't altogether rebuff me. Quite soon, things got to the point where she wanted to meet up with Harold, who was living and working in London, to let him know that this engagement wasn't going to hold good anymore. Sydney and I were becoming very, very deeply in love with each other.

She had digs at 44 Lincoln Road and this is where most of our so-called courting was done. Her landlady was Mrs. Lambert, an awfully nice woman. She was very understanding and didn't mind my visiting Sydney. There was a sitting room on the ground floor and that was where our courtship took place. Mrs. Lambert was very open and kindly in allowing me to visit. Landladies in those days would often forbid a young female to entertain a male visitor late in the evening as Sydney frequently did. We would go back together after the performance at night. Things progressed as the weeks went by, but I didn't have a penny to my name, as most of whatever spare money I'd ever put together had gone into providing myself with a sufficiently variegated wardrobe of clothes, a very important part of the equipment of a young actor in repertory. So I had no capital, no savings, and Sydney knew this. Nevertheless, I realized that no matter the situation, this was the girl for me. It's almost inconceivable now thinking back on it, that I should have had the ambition and the desire, as well as the determination, to marry this girl, but even more, that she should have had the trust and openheartedness to consider marrying me in the state that we were in economically, without a penny in the world.

I knew that I must do something, declare my intentions and all the rest of it. In no time at all, we managed to go down to London for the weekend so I could meet her mother and Sydney could meet my parents. Also, most importantly, so Sydney could make an honest break from her engagement to Harold. All of this happened on a succession of weekends in the month of February. At the weekends we could get a special railway return ticket from Peterborough to London and the journey only took short of two hours each way. My parents were delighted to meet Sydney and thought her a wonderful young woman. We had arranged, having consulted everybody, to announce our engagement on Sunday, March 5 (Sydney's birthday), in order that we could be married three weeks later on March 26, 1939.

I arranged with the management of the theatre that I would get a five pound advance on my upcoming salary. So we were married on that advance—that's all we had in the world. We didn't think there was anything perilous or uncertain at all, we were in love! The local minister from St. Barnabas Church, Hubert Bland, was very friendly and arranged for us to get a special license to get married in his church with only three weeks of notice. In order to do this, however, I had to declare myself as being resident in his parish. My own digs weren't actually within that area so he kindly allowed me to register my address as his vicarage; I'll always remember him thankfully for that.

The newspaper reported that these two young people from the local repertory theatre were going to be married and there was great excitement in the town. The question arose as to whether we could, or should, have any kind of a honeymoon. Mrs. Lambert, Sydney's landlady, had a relative who was a farmer's wife in the village of Bradnop in Staffordshire. She said, "You can go and stay on the farm, they have guests once in a while on a 'bed and breakfast' sort of basis, so why don't we arrange for you to go there."

Our wedding day was approaching and there arose the question of wedding presents. People said, "What would you like for wedding presents?"

After our wedding service at Saint Barnabus Church, Peterborough, on Sunday, March 26, 1939. Sydney is in a lovely leaf-green dress with fur lapels, and I am in a suit, which I had specially made for the occasion (and it cost more than I had ever spent on any item of clothing before this time!).

Well, we weren't going to have any kind of home, so there wasn't any point in people giving us the sort of presents that people sometimes do, silverware, cut glass, or stuff like that. So we let it be known that money would be the most useful thing! So we had quite a good stock of money by the time our wedding presents were counted. We did have three actual presents also, in the form of traveling clocks! People assumed, since we would be traveling around as actors and wouldn't have any permanent home, as we'd be living in digs, that a traveling clock would be a useful gift.

In order to fulfill the terms of this special marriage license, I needed to produce a certificate signed by my parents to certify that they were willing that I should get married, because I was underage in legal terms, not yet 21 years old. My mother and father were happy to sign the papers, but we hadn't actually broken the news to Sydney's family. By this time, I had confessed our age difference to Sydney, but she didn't want to bother her family with the news, as they were already apprehensive at the prospect of their lovely girl having broken her engagement to a perfectly respectable doctor in order to marry a ragamuffin actor! We went to the church on March 26, I in a new suit and Sydney in a beautiful leaf-green dress. It was a lovely bright day and because there had been so much publicity in the local newspaper, the church was packed with local citizens who were touched by this romance between two young actors. It was a wonderfully joyous time, and so, less than three months after our introduction, we were married!

After the ceremony we repaired to the vestry to sign the register and complete the formalities. Our friend Reverend Bland was getting the necessary signatures onto the register, but first he said, "Do you have the form?" Of course, I knew what he meant—the form of consent from my parents. Whereupon all of Sydney's relatives clustered around, "What form, what form?" And so, it came out right there in the vestry after the ceremony had been carried out and we'd been declared man and wife, that I was three and a bit years younger than Sydney.

Following the honeymoon, we traveled to Nottingham, where we had already arranged rather superior digs with a Mrs. Robinson, who turned out to be kind and competent, and rather accomplished as a cook. Her house was located at number 6 Hampden Street and we had two rooms, a sitting room/dining room on the ground floor, and a bedroom on the first floor in the back overlooking the garden.

On days off, several of us from the company would go down to the Trent River, which flows through Nottingham, and either go rowing in boats or swimming. Sydney was always a very keen and a very good swimmer. We went in the afternoons and we noticed after a while that there were several young fellows down there who were obviously miners who worked down in one of the nearby coal mines. One of our fellow players in the company was Peter Cushing, who became very well known as an actor and remained a friend of ours for the rest of his life. He was a very keen swimmer, athlete and overall outdoorsman. One fine day after we met these miners, one of them said to us, "Now 'ow's it you folks get down 'ere to swim then in the afternoon, on a weekday, don't you 'ave any jobs, or do ya just 'ave funny hours like us?" Peter Cushing answered, with great pride, "Oh, well we're actors in the Court Players company at the Theatre Royal." The young miner looked back at us pityingly, "Ah, oh, well. There's no shame in it, is there?"

During this very early part of our marriage Sydney and I had our first spat, our first real row. I can't remember what it was about, but we were upstairs in our bedroom preparing to go to bed and we squabbled about something or other and I said, making a sort of theatrical gesture, "Well, I'm not going to go on with this anymore. I'm going to go out and have a walk." Sydney said, "No, you're not, you're not going to go out." I replied, "Yes I am," to which she replied by going to the door of our bedroom, which happened to have a key inside it, which we'd never used. She locked the door, took the key, and threw it out of the window! I said, "Well, now you've done it, haven't you. What are we going to do?" She then realized that the impulse had rather carried her away and she quickly said, "Well, we'll sort it out in the morning." Well, in the morning Mrs. Robinson came to call us as she customarily did when our breakfast was ready and she knocked on the door cheerfully, "Good morning Mr. and Mrs. Morse, your breakfast is ready." I'm gesturing furiously to Sydney, "You've got to sort this out." So Sydney goes to the door and through the locked door, she says, "Mrs. Robinson, I wonder if you could do something for us. The key, the key to this door here … has somehow fallen out of the window." The window was on the other side of the room so I don't know what the poor lady thought. Sydney continued, "So it must be just down in the garden there, do you think you could go and get it for us?" There was a pause. "Oh, all right," said Mrs. Robinson. Obviously the penny began to drop and she started to understand what had in fact happened. After a few minutes of scrumping around in the garden, with us looking out of the window encouraging her, she managed to find our bedroom key and came to release us.

It was becoming more and more evident in the weeks and months leading up to September of 1939 that there was going to be a war. Adolf Hitler and the Nazis were getting dangerously out of hand. It had been announced in England that there was going to be some form of conscription which would begin after people turned 21. Then the war itself began on Sunday the third of September. All theatres were closed and it was expected that there would be near-immediate air raids from the Germans.

One of the young actresses in the Nottingham company was a close friend of Sydney's called Marjorie Somerville. They had shared digs together during the previous season. As it turned out, the third of September also happened to be the birthday of Marjorie. We had previously arranged to take her out for dinner on her birthday and had made a reservation at a grand pub where they had a good restaurant. We had all heard earlier that day the announcement by Prime Minister Neville Chamberlain that time had run out on the ultimatum they had given to Hitler. No response had been made, and subsequently Britain was at war with Germany. We were in the restaurant for dinner, all of us very much horrified and obsessed with the idea that this Second World War really had begun. We all knew enough about the First World War to know what a horrific experience any war was going to be. To our amazement, we could hear jollifications going on in the bars of the pub down below us on the ground floor: people singing and dancing as if it were their birthday or New Year's Eve! I was so appalled by this. Coming downstairs after our dinner, we were just about to see Marjorie home and then get home ourselves, when there were a bunch of young people, having had a few drinks, singing and dancing in the vestibule of this restaurant/pub. And I said, "How can you be rejoicing? Don't you understand what a horrific thing this is that's now begun?"

I harangued them quite pointlessly, of course, because what they perceived the war meant, in their innocence and ignorance, was that they would be relieved from their dreary, boring, unrewarding jobs in this or that factory or this or that shop and be delivered into a life of unknown adventure.

6

"Flukes and Coincidences"

WE MOPED OUR WAY HOME and then for a couple of days we hung around in Nottingham trying to find out what the future was going to be. Would we continue to have employment now that the theatres had all been closed?

I realized that I was inevitably going to be called up for military service of some kind or another. It was something we had talked about ever since the legislation about conscription had been announced, prior to the start of the war. Sydney and I talked, and I said, "Look, I think the best thing for me to do is to volunteer. Not wait until I'm called up, because if I volunteer, I shall then have at least some degree of choice of what I do and where I go." Sydney agreed that this would be the best thing under the circumstances, so I decided to go to a naval recruiting station. I suppose I was influenced by the fact that Sydney's brother was at that time a cadet in the Royal Naval College and was about to become a regular Royal Naval Officer. In a romantic or melodramatic way I visualized myself as standing on the deck and perhaps growing a beard. So I went to see the recruiting officer, who said, "We'll have to give you a medical examination."

At the beginning of the war, medical exams were a good deal stricter, closer, and more careful than probably they became later on. There had been a couple of cases even in the first days of the war of chaps who'd volunteered and been taken on and then been discovered after their first day of drill to have, in particular, TB—tuberculosis. Therefore, the degree of vigilance was still pretty high because of these scares they'd had. I stripped down for the exam and the surgeon commander went over me with the stethoscope and he said to me, "Have you ever had an X-ray?" I replied, "No," and in fact wasn't even sure what he meant. I vaguely knew what an X-ray was but I had certainly never had one; nobody had X-rays in those days unless for some specific or known ailment or mishap. He said, "I'll give you this chit and you go down to the local hospital, get an X-ray there, and they'll send the results back to me. Then you come in again and see me again on Friday." So, I did just that. I had the chest X-ray shot and reported back to the medical officer as required on Friday. He looked at me and said, "Oh, yes, Morse, yes, right. I'm sorry, but we can't take you, son." With surprise, I said "Good heavens, why not? What's the matter?" I was quite indignant. He said, "Well, I'll tell you what it is." And he had written on a form on his desk. He turned the form around so I could see it and he had written, "The man stating himself to be Barry Morse of Nottingham is unfit to be accepted into the Royal Navy by reason of pulmonary tuberculosis."

Well, so ignorant was I of this whole field, I didn't even know what those words meant. "Pulmonary tuberculosis." So I said, "What's that?" He was a quite kindly fellow and he realized what a blow and a shock this was going to be to me. He said, "You're an actor, aren't you?" I nodded. "Well, perhaps then you'll know the story about Camille." I said, "Yes, yes." He replied, "You know, it's *that*. It's what's commonly called consumption." Well, I was staggered. "I've only been married for six months, what am I going to do?" He said, "Well, I would suggest that you get yourself into a sanatorium just as soon as you can because it's obviously in a very early stage from the look of your X-ray and with prompt and proper treatment, there's no reason why it shouldn't be able to be dealt with."

Of course, in those days there were no such things as antibiotics or any of the things which have since come into use for the treatment of such diseases as TB. It was mostly a matter of how soon the disease was diagnosed and treated. The surgeon was able to put me in touch with various sanatoriums. The standard treatment for this condition in those days was a prolonged stay in a sanatorium. As it turned out, there was a sanatorium in a place called Creaton, just outside of Northampton, and it was arranged that I should go there.

You can imagine what a blow this was to Sydney just as much as to me. But with extraordinary persistence, dedication, and just plain guts, she contrived somehow to get herself a job as an actress in the Northampton Repertory Theatre. The theatres had all reopened by this time. Northampton was a rather superior company and considered a step up. For one thing, they played only once nightly, instead of twice nightly. By changing their play every week, the number of working hours for the actors was quite a bit less. So, at roughly the same time I went into the sanatorium, Sydney joined the new company.

I don't remember the exact distance of Creaton from Northampton, but it is probably six or seven miles. Sydney contrived to come out and visit me pretty well every day, even though she was rehearsing every morning and playing every evening. Her devotion was extraordinary, I see now. At a point when it was a toss-up whether I was going to live or die, in most people's perceptions, she traveled back and forth by bus and even managed—I'm touched just thinking of it—to knit me a sweater. It was October/November, and the arrangement of these sanatoriums was that the patients were separately kept in what were like horse boxes. If you can visualize a horse box, with the door at the front that the horse goes in and out by, that was rather like our cubicles were. They were completely open to the elements on the fourth wall, the idea being that the best kind of treatment was fresh air. I was supposed to be in bed at all times, as bed rest was one of the most important ingredients of treatment for TB. Naturally, just sitting or lying in bed in my pajamas in late October and November I was considerably chilly. So Sydney somehow scrounged some spare time between rehearsals, performances, learning her lines, and organizing her clothes for whatever the current production was to knit me this sweater. It was made of marvelous camel hair wool and I still have it.

It was one more of those almost miraculous flukes that I had happened to have this idea of volunteering for the navy, and the subsequent medical examination, at more or less precisely the time that this spot on my lung was developing. Flukes and coincidences; it's amazing how they channel and divert our lives. I remember seeing the X-rays and it was just a tiny little blot, a smudge no bigger than a pea. Left unattended, it would have grown into a cavity, because TB breaks up the substance of the lung. The medical director of the sanatorium was an athletic, tough-looking fellow named Dr. Starkie. He was very boisterous and cheerful and said things like, "You keep up the bed rest and keep eating plenty of food and we'll get you out of here before long." The bed rest part of it was very frustrating, for someone of my kind of frenetic energy. It was very frustrating to stay in bed virtually 24 hours a day. Of course, I would get up and wander down to adjoining cubicles to fraternize with some of my fellow patients. There were separate wings for men and women and I used to talk to many of the fellows, and the astonishing thing was that because no connection at that point had been made between tuberculosis or any other lung diseases and tobacco, the medical people *never stopped us smoking!* I continued to smoke at least 15 or 20 cigarettes a day and so did many of my neighbors in the adjoining cubicles. No attempt was ever made to discourage us. Of the other fellows in various degrees of seriousness of TB; some of them were very deeply affected and there were deaths, of course, around me while I was there. I can remember wandering along to visit and gossip with some chap a few cubicles along, he lying in bed and me perched on the end of it, smoking cigarettes, of course. A few days later I wandered by there again and his bed was empty. So I said to the bloke in the next cubicle, "What happened to Fred?" And the chap said, "Oh, he's gone." "You mean he's gone home?" "No, no, no," he said, looking upwards. Well, he had died, of course.

The food was rather discouraging and I found that I didn't have much of an appetite. This being at the beginning of the war, there was considerable concern about food supplies, and soon rationing was imposed. The nurses observed that I wasn't eating very much and Sydney would bring me things like chocolates and chocolate biscuits, but that really didn't fill the gap adequately. Soon the nurses started to encourage me to eat plenty of bread and butter because they said that was a good thing for putting on a bit of weight. I was obviously quite a bit underweight, caused by my restlessness and energy, but by eating as much bread and butter as I could stomach I did start to put on a bit of weight. That, combined with a certain amount of bed rest, contrived to get my weight built up and eventually this spot on my lung began to decline and heal.

More X-rays were taken and I remember Dr. Starkie saying to me, "You're very lucky, we've caught this just in time. Although you will be left with a residual kind of condition, at least you're not going to be in a state where the tuberculosis is going to spread and grow." Indeed, it proved to be so. Right around the turn of the year I was being prepared for release and was counseled by Dr. Starkie, "Now you can count yourself very lucky to have escaped the worst of the impact of tuberculosis, but you won't be able to go back to your former profession." Alarmed, I said, "What? What do you mean?" "It's a very unhealthy way of life for someone in your particular condition. You must consider doing something which will keep you in the fresh air." This was the accepted, received opinion, that the only way of dealing with TB was by plenty of outdoor activity in the fresh air. He continued, "You should consider going to work on a market garden or a farm, or doing some other type of outdoor job, but you shouldn't resume your former profession as an actor." Indignant, I replied, "For heaven's sake, I'm not going to do any such thing." He then finished by telling me that, more or less, it would be on my own head.

I was again very lucky that for people of my age, 21, more and more were being subject to conscription or volunteering for the services, and so I was becoming something of a rarity—someone of moderate equipment, experience and training as an actor, who was not subject to military service. Indeed, I now had a permanent exemption from military service. So I got myself a job in another repertory theatre, also a once nightly theatre company, in Coventry in the midlands of England. I wasn't able to get into the company at Northampton with Sydney.

The Nazi forces by this time were completely overrunning the forces of France and Britain and it was coming close to the time when the evacuation of British forces from Dunkirk was achieved, and only very narrowly. It was a very desperate and gloomy time in the course of the war when it looked quite possible that we were going to lose it.

In April of 1940, I got word from the chap who was now running the company at the Prince's Theatre in Bradford (as the company was no longer under the management of Arthur Brough). He was the great, at least great to me, Carl Bernard. By this time he was running the theatre in Bradford with his Paramount Players. Carl had heard of our considerable popularity at Bradford from our time there during the 1938 season. So suddenly a telegram arrived from Carl asking me to phone him in order to discuss the possibility of our going back to Bradford to join his company. This sounded appealing to us, as we wanted to be together again, and we both knew Bradford quite well. In one sense it was a bit of a step back, going to a twice-nightly theatre, but on the other hand the likelihood was that we would be able to ask for, and be given, a higher salary. I talked to Carl and he seemed to be a delightful and enthusiastic fellow. Without having met, we agreed on contracts for Sydney and myself.

The first production we played in was later turned into a movie called *Goodbye, Mr. Chips*. The story followed the life of a dear old schoolmaster from his rather timid, timorous early days as a beginner to his extreme old age when all the boys adored him. It was a sort of standard issue tearjerking play. I was to play Mr. Chips. As you can well imagine, it was a Herculean task to do twice nightly, because it required not only being on the stage virtually all the time throughout the play, but also horrendous quick changes of costume and makeup and wigs as this chap progressed from being 25 to 85! So that was my triumphant return to Bradford, which, I must say, was greeted with immense enthusiasm by the press and the public.

I remember on another occasion Carl Bernard was in the piece and took off on one of his flights of fancy. He loved to do what actors nowadays so pompously call "improvisation." He was absolutely wonderful at inventing dialogue for his character, whatever it happened to be, dialogue that was sometimes rather better than that written by the original author. So Carl was inventing all this elaborate dialogue and got himself marooned at a point where we were all hoping to get back to the actual dialogue in the script. We all looked hopefully to this Scots girl who was supposed to be following the script, and having turned back and forth throughout the script several times and trying to find *where* this dialogue was, she shrugged and said in desperation, "It's all wrong!" And indeed it was.

There are many, many stories about Carl Bernard; he was a true original. He is almost a legendary figure (at least in my book) among pros, as we used to say, because he was the preeminent typical pro. His parents were in our business, and he was brought up in the theatre as a child performer. He was very good looking in a faintly Latin kind of way. In the pictures I saw of him as a very young man he looked rather like Rudolph Valentino. By the time we met him he was in his forties and he had taken to running the Paramount Players. He was our director and also the manager, taking care of all the business, and he also played parts of all kinds and all sizes. Sometimes it was a big leading part, where I would chip in and operate as sort of codirector, and sometimes if I was playing the leading part he would function as director. He was born Charles Bernard Groves but later adopted the stage name of Carl Bernard.

One of the great stories about Carl concerns one of those silly old drawing room comedies of the 1930s in which I was playing the leading part. The leading characters in these plays were usually members of the nobility, and my character was — let's say — the Duke of Ditchwater. Carl, meanwhile, was playing the relatively minor role of Jenkins, the crumbling butler. There was often a crumbling butler in these plays, usually employed simply to explain the plot in the early stages of the play. Carl knew these sort of parts backwards and forwards, of course, and used to call them "yo-yo parts," because in order to suggest great age you came on stage hunched over a bit with your hand trembling up and down as if you were operating a yo-yo.

We got through the first couple of performances of this play on Monday night not too badly, but of course Carl was so brilliantly swift at grasping the elements involved in a particular play or particular performance that he became bored with this very small part. He had only two entrances: In the first act he had to serve some drinks and explain a bit about the relationship in the family, and in the second act he only had to deliver a message, something to the effect of, "Lady Poncenby will be pleased to come and play tennis on Thursday." Well, at the second performance on Tuesday night — the fourth performance we had given — you could see that Carl was getting to be a bit bored with this silly old play, and even more with this silly old part he had to play as the crumbling butler. He came on doing his yo-yo and, only faintly to my surprise, instead of saying this line, "Lady Poncenby ..." he said to me, "Beg pardon your grace, but may I have a word with you?" Of course, that wasn't in the script to begin with, but what could I say? "Yes, yes, of course, Jenkins, what is it?" He said, "Well, begging your pardon your grace, I wish to give in my notice."

What a cataclysmic shock!

The audience absolutely roared with laughter. But what was I going to do? I could see that Carl was in one of his inventive moods, so I said, "Oh, dear, Jenkins, this is such sad and sudden news. You've been with us so long, how long *has* it been now?" He started off in his wavering voice, "I came here first in your great-grandfather's day, sir. Yes, I was a young pageboy; ah, those were the days. In those days, well, in those days the west wing was all blue, all blue it was. Yes. We used to call it the blue wing. Ah, but nowadays things are sadly changed in the manor, sir. The plaster is crumbling down from the ceiling and the wallpaper is peeling off the wall, and this," he looked down at his trembling right hand, "this will have to be looked into." He went on and on and on, all this wonderful stuff! It was absolutely priceless. I sat him down, gave him brandy, and he went on to talk about lots of things in his life and background. He cried a bit and I cried! Then, I remember, as he was bewailing the state of things, at one point he said, "The stock of port wine is getting very low in the cellar, sir, very low. You really must try and remember that there are *two* of us at it, you know." The audience was absolutely roaring. He talked about his mother and how he wasn't getting on well with the young chambermaid and all sorts of things. He did about 10 or 15 minutes and finally when he figured he'd had enough fun for one evening, he went tottering off to the door and just as he was about to exit, he turned and said, "Oh, and by the way, sir, Lady Poncenby says she'll be pleased to come and play tennis on Thursday."

Another time, I remember, we were doing a four-handed play—two guys and two girls—one of those romantic comedies of the times: "bargain basement Noël Coward," we used to call them! In this particular play, Carl Bernard was playing the leading part. I wasn't in it at all. We had done only a couple of performances when Carl came to me and said, "Look, you're going to have to play my part tomorrow night." I'm sure I looked shocked. "What? Good heavens!" I said, "I've scarcely even looked at it. How am I going to...?" Matter-of-factly he told me, "You just need to do the sort of thing that I do, chat along and it'll come out all right." Of course, I didn't have Carl's improvisatory powers and sat up most of the night trying to learn the wretched part!

The reason I had to play Carl's part on such short notice was that we were not doing well at this time. The blitz had begun, air raids were going on all over the UK, and Carl was off to London to see a producer whom he hoped might transfer the whole company to another theatre and give us a chance to do a bit better. In any event, the next day we had an extra rehearsal in the afternoon to try and get me into some sort of shape and we got through the first performance not too badly. We were in the second performance in the culminating scene of the play, where all four characters (the two guys and the two girls) were on stage together exchanging all this badinage, in a set which was supposed to be my apartment, when suddenly there comes a knock at the door. Well, we're all on stage! I thought to myself, the stage manager's gone off his rocker (the stage manager was responsible for door knocks and doorbells and so forth) so we kept pounding on. A minute or two later, even more insistently came another round of knocks! At this point, the leading lady—not one of nature's brightest at the best of times—was seated on a sofa at the center of the set. As the knocking continues, she looked at me and piped up, "John, I think there's somebody at the door!" What could I do? It was supposed to be my apartment. So I went to the door, opened it and—you guessed it—it was Carl! He had got back earlier than he had expected and couldn't bear not being on. He was standing there with one of the stagehands, both wearing flat caps and overalls, like workmen of some kind, and in workmen's type accent Carl said, "Are you Mr. John Jelliby?" I replied, "Yes, yes, I am." "Well," he continued, "We represent the Acme Furnishing Company and we understand that the payments has not been kept up on this here furniture, so it's all got to be repossessed.... Come on, Ernie!" He motioned to the stagehand with him and they came on, picked up the sofa—with the leading lady still on it!— and despite her protestations, carried her off the stage! They then proceeded to strip the stage bare! We got the leading lady back, but never the furniture! Of course, the audience was absolutely hysterical with laughter.

By this time I was getting so much into the spirit of things that I was longing to spring something on Carl. A few weeks later he was playing a sizeable part in a play and I was in it, too. He had a speech in the last act that he was very attached to, all about his youth in Africa, hunting elephants or something. So I said to the stage manager, "When old Carl gets into that speech about the elephants in Africa, ring the phone bell and see what he'll do." Elatedly, he said he would. We always looked forward to any opportunity of "turning Carl on," as it were. Later, we got into the last act of the play and Carl was playing his speech about Kenya, "...There I was, stumping through the jungle when all of sudden, out of the bush, comes a giant bull elephant..." RING-RING. The phone bell started to sound. RING-RING. At first he took no notice, continuing, "...I raised my rifle, took careful aim...." Still, the phone bell went on, RING-RING, RING-RING. So then I piped up and said, "Rodney, your phone is ringing, dear boy." He looked over, "Oh," he said. He went across and picked up the receiver, "Hello? Hello. Yes, just a moment." Carl looked over at me: "It's for you!" He could work his way out of anything.

However, it finally got to the point where Carl was, in fact, more or less broke. We had gone on and on doing these shows, two new plays every week, but the audiences were not picking up to the point where he could pay his costs, so we had to close down. It was also partly because Carl had been offered a job in the newly formed BBC Radio Repertory Company. His marvelous versatility with voice and accents largely led to this offer. I drove with Carl down to his new job, where we parted. And that, unfortunately, was the end of Carl Bernard's Paramount Players, and a great season at the Prince's Theatre in Bradford. We kept in touch with him, of course, for the rest of his life but we would not have the opportunity to work together again.

7

"It's Just a Fad— Like the Yo-Yo"

As a result of my winning the BBC's Radio Prize upon my graduation from the Royal Academy of Dramatic Art, I began work on the radio and then in some of the earliest television broadcasts in the world in addition to my work in the theatre. As a part of the prize, I was given my first acting role in a radio production during the summer of 1937. It led to several other engagements and a leading part in a radio play called *The Fall of the City*. It was a kind of allegorical play set in the distant future written in a form of blank verse. Through Val Gielgud, the BBC's director of drama, I came to know one or two of the people who worked in the then infant branch of the BBC known as the Television Service.

You might think that was an immense opportunity, the chance to break into a great big burgeoning industry. Well, no such thing, in fact! When the BBC started its television service in 1936, the conditions of transmitting the television signal were so primitive that the quality of the picture was very, very poor. Most sets were built with a kind of circular screen rather like the porthole of a small boat. Unless you had your nose virtually pressed to the screen you could scarcely see any sort of picture at all through the great whirlwind of "snow." Due to the more or less experimental state of television, this had the effect of making sets extremely expensive, thousands of pounds. The result was that only very wealthy people had them. So, it wasn't of great interest to many actors because the audience was so tiny. A small transmission tower was erected some 60 or 70 feet above Alexandra Palace, so the picture was only visible in a relatively small area from that transmitter. There were huge parts even of London where you couldn't get any picture at all. It became regarded, then, as a sort of rich man's toy—like having a yacht or a villa in the south of France.

The teleplays that were done in those days were almost all adaptations of out-of-date stage plays. There weren't the finances, or enough of an established industry, for it to be worthwhile for people to write original plays expressly for television. The actual presentation of these plays was very primitive and breakdowns in the machinery were very frequent. It was not at all unusual for transmission to be suspended because some piece of machinery or another would break down in the middle of the show and we'd have to stop. Of course, like radio and theatre, this was all done live. The camera—or whatever piece of machinery it was—would be taken away and hit with a spanner or something while a slide would be put up on the screen announcing a delay. Five or six minutes later, after the ailing equipment had been mended, we would resume.

Because the picture in those early television sets was so bad, we were forced to use grotesquely exaggerated makeups in order that a face would register successfully on this blurry screen. The style of makeup was like an extreme form of stage makeup. It used to be known as the "5 and 9"— Leichner's greasepaint #5 was a kind of pale yellow, and #9 was an orangey-red, and you'd spread those on your face together to produce a rather improbable-looking skin texture. I rather think I still have some Leichner's makeup in my bottom drawer.

But they discovered pretty soon after they started to shoot television stuff that they needed to exaggerate even that stage makeup coloring in order to register successfully for the television picture. You'd walk into a normal room with this makeup and people would think you'd gone raving mad. We used blue for our lips and our eyelids and this bright orange color for the rest of the face.

The sets for these shows would be built in a line rather like a row of shoe boxes and the cameras would move in a very limited way from side to side. But most of the plays would, if possible, take place in only one set. That was the ideal sort of play for those earliest days of television. But there were occasionally instances where two or more sets were used. The biggest peril in all those productions was that something might go wrong with the lighting, or the sound, or the camera itself; so you constantly needed to be wide-awake for the possibility of having to improvise something on the run at short notice in order to get through it.

For one show we were filming a rather more complicated play, part of which was set during the First World War on the Western Front. Several sets were prepared and placed all in a row. The plot, in this instance, began in my own home in the first set where I'm playing a soldier saying goodbye to his mother in the kitchen of the house; then it would go to right next door on a set of the Western Front where the bombs are falling and I'm being machine gunned; and then finally on to the mortuary in the final set or wherever the soldier goes when he's dead. So you can imagine me starting the first scene on the first set bidding a teary-eyed farewell to my poor mother. "Mother, don't cry! I'll soon be back and everything will be just fine…" and so on and so forth. We hug and kiss good-bye, then I leave my tearful mother behind. Quick as a flash I'm out the door at the back of the set, tearing off my civilian clothes and quickly getting into my next costume—the uniform of a soldier. While I'm making this quick change, out front the camera is supposed to move from the first set to the second, in order to be in place for the scene on the Western Front, where the bombs are exploding and the guns firing. Well, as soon as I'm on the set I realize the camera hasn't moved. It is still in its original position on the first set; the crew huddled around, one of them banging at the camera with a spanner! Of course, this is all *live* television. So, quick like a bunny, I tear off my uniform and jump back into my civilian clothes, back onto the first set where my mother is still crying over my departure. "Dear Mother," I cry as I throw open the door and reenter our kitchen, "I'm back!" She looks at me with surprise, and then we improvise this scene where I tell her that the Army has given me a short reprieve and I am able spend a little more time with her before I go, or something. Meanwhile, the crew is still out front working on this disabled camera that won't move!

One of the many peculiarities about it was that we would do two performances of a play, one on a Wednesday or Thursday evening and a second performance on Sunday afternoon. We would rehearse it like a stage play for 10 days, or two weeks for a full-length play, a piece which would run for one and a half to two hours. Another interesting fact was that the plays were not of prescribed lengths. Today a show is a one-hour show, or a 90-minute show, or whatever. In those days the play began at half past eight o'clock and played just as long as it played! If it was 67 minutes, or 83 minutes, well fine, that's how long it played. It seems to me to be a marvelous freedom. Isn't it lunacy in our industry that we've been bullied by the absurd forces of commercialism into carving everything we do on television into prescribed chunks.

Suppose I went into the Royal Academy of Art and proclaimed that henceforth all paintings must be only 30 × 20 centimeters or 50 × 28 centimeters. They would say, and rightly so, "bring on the men with the white coats and take this man away. He's manifestly insane!" But this is what we have allowed ourselves to be bullied into. The result being, of course, that the very pattern of dramatic writing has been changed and dictated by these time frames. I don't think that if Shakespeare were around today he'd appreciate being told that *Hamlet* was too long and wouldn't play on television!

So, those of us who were kids, and were anxious to do anything we could to go through our paces, were the ones working in this new medium. I was among them and through the good offices of the people in the radio department of the BBC I came to do some of these early television shows in that period. An older actor once said to me, "What is this job you're doing during the day then, Morse?" And I said, "Oh, it's up at the BBC, sir." He nodded, "You're on the wireless, then, the wireless?" Everybody used to call the radio "the wireless" in those times. I replied, "No, it's not the wireless, but it's like the wireless with pictures." "Oh, yes," he said with infinite disgust, "you're a bloody fool wasting your time on that twaddle. Don't you see, it's just a fad—like the yo-yo; they'll have forgotten all about it by Christmas." Those were his exact words and that's what a lot of people believed, that it was some kind of freakish toy that was momentarily fashionable among the wealthy and they'd soon get bored with it. Well, the rest as they say, is history! Television was suspended at the beginning of the Second World War and not resumed until considerably after the end of the war. So it really wasn't until the 1950s in the UK, as well as in North America, that television became in any way a popular or universal form of entertainment.

Sydney and I got an offer from one of the best repertory theatres, a once-nightly theatre in Harrogate, Yorkshire, with the White Rose Players. The standard in this company was quite high. I greatly enjoyed a production we did of *Arms and the Man*, one of my earlier experiences in a Shaw play, although I had previously played in a production of *Candida* in one of the other repertory companies. However, Shaw's plays were not often performed in the twice-nightly theatres, because he refused always to allow cuts to be made to his plays, and most of them were longer than the twice-nightly schedule allowed. But, here at Harrogate, we were once-nightly and were able to produce *Arms and the Man*. I played the leading character, Captain Bluntschli, Sydney played the role of the mother, Catherine Petkoff, and playing opposite me in the role of her daughter, Raina, was an actress who became something of a movie star of the 1940s and 1950s, Rosamund John.

Rosamund was the long-standing girlfriend of a most widely renowned and respected actor, Robert Donat. He made an immense success in the film version of *Goodbye, Mr. Chips*, which I had played on the stage. Donat came to see this production of *Arms and the Man* and made the point of coming backstage to see us afterwards. Well, really he had come to see Rosamund, his girlfriend, but he came around and introduced himself to me and was most generously enthusiastic and said he was "staggered by the technical skill and polish that you have in a production which, after all, only had a week's rehearsal." I said, "Well, here I am at the age of 23 and I have played over 200 parts," which indeed I had, "and so," I continued, "that in and of itself will give you a certain amount of assurance, if nothing else!" He was most kind and encouraging and said, "Well, I'm sure you're going to have a marvelous career since, like me, I understand that you are not likely to be drawn into the war." Donat had chronic asthma and was also somewhat older than I.

I went down to London to see various people in the profession who were presenters of shows, partly on the advice of Robert Donat, who said, "You ought to see some people about getting jobs with West End producers, because you have a lot of experience and good background." So I went to see a fellow called Hugh Beaumont. Hugh, though, was not called Hugh by those in the profession. He was a fairly open homosexual and was known to everybody as Binkie. Binkie Beaumont was, I suppose, the most influential and powerful figure in the London theatre at that time. As another instance of fluke and coincidence, I went to see Binkie Beaumont at precisely the moment that he was looking very urgently for someone like me. He said to me, "What are you doing the rest of the day?" I said, "Well, nothing in particular. Why?" And he replied, "I want you to go down to Brighton, to the Theatre Royal, and ask to see Mr. Charles La Trobe. He is the manager of our touring production there." At this point, many productions were touring because the raids had made it very difficult to sustain runs of plays in the West End. There was great bomb damage and air raids virtually every day. Binkie continued: "La Trobe will explain to you what's going on. I'm going to have my secretary give you a letter of authority." The emergency situation had become such that you had to have a letter of authority stating what your business was in going to seaside towns like Brighton, because of the danger of infiltration by enemy agents, or spies. So they paid my fare down to Brighton and I hurried to the Theatre Royal, not knowing in the least what was afoot and why there was all this urgency. The posters outside the theatre announced they were playing a touring production, prior to the West End, of a play called *The First Mrs. Fraser* by a well known author called St. John Ervine. It was starring one of the most eminent actresses of that time in England, Dame Marie Tempest, who by this time was in her 70s but was a great idol of London theatre-goers. Playing opposite her was the wonderful actor A.E. Matthews, and also in the company was another quite well known actor named Milton Rosmer.

Mr. La Trobe quickly explained to me that the young man who was playing the juvenile leading part, the son of Dame Marie Tempest and A.E. Matthews, had been called up to go into the services at short notice and was going to have to leave them at the end of the current week. Mr. La Trobe wanted to know if I wanted to take over this part and asked if I could do a bit of an audition. It was a great opportunity, and he asked Mr. Matthews to come in and go through some of the dialogue with me. Dame Marie, though, didn't deign to come out to vet this proposed new recruit to the company! But A.E. Matthews, who was universally known as Matty, was a wonderful kind and friendly old chap. He, by this time, was in his early 70s, I should think, and he was very helpful. We went onto the set and I went through some of the dialogue, with Mr. La Trobe observing. I played a little scene with Mr. Matthews and he said, "Oh, yes, this boy's fine." Then turning to Mr. La Trobe he asked, "When's he going to join us?" So, it was pretty well taken for granted that I was going to be in. The only snag was that I would be obliged to start on the next Monday!

I hadn't the time to give the proper notice that I should have given to the company in Harrogate. All I was able to do was to ring them up and tell them, "Look, I'm not returning to the company because I've got this other job in a touring production which is due to come into the West End and they want me to take over this part now." There were two women who ran the White Rose Players, and they were not best pleased by my announcement! But, of course, it was a great opportunity.

As for Dame Marie Tempest, I began to rehearse with her understudy, as she didn't deign to rehearse with me! The rest of the company turned up to give me help through the rehearsals and there I was, ready to open in the show at the next stop on the tour at the Pavilion Theatre, Bournemouth, about three days later. I had to open the play with Mr. Matthews. There was a scene that introduced the whole subject of the play between his character and mine. He was playing my father and Dame Marie was playing my mother. We started up the play and he was very helpful and encouraging. We got through the first scene, and then we arrived at the moment when Dame Marie Tempest was due to enter. I had to welcome her in and say something to the effect of, "Oh, hello, Mother, did you know Father is here?" The play was about an estranged older couple and their sons, and I was playing the younger of the sons. I had to go to the door, up a couple of steps set-up in order to give Dame Marie Tempest a suitably grand entrance, and take her hand to welcome her in. Well, she had never set eyes on me before, although I had seen her in other productions in years past. The door opened and I go to take her hand; she looks me up and down and there is quite a sizeable pause while she is taking me in! Then, in a scarcely muffled stage whisper, she said, "Oh yes, I think you'll do," and then continued on with the rest of her dialogue! She sent for me after the first performance that I'd given and gave her qualified approval. She was never very generous, exactly, with her encouragement to colleagues; she was a considerably grandiose kind of lady. But she did give her approval to my efforts and so off we went on this tour.

During this time Sydney had remained in Harrogate. Well, once again a fluke came to our aid! It turned out that the young lady who was playing the wife of the elder of the two brothers in *The First Mrs. Fraser* was leaving the show for family reasons. So, it became possible for me to arrange through the management that Sydney should be engaged to play this part in the production on the tour. The tour played all over the place, waiting for the air raids to diminish in London so that we could come in to the West End for a run. Well, of course, it never happened. The raids went on and on and on almost uninterruptedly in London for many, many months for the rest of 1941 and into 1942. We played not only the seaside places like Bournemouth and Brighton, but some of the places where there were air raids, such as Manchester, Liverpool, and Sheffield. At that time, it got to the point where Dame Marie Tempest was becoming somewhat frail, "bearing her years," as they say, with some difficulty.

On the other hand, Matty, who played my father in the show, was as spry as anything. Upon joining the show I was seeking digs on my own, but Mr. Matthews in his wonderfully warm, welcoming and friendly way, said, "Look here, when we get to the next town you come with me and we'll look for digs together. I've played all these places before in years gone by and I'm sure we should find somewhere pleasant—so you come along with me. When we get to the station we'll just set out and walk." That was the way he was accustomed to looking for digs! Well, when we arrived in Exeter, the next town on the tour, we set forth from the station. "Oh, I know this town, somewhere not far from the Cathedral I remember some very pleasant digs." So we set out on this fine Sunday morning carrying our bags. Finally we arrived at the house, the house that Matty firmly believed was a theatrical boarding house, the house where we would get our rooms. Matty looked up and said to me, "Yes, yes, of course, I remember the landlady's name—Mrs. Frugebush!" We approached the door and rang the bell and a chap came to answer it. Matty was always wonderfully charming and friendly and he greeted the man. "Good morning. Is Mrs. Frugebush here?" The chap looked at Matty quizzically. "Mrs. Who? I don't think I've ever heard of her." He called out to the back, obviously to his wife, and said "Florrie, do you know anything about a Mrs. Frugebush?" And the answer came back, "Oh, no, no, she died years ago!" Obviously it had been some years since Mr. Matthews had played Exeter.

Then we asked more about where we might get digs and were told that a theatrical boardinghouse was just down the street. So along we went, still carrying our bags, to the next house. Matty, in his charming way, talked to the landlady and said, "This is my young friend, my colleague, we're playing here at the Theatre Royal this coming week and we're looking for lodgings."

"Oh, yes," said the lady and asked us to come in. We sat down to talk and discovered that indeed she had two bedrooms with a shared living room. (Matty was quite prepared to share a living room with me, a new kid in the company.) He said, "Can we have a look at my bedroom then?" We went upstairs and were standing around in what appeared to me to be perfectly adequate rooms. Suddenly, without warning, Matty started to exhibit signs of faintness. He put his hand to his forehead and said, "Oh! We've been walking around a long way this morning and I feel a little bit dizzy. I wonder, madam, if you'd be kind enough to get me a glass of water." She immediately bustled off down to the kitchen to get Matty a glass of water. Whereupon, the moment she departed he threw off his supposed dizziness, darted across the room and turned back the bedding to check the sheets to make sure they were all nice and clean! He put them all back in time for the landlady to appear with a glass of water, which he gratefully accepted and then "recovered" his composure. This, apparently, was an old dodge of his for finding out whether the bed linen was properly laundered and decently clean.

Unfortunately, we had to suspend our tour because of Dame Marie Tempest's illness. It was just after we'd played in Sheffield, which coincidentally, was where we had been playing on the eve of the outbreak of the Second World War some two years before. By this time, due to the courtesy of Mr. Matthews, I had acquired an agent. I had never had an agent before. It was very different in those days than it is now. Actors who didn't work in London didn't really need to have an agent. Provincial theatre was a whole different world. To begin with, British Actors' Equity—our professional association—didn't have any jurisdiction in provincial theatres, they only had control over companies by and large in the West End. Also, actors who worked entirely in rep got their jobs mainly by writing letters and sending credit lists and photographs to potential employers in other repertory companies. It was pretty well all done by mail, and partly by word of mouth. Repertory company managers would go around and look at other companies from which they might recruit people in the future. So I had never had an agent up to that point. Matty took a sort of parental interest in my career, thought that I was a promising lad and said to me one day, "You don't have an agent, I believe?" "No, sir, I don't," I responded. "Well,

I'll tell you what we'll do. When we get to play somewhere near London I'll get my agent to come down and see the show; he's an American, a wonderful fellow—the best agent in London!" I thought, "Wow, that's good!" Dear Matty was as good as his word and when we played Reading, he got this extraordinary guy named Al Parker to come to the show.

Al Parker himself had an extraordinary career. He had been a film director back in the silent days, and had directed one of the early films of Douglas Fairbanks, Sr. He went on to direct many other well-known films of that day. Then, before the war, he had been sent over by Fox Films (with whom he was under contract) to open up studios for the production of films in London. He took over a space in the Wembley district to do just that, then the war broke out, and that venture was abandoned. By this time, Al Parker had become very enamored with the English way of life, and London in particular, so he decided to stay in England and become an agent. Al had known A.E. Matthews years before when Matty had worked in the States, so it was natural that he would represent Matty. But since he'd only recently started up in business, he didn't have many clients in his agency. He had, for example, the then child actress Glynis Johns as a client, and a young man he'd spotted somewhere whom he thought had a future in the movies—and by Jove he did!—James Mason. So when Matty persuaded him to come down to Reading to see our performance, Al Parker, much to my amazement and delight, offered to take me on as one of his clients. Therefore, when we got to the end of our tour, I had an agent ready and willing to seek other work for me.

I went back to doing a certain amount of radio because of the contacts that I had established before the war. Al Parker succeeded in getting me ever-bigger fees for my radio jobs and I became something of a regular on BBC productions. Al was also determined that I was going to be in the movies. Well, there weren't all that many movies being made during this time, of course, during the blitz, and many studios were closed down. But there were some still working, among them the famous Ealing studios where a great many well-known comedies were made, including films featuring the then very popular music hall entertainer Will Hay. He had come to great prominence and success as a movie actor by the adoption of a sort of quizzical character. A movie was being planned called *The Goose Steps Out*, in which Will Hay was to play an eccentric schoolmaster, and some of his stooges were enlisted to play his unruly students. In the film, Will Hay's character was supposed to have finagled his way into a German college where all these Nazi youths were being trained. You would think the idea of making a comedy film about Nazi Germany would have been greeted with complete disgust as being in the worst possible taste. Al Parker took me down to see the senior producer at Ealing, Michael Balcon, and the co-director of the film (with Will Hay), Basil Dearden.

Basil Dearden looked rather like Napoleon in general appearance, short and with aquiline nose and jutting chin. So, I was taken down to see if I was suitable to play the character of a student in the film. There were three student characters who were all meant to be 18 or 19, supposedly at this Nazi-controlled German university. Al Parker showed me into the office much like a prize fight manager, saying "There now, look at this! See this boy? Barry Morse is his name, you'll be hearing a lot about him. He'd be just perfect for one of these characters—he's got a fine figure, a very hand-some profile…." He gestured to me. "Go stand by the window there, Barry, will you, and show Mr. Balcon your profile." Well, I got this part and the film went on quite a long while because, as his stooges, we three actors, were in virtually every scene. Our principal function was to stand around and look amused whenever Will Hay did or said anything. Among the others in the cast was the then very young Peter Ustinov. He played another of the students who served as foils to Will Hay. So this gig was quite profitable, as it went on for some eight or ten weeks.

Shortly afterwards there was a play being produced in the West End which was called *The School for Slavery*. It was based upon the Nazi occupation and the terrible persecution that resulted from that occupation in Poland. The play wasn't the best play in the world but it was very deeply and sincerely felt. It was written by a quite famous film writer named Lajos Biro. He had come to prominence as the writer of various well-known British films of that time, including the famous film *The Private Life of Henry the Eighth* in which Charles Laughton starred. In *The School for Slavery* my character was part of the invading force representing the German government and the Nazis who were occupying this particular town in Poland, which was an academic center. This young man, a Nazi by faith and declaration, falls in love with the daughter of a university professor. The play was to be presented in the West End at the Westminster Theatre. Of course this was a tremendous opportunity for me, playing a leading role *in the West End!* It was directed by a well-known director called Maurice Browne, who'd been the producer and director of many plays over the years, notably the great play about the First World War, *Journey's End*. Upon opening, *The School for Slavery* received respectful, rather than glowing, notices. They were respectful mostly by virtue of its subject matter. As far as I can recall, it probably was one of the first new plays to be produced in London which dealt with a wartime subject, but not a British subject. There were other plays that dealt with life in England in wartime, but this was an investigation of life in Poland in the depths of the war.

My next job in the West End was in another interesting wartime play, this one written by a very distinguished and famous barrister, Sir Patrick Hastings, KC. He'd been involved in various famous trials and he had a relation who had been working in an armed merchantman ship. There was by this time so much going on in the war at sea that convoys were beginning to be used to carry cargo to and from the UK. This play was called *Escort* and was about the adventures of a ship doing this sort of convoy/escort work. It had an all male cast because the whole play was set onboard this relatively small ship. The set became quite important and was unusual in that it actually moved. It reproduced the pitching and rolling of a ship, which was considered to be quite a novelty. The cast was not large, as the crew of such a ship wouldn't have been very large. There were about 12 or 14 of us and I played a shifty, unreliable sort of character, a lieutenant who was psychologically quite interesting. The captain of the ship was played by a delightful chap, considerably older than myself, by the name of John Stuart. John came to the production by way of being a movie star. He was very handsome and had a gentle way about him. He had some prominence in early English movies, dating back to the silent days. Our director was the redoubtable Basil Dean. He had directed a number of quite well known theatrical hits in his day and was something of a bully. He had been known to reduce actresses to tears and hysterics. Well, we didn't have any actresses, but he *was* a tough nut. Everybody said, "Oh, boy, you're working with Basil Dean, are you—you'll have a rough time with him," and so on. But curiously enough, I didn't. I suppose he somehow subconsciously knew that I was not going to put up with any rough handling. I think he saw something of a glint in my eye! He did pick quite heavily on John Stuart, who was a very good-natured fellow. The play was (again) moderately respectfully received—it was on a subject in the public interest, as it were.

In those days, however, there weren't the mammoth long runs that there are nowadays running into numbers of years. At that time, I believe the record in the English-speaking world was still held by a musical of the First World War which ran three to four years.

Basil Dean, in addition to directing *Escort*, was the overall director of an organization called ENSA, the Entertainment National Services Association. This was the group that was in charge of producing entertainment for the armed services, whether at home in the UK or overseas. Companies would be organized to go and play at military bases or naval dockyards or air force bases or whatever. As you can imagine, morale among the civilian population was regarded as being very, very important and all sorts of things were being organized to try and keep the spirits up. There had been, among all the other raids, one of the most serious air raids outside of London, that on Coventry, in the course of which Coventry Cathedral had been virtually destroyed. And so ENSA decided that they would present a sort of patriotic pageant in the ruins of the cathedral. A well-known woman author Clemence Dane was commissioned to put together this dramatized anthology of patriotic material to be played in the ruins of Coventry Cathedral and called *Cathedral Steps*.

Because I had recently worked with Basil Dean in *Escort*, he asked me to be one of the company, which was made up of very substantial stars of the day, well-known people like Leslie Howard, Dame Sybil Thorndike, and Lewis Casson. All the leaders of the profession were dragooned into this enterprise. So, we all went up to Coventry on a Sunday and did this show in the afternoon. I was assigned King Henry the Fifth's wonderful speech, "Once more unto the breach dear friends, once more; or close the wall up with our English dead...!" and so on. All sorts of stars did other things connected with English history and it was greatly welcomed. It was resolved that we should do it again on another occasion. The authorities decided it should be done on the steps of St. Paul's Cathedral in London, as at that time, during the course of one or other of the raids, St. Paul's had almost miraculously escaped destruction. Indeed, a bomb had fallen on the cathedral but had failed to go off! There's a famous photograph of a huge nighttime air raid when St. Paul's is silhouetted over a sea of flames, as all the buildings around it have been hit and set on fire. So we brought that patriotic anthology to St. Paul's. It had to be done during daytime of course and it had to be hoped that there wouldn't be an air raid at the time when this was going on. It was a very moving occasion. All the roads were closed off and tens of thousands of people were packed all the way down Ludgate Hill and Fleet Street as far as the eye could see. Among our cast for that performance was that great old actor—largely infirm and unable to appear on the stage but still appearing once in a while on the radio— Henry Ainley. He had a glorious voice. Henry had been a huge star when he was a younger fellow. Actress Ellen Terry had once pronounced him to be the most beautiful man—or woman—she had ever seen. I'll always remember standing there in the vestry of St. Paul's, getting ready before we all came out onto the steps. This dear old man, who had not appeared in front of a live audience for quite a few years, could hear the crowds outside and the shouts of all the people.

He said to me in a quiet voice, "Is there an audience out there?" And I replied, "Yes, sir, yes there is. Many, many thousands."

"Oh, good heavens," he said looking quite worried, getting quite nervous and trembling.

I had worked with him a few times on radio and they would engage dear Henry Ainley to do these radio plays because he had a beautiful voice. We all read from scripts on the radio; no one learned lines. But by this time, his mind was kind of confused. The first radio show I did with him, he insisted on reading things like stage directions and character names—as well as his actual dialogue! He'd read everything on the script! So we had to start scratching out the things that we didn't want him to say.

It was in 1943 that Sydney and I were to have our first baby. Great excitement! We had been married by this time four years and we'd decided that this was the time. Sydney was never more beautiful. As happens with so many women, pregnancy agreed with her, she was glowing and fitter than she'd ever been. It was a marvelously happy time of expectancy. Our doctor, who shall remain nameless—aside from the fact that I think I have almost purposefully forgotten his name—was in Windsor. He had arranged for Sydney to go into a hospital in Windsor when the time came for the baby to be born. Of course, we'd never been through this experience before, we didn't know a great deal about it, and the baby was due on August 23. That was the projected date, but as we know now projected dates are largely a matter of medical guesswork. There is no absolutely infallible way of predicting what a baby's birth date is going to be. We were told by this doctor that since the baby had not arrived on the due date—the date that he predicted—Sydney should go into the hospital nonetheless and he would induce the birth. Innocent as we were, trusting as we were, we agreed to this and Sydney went into the hospital and the birth was induced. What we didn't know at that time—I know a good deal more about it now and I've become a good deal more watchful and skeptical, frankly, of medical "omniscience"—was that the induction of the birth of a baby is a very delicate process and needs very careful timing within the cycle which governs the whole of the birth process. The baby boy, having been born on August 25, was named Barry Richard Charles Morse. Barry, of course, after me, Richard after Sydney's younger brother, and Charles after my father. Unfortunately, he proved to be what was termed a "blue" baby. In other words, he had suffered damage to his heart in the process of being born which proved irreparable and he was dead within 48 hours. What we didn't know was that the doctor had arranged this induced birth so that the baby should not be born more than a couple of days past his projected date *because he wanted to go on holiday!* It was a terrible, terrible blow to me, but even more to Sydney. She had suffered no damage herself, and later events would show that our babies for some reason or another had a tendency to be rather later in birth than the projected date and also rather large in size.

Our son's death was something very hard for us to rise above, but that's how life sometimes goes and that's what we had to bear.

8

"The Voice of the Turtle"

I CONTINUED TO WORK ON FILMS and one of the next that I made was called
Thunder Rock. It was a most interesting film based on a play by an American writer called Robert Ardrey. In a way it was curious that this piece
had been made popular as a play, and now as a film, because it was essentially a pacifist film about an American who, in the period just before the
Second World War, decides that he wants to get away from what he thinks
is the deteriorating society of the modern world and takes a job as a lighthouse keeper on one of the Great Lakes. It's a most interesting story and
the leading role in the film was played by a chap who was becoming very
popular both in the theatre and in film, Michael Redgrave, father of the
Redgrave family which has become quite a show business dynasty. He was
married to Rachel Kempson, who was distantly related to Sydney. A secondary, but quite good, part was played by James Mason.

In 1944 the important stage play I worked on was a piece called *Crisis in Heaven*. It was written by Eric Linklater and was a kind of allegorical fantasy. The story assumed that in Heaven all the characters that ever
existed in the whole history of mankind are assembled together in a whole
nationhood, as it were. It is a marvelously fanciful idea and it dealt with
international affairs. The characters in the piece consisted of notable figures
from a number of different countries of the world and from all periods of
history ranging from Abraham Lincoln, Helen of Troy, Voltaire and Aristo-
phanes to Alexander Pushkin, the Russian poet. These characters were
embodiments of the particular kinds of human characteristics which they
represented; for instance, Helen of Troy was physical beauty and rather
indolent power, and Alexander Pushkin represented poetic imagination and
high spirited human enthusiasm. It was a very worthwhile and very well

Onstage with Dorothy Dickson in *Crisis in Heaven*.

conceived and well-written play. It was produced by Binkie Beaumont (who had also produced *The First Mrs. Fraser*). John Gielgud, whom I'd known for some time, directed the play.

In the context of that period, this was what you might call an all-star cast. Everybody who played all these great characters was quite well known in their own right. We were all billed equally, above the title in alphabetical order. Gielgud was very intellectually searching and directed the play in a very vibrant kind of way. I had the majority of my more passionate scenes with the actress who played Helen of Troy. In the script, Pushkin develops an enormous passion for Helen of Troy and there is a sort of seduction scene that was marvelously poetic. Helen of Troy was being played by a musical comedy star of the day named Dorothy Dickson. She was not the most instinctively inspired actress, but she had been successful in various musicals and was quite beautiful, albeit getting towards her senior years by this point. She relied very much on directors to give her some kind of basis for a performance. Thus, I played opposite a lady who was giving a not too heavily veiled impression of John Gielgud! Gielgud had a marvelously fluted, mellifluous voice, and lots of younger actors tended to give partly unconscious imitations of him in their way of speaking. Dorothy Dickson finished up giving a performance that was rather like John Gielgud in drag!

One evening Sydney and I were out after a performance during an air raid warning. Of course, nobody paid too much attention to that; we had grown used to it. However, there had been a lessening in the frequency of raids in the recent weeks. That particular night, not only was there an air raid warning on, but we could see aircraft being shot. That was something that you didn't often see and we saw two or three! We thought, *Wow, they must have come up with some new technique or weapon that is able to shoot down planes*. We could see this tail of fire coming down and, shortly after, an explosion when it hit the ground. Well, we weren't to know until the next day, but that was the beginning of the launching of what were known as "flying bombs" or "buzz bombs" or "doodle bugs." They were a form of pilotless aircraft which Hitler had developed and were being fired over from France and aimed at London. A flying bomb, or V-1 as the Germans called it, was calculated to have its engines cut out when it got over London so the thing dropped to the ground and exploded. There was later a more powerful and sinister weapon called the V-2. They were shaped somewhat like a small aircraft and it turned out to be a rather dangerous secret weapon of Hitler's.

In succeeding days and months the flying bombs became a daily and nightly occurrence. By this time we had acquired the first apartment of our own in London. It was flat number 3 at 21 DeVere Gardens in Kensington, just a stone's throw from Kensington Gardens and Kensington Palace, so we were right in the middle of this attack on London. Inevitably, it led to the play not running very long as attendance fell off with the threat of the flying bombs and, indeed, many shows closed in London.

There was a notable "off–Broadway" type theatre during those years simply called the Q Theatre, because it was in the district called Kew (where there is a bridge over the Thames and the famous Kew Horticultural Gardens), a lovely part of London. It was housed at the foot of the Kew Bridge in what had been a roller skating rink—a rather unpromising looking, cavernous building which had been adapted into a smallish sized theatre with only one level. There were no balconies or circle, or anything like that. It was run by a remarkable couple named Jack and Beatrice DeLeon. They were brave theatrical pioneers and ran this theatre for a number of years, it having been established in 1924 and the venue for many very courageous productions. Their policy was to mount, as often as they could, adventurous productions of new plays, plays that in some instances were not considered to exhibit sufficient commercial promise to be presented in the West End. Other plays were of unusual, or daring, subject matter which couldn't be presented in the West End; and occasionally revivals of what had become respected semiclassical popular plays. Some of the plays that originated at Q would eventually transfer to the West End, thereby proving quite commercially valuable to the DeLeons.

When the DeLeons weren't producing a new play at Q, they would sometimes arrange to do a new production of a play that had already been done. *Thunder Rock* was one such play. In this instance I was playing the central role of the lighthouse keeper. In the production, one of the ghosts—the Viennese doctor—was played by a good friend of mine, the great Czech actor Frederick Valk. He had a marvelously whimsical sense of humor and a wonderfully impressive voice, still imbued with the native tones of his Czechoslovakian origins. One of the scenes in this play takes place when this old European doctor is trying to encourage my character to break from his cynical attitude about the future of the world by saying, "Young man, you must not despair of the human species. Think of the marvelous things that have been accomplished so far—and if you look into the future you'll see all kinds of wonderful things yet to be." During the course of the scene he had to rattle off the names of great people in history who had overcome discouragements and setbacks to contribute to the growth of civilization. At one performance he began, in his most serious way, with his trademark Czech accent, "Consider, Mr. Charleston, the great men in human history who have always carried such great hope within their hearts—think of the great figures of the past who have done such great things and made such wonderful accomplishments in the name of humanity: Leonardo DaVinci, Ludwig van Beethoven, William Shakespeare, *Jack DeLeon*...." Well, it was all we could do to hold off from breaking up!

Another show was a production of what many people think is Terence Rattigan's best play, *The Browning Version*, which is a tragic story about a failed schoolmaster. I played that role, a wonderful part. On another occasion, Jack DeLeon adapted Goethe's *Faust* for the stage. Joseph O'Conor, a lovely actor with a great sort of nobility, played Faust. I played Mephistopheles with a sort of baffled, comedic fury. Despite all his resources and all his ingenuities, Mephistopheles is constantly being defeated. One of the things I did was to play him with a limp, as though, somehow or other, his cloven hoof was bothering him a bit.

We used to play on Sunday nights at Q. Most other theatres at that time, and, indeed, still in London, don't open on a Sunday. On one particular Sunday night, near the end of the war, my old friend Peter Cushing, his wife, Helen, and my Sydney had come down to the Q to see the performance. Peter and his wife lived not far from us in Kensington and so the logical way for us to go back there, after the show, was on the number 27 bus that came past the foot of Kew Bridge and also went all the way up to Kensington. So we were making our way back quite late at night and there was an air raid warning on.

Of course, by this time we didn't take much notice of air raid warnings because it was a matter of fluke with the flying bombs as to where they fell. They were rather unpredictable and if you took notice of every air raid warning that sounded you wouldn't get much done. Since all of us except Sydney smoked at the time, we got on top of the bus where passengers were allowed to smoke. We were riding along through Hammersmith and flying bombs were apparently coming over. You could hear these flying bombs if they were at all close because they made a growling kind of exhaust noise when they came closer to the ground. The only clue to the danger was when the exhaust noise stopped and the engine cut out. That meant that the bomb was about to drop and it would fall perpendicularly to Earth. It was rather eerie.

Well, we were not paying too much attention when we heard the approaching sound of one of these flying bombs, ominously close, we thought, to where we were—and then it stopped. There was silence! We started to get up, thinking what should we do? Should we try to get off the bus, or what? The bomb was very close over our heads and about to drop. We were undecided what to do. Our lives were almost literally in the hands of the bus driver, who had three options: stop, go backward, or go forward. He elected, he told us afterward, purely by instinct to go forward as fast as he could. He put his foot down and the bus shot down the road at top speed. It was the right and sensible thing to do. When it was about 100 yards ahead of where we had first heard this engine cut out, we saw the bomb actually come down and hit a church, St. Mary's, which was almost completely destroyed, as well as a couple of houses nearby. Mercifully, there were very few casualties because it was late in the evening and the church was not occupied. It has since been rebuilt and I very often go past it, and every time I do I think of that occasion and what a marvelously narrow escape we had. It was due only to the presence of mind and instinct of our bus driver. We all piled downstairs and shook him by the hand, thanking him gratefully.

The next West End production that I did was called *The Assassin*, written by a well-known American author, Irwin Shaw. The play was based on actual facts, about events in France after the Vichy government took power in World War II. It was produced at the Savoy Theatre in the Strand, a lovely big theatre, in January 1945, and concerned a young Royalist, a Monarchist, by the name of Robert DeMauny. It was a fine play on quite a wide scale in terms of the dramatic presentation. There were many different sets and a fairly large cast. There were a number of senior actors playing some of the other characters in the piece, among them again the father of my dear old friend Doreen Oscar (my friend from the RADA), Henry Oscar. Because it was a very elaborate and large scale production, it was sensibly decided that we shouldn't attempt to "run it in" out of town. We were going to open immediately at the Savoy Theatre in the Strand. The director of the show was a chap who eventually became a good friend of ours, Marcel Varnel. He was French by origin but had lived and worked a long time in England and as well as directing in the theatre, to great success, he directed a number of very popular English films. *The Assassin* was a great opportunity for me because I had star billing, my name above the title, and was playing the leading role in what was regarded as a very high quality production of a very high quality play. I got very good notices. Quite good for a 26-year-old actor!

The war ended on May 8, 1945. On that day I was on my way back from the Savoy Theatre after a matinee to our flat in DeVere Gardens, Kensington. In order to make that journey, I had to take a bus which went to Kensington. But to do this, there was this little alley and some steps that led up from our stage door. As I came out of the stage door in order to get to those steps I saw a bus going along the Strand and there were sailors and soldiers dancing on top of it—they'd managed to get themselves up there somehow! I thought to myself, "Wow, the war really is over." It was almost impossible to believe at first. So everything to do with the war was, at least for the time being, shelved. Nobody wanted to know or hear anything about the wretched war anymore. It had been so dismal and so miserable—and so tragic—for so many people, that once the war ended our box office receipts plummeted and the play inevitably closed.

Following the end of the play, the director, Marcel Varnel, gave me a good part in the film *A Soldier for Christmas*. Perhaps because of the widespread feelings about the war, the film was released under the title *This Man Is Mine* in the UK but did retain the original name for release in Canada and the USA. The two female leads were played by Glynis Johns

On the bill with Irina Baranova and Leonide Massine!

and Nova Pilbeam. Nova had been a child movie star and had played in a few historical English films, one of which, *Tudor Rose* had considerable fame—all about Mary Tudor as a young girl. Nova was destined, as they say in the cheaper fiction, to work with me quite a lot after that.

When the film wrapped, I soon after became involved in a rather remarkable stage production along with Irina Baronova, the famous Russian ballerina. Believe it or not, I can claim—honestly—to have danced with the famed Irina Baronova in an extraordinary stage production! It was a musical ballet murder mystery. This show was directed by Marcel Varnel, by this time my friend and colleague, and it was called *A Bullet in the Ballet*. It was based on a comedic murder mystery book which had been published a few years earlier and had to do with a murder committed within a ballet company, with the resulting disruptions and investigations. Somebody had the bright idea of putting together a stage production and I was asked to play the detective in this piece. But much more important than me were two great ballet stars. The show incorporated three ballets, different in style, in period, and everything else. The star and choreographer was the great Russian ballet dancer Leonide Massine. He was immensely famous and revered in his day. There was a complete ballet company and orchestra required, a very ambitious project overall. Once we were rehearsing it occurred to me that it would be a good "stunt" if the young detective was onstage during the ballet during which the murder is supposed to have been committed. Therefore, he would have a kind of "participant's eye view" of exactly what happened on the stage during that ballet. The ballet *Petrushka* concerns a group of puppets who are appearing at a country fair. Petrushka is actually the name of the clown figure played by Leonid Massine, while the second lead is a doll played by Irina Baronova. In this ballet there are a lot of other characters but also there is a performing bear, with a bear master, and the bear is held on the end of a rope and makes clumsy attempts at dancing. It was supposed to be one of the attractions of this fair. So I said, "Why couldn't I appear as the bear and the audience can see me getting into the bear costume; I can do this clumsy dancing, and it'll give a marvelous kind of subtext to the operations of the ballet." Everyone agreed and Massine was kind enough to accept me into his ballet company in the role of the bear, and Irina Baranova, who was a beautiful, vivacious young dancer, thought it was a great lark. And so I actually appeared in the ballet company dancing with Massine and Baranova! Perhaps *dancing* is not quite the right word, but we were at least on the same stage.

It became obvious, pretty well from the word go, that this was a wildly uneconomical proposition and couldn't make money. So after this tour,

A couple of days after Melanie's birth. Sydney is looking gorgeous and radiantly happy, and I'm now a proud father.

which was highly enjoyable, it all came to an end and we didn't bring the show into the West End for a run.

Having had the terrible, tragic disappointment earlier over our first baby, we had decided to wait a couple of years before we tried again. However, at this time we discovered that Sydney was indeed expecting once again. Sydney was more beautiful than ever and blazingly well during this time and everything seemed to be pointing in the right direction. On June 8, Sydney felt that the baby was on the way. Being a bit over trained and anxious as I was, I rushed her down to the nursing home in a cab, checked her in and sat there. After a few hours, it was determined that the baby wasn't coming yet. So I took her back home again. Our baby was actually born on June 13 and everything went beautifully. We had a baby girl, who weighed in at 11 pounds 9 ounces! I always remember this very vividly—baby Melanie Virginia Sydney Morse made the headlines as one of the biggest babies to be born in the UK that year. The Virginia was for a cousin of Sydney's who had died in childhood and Sydney, of course, after her mother.

During this time I was continuing my work on BBC radio. They decided to do a production of Shakespeare's *Hamlet* and I played that title role for the first time in my life and the only time, unfortunately, in any medium. I never had the opportunity to play the part in the theatre or on television. But I did play it in this radio production and I took it very seriously, I remember. I went into weeks and weeks of study of the text and even went down for a spell with Sydney to a farm in Devonshire so I could get myself thoroughly fit. I went out and jogged, exercising vigorously for about a week to get in shape for a *radio* production!

I also played in a radio series about a gentleman private eye character, written by the successful author Francis Durbridge. The series was a weekly half-hour show built around that character called, simply, *Send for Paul Temple*. It became hugely popular and for the first time I began to receive a considerable volume of what nowadays (well, even then) is called fan mail. The character became immensely popular, but it threatened—as sometimes happens in our trade—to become permanently associated with me. If you become very successfully identified with a particular character, the audience will start to believe that you can't do anything else. There have been other instances where there was a danger of that happening to me, and it has happened to numbers of other actors. They get so deeply built into a particular character and a particular show that the audience after a while almost refuses to accept them as anything else.

There was one marvelous episode to do with *Send for Paul Temple* that I must mention. In those days, the BBC announcers were all terribly posh, speaking in this rather strangulated upper-class chinless twit kind of way. They were all compelled by the director general of the BBC, a fearsome character named Sir John Reith, to wear evening dress after six o'clock in the evening. So there they all were in the studio—nobody could see them—wearing dinner jackets, boiled starched shirts and winged collars and such! We, the cast, didn't go in for all of that; we wore more or less what we wanted. One fine night when we were doing the live broadcast of an episode of *Send for Paul Temple* one of these upper-class announcers came on, and in his most posh voice began, "Tonight, the BBC is proud to present episode number fourteen of *Send for Tall Pimple....*" Well, we were all on the floor rolling with laughter! The show went out live and couldn't be corrected. Unfortunately, I suppose it wasn't recorded and so such blissful moments as these disappeared forever.

A couple of years had passed since the birth of our daughter, Melanie, and Sydney and I thought it was about time to try again. So we did and, lo and behold—again on the thirteenth (but this time the thirteenth of September 1947)—our son, Hayward Barry Morse, was born. We gave him my father's middle name, as our first baby had been given my father's first name, Charles, and the middle name of Barry, since I had never had Barry as a true baptismal name.

I continued to do a lot of work on the stage during this period. One such play was called *Written for a Lady* by Leo Marks, which I did in 1948 at the Garrick Theatre in the West End. Playing opposite me was a lovely and gifted actress by the name of Margaretta Scott. Understudying me, and playing a small part, was a young lad who became one of our closest friends—Eric Bretherton. Eric was a marvelous chap who came originally from Southport, just outside of Liverpool, and had served during the war in the merchant navy. He decided, with rare courage, that he was going to take up show business after the war.

This production led me into a venture as an actor/manager, producing, directing, designing the set for, and playing in *The Voice of the Turtle* by John Van Druten. He had written a number of other quite successful and popular plays and it seemed to me to offer a marvelous commercial opportunity, partly because it was only a three character play and not very expensive to produce, although the set was rather complicated. It had a sort of timeliness about it, in a way.

The austerity that was brought about by the war, in particular the rationing, persisted long after the end of the war. Rationing was not put an end to until 1952, seven years after the war was over. So at this point, in 1948, the general austerity and rationing was still pretty much like it had been during the war. I got the idea that I could produce this play, and play in it; and I could quite readily cast the two female roles. The play itself is set in New York and is simply the development of a romance between a U.S. soldier and a girl. The soldier comes to pick up a girl at her apartment, which she shares with another girl. The girl with whom he has the date is a rather flighty, tarty sort of character. She doesn't really appeal to him very much, beyond the rather obvious ways! But he does become very interested in the other girl, named Sally, who is a quieter, shyer sort of young lady. It is a very well made play and sensitively written. Since Sydney and I had been earning quite well in recent years, it occurred to me that we could use some of our savings and actually launch this production. So we formed a company, a properly registered, limited company called Melward Plays, Ltd. You can guess where that name comes from—Mel from our daughter Melanie, and ward from our son Hayward. We had marvelous help and advice from within the profession from my agent, Al Parker, who was wonderfully cooperative and helpful, and also from a chap I'd come to know who was one of the producers of *The Assassin*; Stanley French was a great help with the "business end" of the business.

Our production of *The Voice of the Turtle* opened in February 1949, after several months of preproduction. I'd already had it in mind—and had discussed it with Al Parker and Stanley French—about the desirability of Sydney playing one of the two ladies, Olive Lashbrook (the tarty lady!), as Sydney was always very good at playing tarty ladies. It was something totally outside of her own personality and character; she rather loved being flaunty and cheap onstage. The other part, Sally Middleton, we decided should be played by Nova Pilbeam (the actress who'd played in the film *This Man Is Mine* with me). Nova was a marvelous pro and was well known in the UK for her various film roles, so she was a logical choice. I played the role of Bill Page. All the characters are American and I was able, with my knack—and that's what it is, really, a knack, just like riding a bicycle—for making other people's noises, to get the right sort of U.S. noises out of Sydney and Nova. This would turn out to be something of a novelty for audiences in the provinces as well, to see a stage play in which all the characters were American.

Gradually we pulled all the pieces together and, in order to keep the economics in order, I decided to direct the piece and design the set. The set was something of a challenge because it is a New York apartment of which we see a whole cross-section. Three rooms are on the stage at the same time. On Stage Left was the kitchen, in Stage Center the living room, and on Stage Right was the bedroom. I started to rough out, from the author's stage directions, what our set could be like. It was a rather unusual kind of design at the time, in that one of the attractions of the play was that the action moved from one room to another. As the play program states, "The action takes place over a weekend in early April in an apartment in the East 60s, near Third Avenue, New York City, during the course of the war." To promote this setting I went around and talked various companies into providing equipment for our setting in exchange for a credit in our program. It was a good form of promotion and advertising for them. Advertising wasn't as widespread or as energetic as it is today, particularly in those austere times. I wanted to present a set which looked—in the North American sense—quite luxurious, which would be fairly exotic to an English audience, in particular the kitchen fittings. Such things as a "fitted kitchen" did not exist in the UK in those days. So I got this company who were manufacturers of kitchen units to supply the most luxurious fitted kitchen unit that they could, with a sink built in, a fridge, an electric stove, all of which I incorporated into our set. The sheets and furnishing fabrics which covered the armchair and sofa in the living room, and the bedcover in the bedroom, were all very fine looking and supplied by these various companies. The gowns for Nova and Sydney were provided by Pinewood Studios. I went to the film studios where I knew people and where I had worked and got them to agree to let our actresses be outfitted from their rather extensive wardrobe departments. This was necessary because at this point there was clothes rationing in effect. One couldn't go out and buy luxurious clothes as and when one wanted. Everything from stockings and pajamas for Nova, ladies' shoes, champagne, right down to cigarette lighters and cigarettes (I'm ashamed to admit that Nova and I both smoked in the play) was provided by various firms, all duly credited. That was something of a novelty in theatre production in those days.

The uncommonly elegant set I designed for _The Voice of the Turtle_. Sydney is on the phone to the left, and I'm sitting center stage on the sofa with Nova Pilbeam. The fitted kitchen is on the right.

Our manager and stage director was a chap called Aubrey Denning and our stage managers (in charge of preparing the sets, getting the props in the right place, and ringing the phone bell when it needed to be rung, etc.) were Eric Bretherton and Pauline Growse. Eric and Pauline were at that time "together," as we say. Just after the tour Eric and Pauline married and remained friends with Sydney and me for many years. As well as acting as stage managers, Eric understudied me and Pauline understudied the two female parts. So our whole company consisted of me, Sydney, Nova, Eric, Pauline, Aubrey, and a carpenter who traveled with us—Ernest "Ernie" Williamson, who was a great character. It was he who was responsible for erecting the set. As you can imagine, traveling and reerecting this quite complicated and elaborate set week-by-week was a sizeable job for a stage carpenter.

The tour began in February, not long before our tenth wedding anniversary, and a jolly old time we had. There was a rather interesting part of the play that called for a bit of ingenuity. My character, Bill (a sergeant in the army), at one point in the play offers to get lunch and goes into the kitchen.

During this time Sally, played by Nova Pilbeam, makes a phone call, then comes back into the kitchen as Bill is breaking eggs into a bowl. Bill, we gather, is rather a domestically-minded sort of chap. He says to her, "Come and learn how to make scrambled eggs properly," and Sally replies, "All right."

"First you break the eggs," Bill instructs. "Oh yes, I do know that," she says. "Do you have an egg-beater?" Bill asks.

In the UK in 1949 eggs were still rationed—two eggs per person *per week!* So there was never any question of actually *using* eggs, though I didn't want to give up this bit of business in the play because it's rather charming. So I thought of a way of getting around it. First I got everybody I knew to save their egg shells as carefully as they could while we were rehearsing, and during the time coming up to the production of the show. Friends in the company, the stage management people, and our family would all save their shells as completely as they could. These shells would be stuck back together again with sticky tape, with a piece of tinned apricot inside—a bright yellow approximating the color of an egg yolk. Then, when we got to this piece of business in our handsomely equipped kitchen onstage, I would get the bowl, take a couple of these so-called eggs out of the fridge and proceed to break them into the bowl. Out would come the yellow "yolk"! Well, it caused a tremendous sensation with the audience wherever we went; it was quite rewarding. The audience would be so appalled to see, as they thought, perfectly good eggs being wasted as a part of the action on the stage. There would be a sort of a gasp that went right round the audience every night, and indignant mutterings! We actually got letters telling us how disgraceful it was that we should be allowed to waste eggs in this way. We got quite a lot of publicity by making it public that, in fact, we weren't using real eggs. This shows you how simple it is, sometimes, to totally deceive an audience.

We played over 30 cities and well over 250 performances of the show in a tour lasting about eight months. We played all sorts of theatres, popular and less popular, grand and prestigious, smallish and obscure—because we could afford, with our modest-sized company, to play in smaller theatres where larger scale productions couldn't afford to go. During portions of the tour we played some places where "straight" plays very seldom went. Theatres like the Empire West Hartlepool up in the northeast of England. In those days those sorts of theatres, which had formerly been music halls, were given over all too often to salacious musical revues. The previous week's presentation had been called *Strip, Strip Hooray* and an upcoming production was to be called *All Nudes Is Good News* or some such title as that! So we were able to play in some of these places where, much to the

NOVA PILBEAM
AND
BARRY MORSE
in
"FLOWERS FOR THE LIVING"
BY TONI BLOCK

This was just one of several plays in which I performed with Nova Pilbeam. Note all the hair I've got, and Nova jumping up into the air.

surprise and sometimes delight of audiences, they got an intelligent play instead of this parade of half-clothed girls. As well, we played some of the more prestigious theatres in cities like Liverpool, Brighton, etc. We were literally all over the UK, including up in Scotland, where we played Edinburgh, Glasgow, and so forth. It was, of course, a valuable "shop window" for me, emerging as a proper commercial director and something of a box office name. The standard of production was very good, and I can say that honestly, without vanity. It was a worthwhile venture in all sorts of ways, not the least of which was that we enjoyed it.

I played in another stage production that year in the West End called *Flowers for the Living*, which was quite a brave play for its time. It was a play of some considerable social significance written by a young woman named Toni Block. The play was a celebration of the social changes which had been brought about by the war. The implication of the title was that some of the fruits of knowledge which had come out of the war should be directed towards the living, that the outcome of the war need not necessarily be exclusively devoted to providing flowers for the dead. It was the story about a young man named Stan Roberts (whom I played), who had been born and brought up in a working class Cockney family. As a result of his experiences and his observations during his travels in the course of the war, his mind had been broadened considerably more than would have been the case if there hadn't been a war. The story dealt with his social advancement in that he took up with and wooed a girl from a "superior" social class. It was a very good cast, many of whom were thoroughgoing Cockney characters. I was able to make good use of my "native wood-notes wild" to some extent, although what I hoped to try and present was a chap who had had some of the "Cockney-ism" rubbed off him by his travels and experiences in the service. This was being presented five years after the war, when we had our first Labour government and some people were beginning to realize that old social barriers and awful class distinctions which had been so rigid before the Second World War were, at least to some degree, being removed and erased. In the cast—and we were beginning to be recognized as something of a partnership—was Nova Pilbeam from *The Voice of the Turtle*. Both she and I were reasonably recognizable younger names in the theatre.

In 1950 there was a special broadcast put out to celebrate the eightieth birthday of Queen Mary, the widow of King George V. Queen Mary had been a very keen theatregoer throughout her life, but was now somewhat frail. It wasn't believed that a command performance could be organized in the theatre to celebrate her birthday due to her health, so it was decided that the BBC should present a radio evening for her as a command performance. As she was an enthusiastic reader of who-dunnits, it was decided that as a part of this Royal Command Radio Evening a dramatized who-dunnit would be presented and, of course, the logical person to go to was Miss Agatha Christie, later Dame Agatha Christie. They hit upon a long short story of hers which was called *Three Blind Mice*. It was adapted for radio and shortly before the occasion of this broadcast, Martyn C. Webster, who had been the director of the *Send for Paul Temple* series (and was also a staff director at BBC) called me up and said, "You've gotta be in this Royal Command Performance we're going to do for Queen Mary." I replied, "Oh, dear, I suppose that means no fee, does it?" He said, "I expect so, but you'll get a letter from Marlborough House or Buckingham Palace or someone...." Nevertheless, I accepted and played the leading role in this piece, that of a plainclothes detective who becomes embroiled in a murder mystery. It all went off reasonably well, and we went round to the pub afterwards. It was a custom that we quite often followed after we'd done a performance. We'd all repair, with the director and sometimes other crew members and technicians, to a pub near Broadcasting House in Great Portland Street to have a drink and mull over how it went.

By this time I had become what was known as an actor/manager. I had put money into and produced, as well as directed and played in, a play which we toured throughout the previous year in 1949. So we were sitting there in the pub talking about the show we'd just done and it was Martyn

Webster who said, "You know, *Three Blind Mice* wouldn't make a bad stage play would it? The script we used tonight could be readily adapted and perhaps expanded a bit. It could be played all in one set—you could play the part you've just played, there's a part that Sydney could play, and it might be quite a worthwhile kind of commercial proposition." I very pompously drew myself up to my full height and told him, "Martyn, my dear fellow, that's not the quality of work that I'm interested in." I turned it down. The project was subsequently taken up and adapted, then produced commercially by someone else. The name was changed to *The Mousetrap*. It holds the distinction of being *the longest-running play in the history of the world!* Indeed, it has played for more than half a century. Our dear son Hayward played, or as he sometimes says, "served a spell," in *The Mousetrap* just a few years ago himself. So, I have the rare distinction of rejecting the possibility of producing and playing in *The Mousetrap*. Of course, I would have been a multimillionaire many times over. I count this as one of my principal claims to fame!

9

"Tell Me All Your Troubles"

NOËL COWARD WAS VERY KIND TO Sydney and me many times. Back in 1942 he was making his very notable film called *In Which We Serve*, which was all about the Royal Navy. It was codirected by a chap who went on to become one of the most eminent British film directors—David Lean. Coward wanted me to play a part in it of a young naval fellow, who was called Flags because he was a signaling officer.

At this time I was considered to be a bit of a hot prospect, and was led to believe by my agent, Al Parker, that I was reasonably assured to get this part as Flags. But I hadn't got it yet.

In the course of the film the ship in which they are serving is sunk and they have to spend quite a long time clinging to a raft, soaking wet and being battered about, in the open sea. Some of it was to be shot in a tank, but some of it also was to be shot in open water.

As this was in 1942, and the war having been going for three years, the producers naturally wanted to know why this young fellow offering himself for the part was available. Why was I not serving in one of the armed forces? Well, they found out I had been certified as suffering from TB, and because of that they couldn't get insurance on me for all this time in the water, exposed to the elements. The result was that, no matter what they thought of me, I ceased being even considered for the part.

Coward, bless his heart, was marvelously understanding about the huge, almost disastrous, disappointment it was not to get this quite prominent part. By 1950 he had constructed a musical called *Ace of Clubs*, all about the doings in a nightclub, and there was a character in it—a rather sleazy character, but quite small—which he wanted me to play. Well, at this time I was directing what we hoped would be a West End production, *Pommy*.

97

Set in Australia, *Pommy* was written by W.P. Lipscomb, a well-known writer both for the theatre and for films, and had to do with events on a sheep station in western Australia. The word *pommy* is Australian slang generally used to derisively describe Brits. This play was going on tour and I was invited to direct it. The cast was made up of all sorts of different actors, among them Cyril Cusack, Ronald Howard (the son of the film star Leslie Howard), and the Australian actor Bill Kerr.

So when I read the script of *Ace of Clubs* for the first time and saw this rather incomplete and not very prominent part that they were asking me to play, I decided I was going to have to turn it down. I delayed for quite some time making any reply through my agent. I just said, "Let Mr. Coward know that I'll be in touch with him personally."

Ace of Clubs was not, in the event, successful. I thought it was considerably below Noël's usual standards. In fact, it had been written by Coward to create a star part for the chap who was the love of his life at that time—and for the rest of his life—Graham Payn.

I was rather embarrassed to have to say that I had reservations about the script. And I had even more reservations about this subsidiary part that I was being asked to play. I thought it would be a bit of a step backwards for me, but they persisted in pursuing me to play it.

Eventually I decided that the only solution would be to just go to Coward's house—he lived down near Belgrave Square, not very far from where we were living in Kensington—and deliver my message personally. So one evening I said to Sydney, "Look, I'm going to go down there and just make a clean breast of it in an evasive letter—or rather *not* make a clean breast of it—but I'll just go down there personally and shove the script and the accompanying letter through the letterbox. He will have a polite answer, and I shall be off tomorrow anyway."

In fact, I was due to leave the next day, to catch up with *Pommy*, which was still playing in the provinces. This was still a few weeks prior to the opening of the Coward musical. So I wrote the apologetic letter, trying as tactfully as I could to make the excuse that I was bound to keep an eye on this play I was directing and which I was hoping would be heading for the West End, which was true, of course. Therefore I couldn't undertake to play in another production destined to come into the West End at about the same time.

I got myself together, got a taxi, and went down to Coward's place in Belgravia. I went with trepidation up to the front door, noticing somewhat to my unease that there were lights on in the place. But I thought, *Perhaps he's not in, and if I move smartly and shove the package in through the letterbox and take off before somebody comes to pick it up, I'll be out of sight and earshot.*

There I was, surreptitiously slipping my large envelope into the letter-box, when the door is thrown open and there he is! Noël Coward himself, looking for all the world like one of those caricatures of him, with a cig-arette and wearing a silk dressing gown, and he said, "Hello, hello, hello. Do come in and tell me all your troubles."

What had happened was that he had been forewarned about my arrival. Coincidentally, just after I had set forth to go down to his place, he had telephoned me. Of course I wasn't there, but Sydney answered the phone. Well, Sydney was incapable of untruth. She couldn't, or didn't, think of any kind of evasive answer. Noël said, "Where's Barry?" and she told him, "Actually, he's on his way down to see you. He just left in a taxi." "Oh, really?" he said, and hatched his plan.

He forestalled me, opened the door and took me in, and we sat and talked, I rather uneasily and he rather enjoying the whole joke of the thing. He didn't actually really care if I played this small role or not. I succeeded in more or less persuading him that my main responsibility had to be to *Pommy*, so I managed to talk my way out of *Ace of Clubs*. When the time came on May 15, 1950, I sent Coward a wire of good wishes for the open-ing of his show. Unfortunately, the play was rather frigidly received and didn't last very long.

That was one of my brushes with Noël Coward, but he was to continue to be very friendly towards Sydney and me and he figures in the first pro-duction that I did in the theatre in Canada a year or so later; but we're not quite up to that yet.

Meanwhile, *Pommy* was playing, but, in the event, it did not come into the West End, which I think was rather a pity. It was an unusual, refresh-ing and quite worthwhile comedy with some lovely performances in it.

I was asked to play in and direct a play called *Springtime for Henry* by an organization called the Inland Waterways Association. It was an organization designed to restore and popularize the extraordinary network of inland waterways which there are in the UK. It's not widely known, even by British people, that there is a marvelous network of canals linking (in some cases) the rivers of the UK, which were created and built just before railways came into popularity, in the early part of the nineteenth century. The leading spirits of the Inland Waterways Association were Robert Fordyce Aickman, a notable writer, and Peter Scott, only son of Captain Robert Scott of the Antarctic. He was a notable figure, widely known as a naturalist and also as an artist who did marvelous paintings of nature and wildlife.

They had conceived the idea of having an Inland Waterways Festival, which would have as its leading event a Rally of Boats. They decided that they would ask me to direct and play in a, preferably, light-hearted comedy type of piece as a feature of this Rally of Boats. They realized that if they were going to invite people to come from the four corners of the UK to the town which is more or less the geographic center of England, called Market Harborough, they'd better serve up something for them when they got there. So I was introduced to Peter Scott and—seeing that I was a great enthusiast for all kinds of improbable causes—he asked me if I would join with him to set up this Festival Rally of Boats.

Peter Scott was a very charming and outgoing kind of guy, and after some persuasion from me, Peter (who had never acted before), said that he was willing to play in this piece. *Springtime for Henry* is a four-handed play—two men and two women—and so it was agreed that he and I would play the two male characters, and that we would engage actress Carla Lehmann and Sydney for the female roles.

In August we went up to Market Harborough where we played *Springtime for Henry* as the main entertainment. It was a wonderful event. People came in all sorts of boats—troops of Sea Scouts came in their converted lifeboats, elderly couples came in their covered canoes, and others from far and wide all over the UK. When they arrived we had all kinds of exhibitions of paintings and photographs, and Peter himself gave several talks. It was a great success.

Peter's boat was named *Beatrice* and he had brought it up to Market Harborough to show off to everybody, and of course to have somewhere to stay in. *Beatrice* was actually a type of narrowboat. A narrowboat is some seventy feet long, and quite narrow, so they are able to navigate their way into and out of the various locks that these canals have. We were invited by Peter after the festival to join him on *Beatrice* for a lovely canal journey back down through the southwest of England to Slimbridge. And we did. That journey of more than one hundred miles took nine days in August of 1950 and it was a memorably happy time. Peter himself wasn't able to be with us all the time, but Sydney was there, and Peter's wife—a lovely lady called Elizabeth Jane Howard, a notably popular novelist—was also with us. Robert Fordyce Aickman, the other leading spirit of the Inland Waterways Association, was also on board. Various other people came and went for odd days, but Sydney and I were in *Beatrice* as part of her crew for the whole journey, sailing through all sorts of wonderful backwaters that I never even knew existed. It was a great holiday/adventure and the Festival Rally of Boats was hugely successful and has resulted in the canal system being immensely revived.

In early 1951 I went into a tour presentation of a two-handed play called *The Four Poster* by Jan de Hartog which was, in a way, the biography of a bed. It traces—throughout the whole of their married life—the adventures and misadventures of a young couple who obtain this particular four poster bed, which they keep throughout the whole of the rest of their days. The play is a chronicle through many years and the two characters get progressively older. It was rather a challenge for two actors, with two quite demanding parts. Once again, I was invited along with Nova Pilbeam to play these two parts. We had now become quite established as a theatrical duo and were great friends; however, the two of us never had a personal relationship. This production was quite successful and we toured for several months. It was the last theatre production that I did in England for many years; our family stood at the cusp of a real life-change.

Sydney came from a Canadian family and her mother, Dolly, was born in Vancouver, British Columbia. Dolly's father, whose name was Robert Palmer, had been the first city engineer of Vancouver. After the Second World War, Dolly went back to Canada to visit various members of her family, including her son and daughter (Sydney's brother Bob and sister Jennifer). During her visit she became rather ill and was advised that she shouldn't attempt to go back to England for the time being. Also at this time our daughter Melanie had a tendency to "chest troubles." At about the age of three she developed measles, after which she contracted pneumonia and was seriously ill and in hospital for quite some length of time. It was suggested to us that living in London was not the most healthy of climates for her. Due to these reasons we started to think about the idea of making an exploratory trip, or an extended stay in Canada.

Another consideration was that Britain was in what, for a number of years, was called "austerity." The UK was economically very badly damaged by the Second World War, and continued to be in a severely depressed state, certainly in the arts fields, for quite a long time. That was not particularly encouraging for a young family with reasonably wide ambitions, as we had.

Then there was me and my standing in the profession. When I started to talk about the possibility of going to Canada, most people thought I was crazy, in particular Al Parker, my agent. He had brought me forward in the profession to the extent where I was being recognized as one of the up and coming younger actors. Sydney and I were able to live in a fairly comfortable way with a nice apartment in Kensington and a live-in Nanny. Therefore, when I started to talk about the possibilities of visiting Canada with a view to perhaps settling there, it drew responses like "You must be crazy!" Indeed, I knew nothing about—nor did I know anybody who knew anything about—our profession in Canada. As far as I could gather our profession virtually did not exist there. Almost all theatrical productions that played in Canada originated in the USA (most tours organized from New York) or in some cases tours originated from the UK. There was hardly any native professional activity at all.

Also, there was a limitation that if you were visiting Canada, no matter what the size of your family group or for how long you were proposing to go, you were only allowed to take a sum total of fifty pounds. I thought, *How can we swing this? I can't possibly be visiting Canada and living not only perhaps with, but even* on *my in-laws.* I felt there was some kind of challenge attached to having "a go" in Canada, even though I was totally ignorant of what opportunities there might be. Nobody in Sydney's family in Canada had any connection with show biz in any way, so there wasn't anyone to ask advice from. Nevertheless, I wanted to find someone to consult who might know what went on in Canada. I thought, *Ah! The BBC, they'll know whether there's anything going on in Canada.* So I went to pick the brains of Val Gielgud.

I said, "I'm thinking of making this trip to Canada and I'd just like to know if there's any possibility of my being able to do any professional work there."

"Oh, yes, there is the BBC's counterpart in radio—the CBC, the Canadian Broadcasting Corporation," he replied, "and they do very good quality radio. I'll write a letter of introduction for you to my opposite number."

We gave up the flat in DeVere Gardens and set forth, with our children and our huge consignment of luggage. As you can imagine, we had virtually everything we owned with us. We were seen off by all sorts of friends and relatives, some twenty or more who had gathered to wish us well and to say goodbye. In those days transatlantic travel was not quite as easy a prospect as it's become in the years since; and the very real thought in the back of everybody's minds was that this might be the last time that we would all see each other.

10

"Just Mounties and Polar Bears"

ON FRIDAY, APRIL 27, 1951, we sailed for Canada in the good ship *Franconia*. I don't remember much about the journey itself, beyond the fact that it was very encouraging to see that Melanie, who had been so ill such a short time before, was already benefiting from the sea air and the general excitement of being on a big ship.

We landed at Quebec City late on the night of the fourth of May. We disembarked, and traveled down to Montreal by train, where we were met by all the assembled family in the Montreal station. We started to settle ourselves down for—well, we didn't know quite what. I started to go around and visit people with the view to doing various jobs. Within a week or so I had met a young woman called Joy Thomson, who ran a theatre in the heart of Montreal called the Mountain Playhouse. The decision was made that we would open with a play of Noël Coward's called *Present Laughter*. I was the first to play the lead part after Coward himself had played it for the opening production. The leading character in it, Gary, is a flamboyant and rather *overly* theatrical actor. There was a lovely part in it for Sydney, and it was agreed that we would appear together in this opening production. That is what ultimately led to our careers blossoming in Canada, and to our eventually becoming Canadian citizens. I always like to boast that I was "English by the accident of birth—but became Canadian by the exercise of choice."

There was a whole group of us in those years: Sydney and I, Christopher Plummer, James Doohan, Joan Blackman, Corinne Orr, and numbers of others. It was almost a repertory company of people who worked together in radio and the theatre. There were other people involved in that production of *Present Laughter* whom I am still friends with, who live still in Canada, such as Corinne Conley and Bonar Stuart.

On June 11 there is an entry in my diary which reads, "Open *Present Laughter*!!! (God, what a night)." It was one of the most triumphant first nights that I've ever been involved in, and we got extravagantly good notices. To help with our publicity for this production, Noël Coward very kindly came to our aid. I had been in touch with him by telephone and told him that I was doing this play of his as my baptism by fire in Canada, and I asked him if he would agree to our conducting a transatlantic telephone conversation, to be recorded and broadcast by the CBC. He said, "Yes, of course. Give me a time." It all went off charmingly, and he was delightful and funny, and said something like, "Oh, Barry, my dear! You're in the colonies are you? Is it snowing?" It was the middle of June! The play was originally scheduled to run only a couple of weeks, but it kept on being extended because it was selling out. It ran all the way on through the middle of August and ended up setting a record for the length of run of a play in English in Canada.

In Montreal I also met Rupert Caplan, who was in charge of radio drama at the CBC. I met him in May, and he had received a letter about me from Val Gielgud. It was on the second of August that I made my first appearance. The play was still running in the theatre, but CBC were very kind and offered me a continuing part on a daily program which was Canada's first radio soap opera, called *Laura Limited*. Laura Limited was the name of a fashion house business run by the leading lady character, and they introduced a character who was to become her follower, more or less her boyfriend, which I played. He was an English chap who came to Canada for some reason or other and began to be interested in Laura, and she in him. It was broadcast somewhere around lunchtime, because that was the time when the largest domestic audience could be achieved, and the show was aimed largely at ladies. We didn't rehearse very long, and it was all done from the CBC studio building on Dorchester Street, which had formerly been the Ford Hotel, in Montreal. Among the cast who played in it was Christopher Plummer as, I think, a rascally younger brother of the central character, Laura. Sydney and I first knew Christopher as a lad living and working in Montreal. Also in the serial was the young William Shatner, later of *Star Trek* fame. He was just trying to get his foot in the door in the performing field. He wasn't troubled by having to wear a toupee in those days, of course, and it was on radio, anyway. I started to play on this series pretty well every day, and continued to work in the theatre in the evenings. And so it went on through the rest of that summer.

At this time I would say "Yes" to almost anything anybody asked me to do. Sydney used to have a stock joke; she'd say to me, "Thank heavens you're not a girl, because you don't seem to be able to say 'No'!" Whatever anybody asked me to do, I would always say, "Sure, why not?" The pattern was that most days I would go down to the CBC, traveling on the streetcar, for one or other of these shows. There was scarcely a day I wasn't at CBC for some rehearsal or performance of a radio show. From the early part of December onwards, I started working in Toronto, and was commuting fairly regularly. The center of operations for English language broadcasting was in Toronto. A great deal of French language broadcasting was done from Montreal, but most of what would have been considered leading shows in English were done from Toronto. We discussed the possibility of moving to Toronto, and in due time we did, but at this point we felt we shouldn't uproot the children so soon after they'd settled into their schools in Montreal. Partly because my dear mother-in-law, Dolly, was living with us and had been so kind as to organize living accommodation for us before we came, and partly because of the children being newly settled, we felt it was better all round if I commuted to Toronto.

In 1952 I ended up playing in 152 episodes of the *Laura Limited* soap opera. That, quite aside from all the other things I did, greatly helped our income. We did another production of *Present Laughter* in Montreal and, although it didn't run for many performances, it was popular. I wrote to Noël Coward to tell him about the success we'd had, and there were plans for us to do his play *Private Lives* at the Montreal Playhouse during the summer of 1952, which we did indeed do. Sydney played opposite me, and we had a great time and a huge success. I was becoming Canada's apology for Noël Coward!

I first met my friend David Greene on a production of *Private Lives*, in England, in which he was playing the pompous boring husband. David was a terrible giggler. We nearly got fired because—he always said—there was something I did during the breakfast scene that would set him off, and he would giggle uncontrollably, at a moment when he was supposed to be being terribly pompous and all that. The management was very upset about this, but we didn't get fired. Later, David was very keen to start directing. This was at the point that the CBC were seeking to engage people to become directors. I told David about it and that was how he got launched as a television director in Toronto. He went on to do many very good productions in Canada, and eventually moved down to the States, continuing his success.

My agent in London, Al Parker, was continually imploring me to return. He couldn't see at all why I would want to turn my back on what I must immodestly confess was a quite successful career in the UK. Our decision to move to Canada had been a very difficult one. I was earning quite handsomely, relative to the time, of course. Naturally, Al was rather incredulous when it was beginning to look as if we were going to stay in Canada. I explained to him how things were developing, and how I was becoming a prominent part of the development of our trade. He said to me once, when he was getting rather exasperated, *"For Christ's sake, Barry! What is there in Canada? It's just Mounties and polar bears ... isn't it?"* But he was very supportive and sympathetic, because he realized we had other considerations, as well as the purely professional ones.

At this time I got to know Mavor Moore, a writer and actor who lived and worked mostly in Toronto. He said to me in early 1952, "You know, the CBC is planning to launch a television service in this country." I said that I had heard something about it, but I wasn't sure if it was a firm plan. He said, "Yes, indeed. It's going to go on the air at the beginning of September. You must be the only person in this country with any first-hand experience of working in television. I think it will be very worth your while staying on to see how it all goes." At the point when we arrived in 1951 you could have put the whole of the English speaking dramatic profession in the country—actors, writers, producers, name what you will—into a quite small bus! Literally. And here we were now at a point when television was about to begin, and the theatre was beginning to develop, and it was beginning to be recognized that Canada had a considerable future in these fields. And I was a part of it.

On June 16 we opened *Private Lives* at the Mountain Playhouse. Sydney and I played the two leading parts, and Sydney's sister, Jennifer, helped us with the set for the show, which was very beautiful. Our dear friend Jack Creley played the part of the dull husband, although he is in fact anything but dull. It was immensely praised and popular. Noël Coward did another telephone interview to help with our publicity. He was marvelously charming, enthusiastic, and supportive—which was natural, because we were doing one of his plays, but it contributed immensely to the success of the production.

Then came a production of *The Man Who Came to Dinner*, which was a popular potboiling comedy of the time, and I played the leading role in it of an irascible, crusty old man. I think I had a beard. This character is a critic who comes to a small town to give a talk and is supposed to be going to have dinner with some family in this town, but he falls on the path leading up to their front door. The result is that instead of just spending an evening having a dinner, he has to spend two or three weeks in these people's home, in a wheelchair. It's a rather farcical relationship that grows between him and the family in whose house he happens to fetch up. Playing the son of the house—a relatively small part—was William Shatner. Now, Bill, at that time—and he reminds me of this whenever we meet—was very much under the influence, as many young actors were, of The Method, in particular, someone who's reckoned to be the greatest practitioner of The Method: Marlon Brando. Well, Marlon Brando's characteristic acting style really consisted mostly of mumbling into the carpet. Influenced by him, many young actors adopted this mumbling method. In this case William Shatner was called upon to provide a lot of the feed lines for my character's witticisms. So, of course, it was very important that his dialogue be absolutely clearly heard. But poor Bill, under the influence of Marlon Brando, would persist in mumbling his lines. So I would very often make him say the same line *twice* by saying things like, "What's that you say, son? I can't hear you, boy!" and so he would have to say it again!

So there we were, and television was just beginning. Mixed up in one of these early television shows were our children, in a play called *Noises in the Nursery*. It involved two young children, played by Melanie and Hayward, then 7 and almost 5 years old respectively, along with Sydney and me and broadcast live on September 1, 1952. It had to do with things children heard in their nursery, and the way *they* interpreted them, as compared to what those sounds actually were.

This was followed by another stage play called *Dinner for Three*. It was presented—that is to say financed—by a very nice fellow called Louis Levin, who was married to a lady who had been an actress in Vienna; they now lived in Canada. His wife's name was Elfi Koenig. Louis put this play on largely to promote his wife as an actress. The piece was an impossibly silly romantic comedy written by Herbert Kramer. It involved a slightly rascally lover of this irresistibly beautiful young woman, whom Elfi played, and her rather pompous and dull husband. Well, I played the rather dull husband, and the lover was played by Herbert Kramer. He had appeared on the North American scene, having come from Austria or Germany—we never really found out—and suspicions began to arise that he might well have been some kind of Nazi, because he certainly behaved like it. He was very pushy and assertive. Why had I got myself involved in all of this? Well, it was because Louis Levin, bless his heart, was a pleasant fellow and his wife was an awfully nice woman, and he was financing this project and offered to pay me very generously for this third role. The production was also directed by Herbert Kramer. He was rather paunchy and had a *very* heavy and rather Hitlerian kind of accent, and I remember he had to speak the line, "There iz nothink more attraktif than dinner for tree." That's the way he spoke! And he also introduced a couple of musical numbers

Hayward and Melanie ("the Morsels"), along with Sydney and me at home in Toronto.

into this piece. He had an awful, unpleasant, grating voice, which went along with his grating and unpleasant personality. Well, it was a foregone disaster, of course! But I, perhaps rather cynically, agreed to do it—mostly because of the financial rewards involved. I should have had more confidence in myself and just turned it down out of hand.

We opened on October 13 at the Grand Theatre in London, Ontario, a lovely old theatre, and I've played there again in more recent years. *Dinner for Three* was promoted as being a world premiere, and so many press people came, including a dear chum of ours, Herbert Whittaker, the then critic of the *Toronto Globe & Mail* newspaper, and one of the most respected critics in Canada. His review started like this, "Last night I attended the world premiere of a presentation called *Dinner for Three*. It was an experience I shall never forget." And he went on to itemize all the various shortcomings, not to mention *horrors*, of this play. He was kind enough to me, and he was kind enough to Elfi Koenig, but he had some appalling things to say about the material and about the leading man. Well, the leading man, Herbert Kramer—who directed and was more or less managing this whole thing—extracted from that review the very words, "An experience I shall never forget." and quoted them in ads, as if it had been the triumph of this critic's working lifetime! We played down there only for about a week, and came back up to Montreal, where I was again doing various radio shows. We opened *Dinner for Three* at the Gésu Theatre in Montreal, and played it there for only a week. It continued to be just as terrible as it had started to be! So *Dinner for Three*, which was announced as being "Prior to Broadway," came to an untimely yet merciful end in Montreal and has yet to reach Broadway. In my diary in mid–November there is the notation "Finish *Dinner for Three*," with three exclamation marks after it!!! So that was the end of that.

At this time, it became inevitable that we should center ourselves in Toronto. People kept saying to us, "You keep coming down here to do shows, why don't you come and live here?" On February 2, 1953, I traveled to Toronto, while Sydney stayed behind in Montreal for a little while to tie up loose ends there. Our family life during this time was helped by having Sydney's mother, Dolly, with us. She and Sydney between them were marvelously organized at caring for the family and Sydney was still doing a certain amount of work as an actress. The children were occasionally working with us, but only very rarely, as we never wanted them to turn into *professional* children, so we only allowed them to do things which didn't interrupt their school life. But the heroine of the whole time, really, was Sydney. She had, always very clearly, in her mind that her first duty was to the family and to the children, and to me, of course. I don't think she's ever been given enough credit among all the wonderful things our family has managed to accomplish, for being the anchor and motive power. People often asked us, "What is the secret of a long and happy marriage in your very precarious and perilous profession?" Sydney would say, "Well, it's rather like playing a musical instrument. You have to practice a lot, and never for a moment think of giving it up if you happen to play a wrong note." I won't pretend that I (and perhaps Sydney, too) didn't occasionally play a wrong note. But we never allowed that to disturb the larger harmony.

11

"Pioneers and Bureaucrats"

I CONTINUED TO WORK MORE OR LESS all of the time. The working day, all the hours rehearsing and performing these different shows, didn't take into account such things as thinking about one's performance, and, first and foremost, learning the lines. Thankfully, I seem to have been gifted with blotting paper instead of brains in my head, because they all do go in fairly readily. I used always to carry my script around in my hand, and Sydney would say, "Why do you always carry your script around in your hand? Are you hoping that the lines will eventually go up your arm?"

In early 1953 I appeared in Robert Louis Stevenson's *Ebbtide*, and a very interesting production that was, one of many productions I did with my old friend David Greene. One of the other leading characters in it was played by a chap who later became quite well known, Lorne Greene. *Ebbtide* is about a bunch of merchant seamen who get wrecked on some island. I played a marvelously grotty character, a scruffy and verminous Cockney deck hand. At that time the commercial sponsor of many television dramas that the CBC did was General Motors. The advertisers and the advertising agencies would try and influence the content of the performances, trying to remove things that they thought might upset their viewers. Of course, they only bought commercial time, they didn't have any real control over the content. I had a big fight with the advertising agency for General Motors because they observed during the run-through of this performance of *Ebbtide* that I spent a good deal of time, as this character, picking my nose. They thought this was rather revolting, and might upset potential Cadillac purchasers. So they tried to stop me doing this! I told them, with a good deal of pleasure, to go away and pick their noses. We had quite a showdown. I'm glad to say my friend and director, David Greene, upheld me in all of that.

Hereabouts I started to work with another old friend, Patrick Macnee, who later came to fame as the leading character of John Steed in *The Avengers* television series. He had turned up in Toronto, and we started to work together. Indeed, he stayed with us in the apartment we had in Toronto while he was looking for somewhere to live. I'd been camping out at our new home in Toronto since March 25, and on April 10, Sydney and the Morsels—as I used to call Melanie and Hayward—arrived, and we settled into our new home. The next day was our performance of *Ebbtide*, which had up until now been in rehearsals.

The CBC's headquarters at that time were on Jarvis Street. The radio department was housed in what had been a school building. It had been built, I suppose, around the turn of the century to house a girls' school called Havergal College. That was where the CBC's radio programs were produced and transmitted from. The principal drama studio was the famous Studio G, which had been at one time the assembly hall for Havergal College. Various of the rooms had been made over to other purposes, including one I always remember with great amusement, the office of the CBC staff announcers. Among them was Lorne Greene. Their office, where they all examined what shows they were going to do, had been one of the dormitory rooms of the girls' school. They had carefully preserved a sign, alongside a bell-push in that room, which read, "If you want a mistress in the night, ring this bell."

Among my other new involvements were the radio broadcasts put out by the CBC for its *Schools* programs. CBC transmitted educational programs to schools all across the country. They were historical or literary oriented, and included every kind of subject under the sun. Because they were live, they all had to be put out early in the morning. We used to have to turn up to rehearse at about 7:00 a.m., in order to go on the air as we frequently did by 9:00 in the morning. The *Schools* programs were largely organized by a lady called Lola Thompson. She was a very cheerful and friendly lady who had been a dancer. She was able to provide considerable volumes of work for us actors, and there were a team of us who became almost like a regular company, playing in so many of these productions to do with Canadian history or the classics. Turning up at 7:00 in the morning to rehearse was something actors by and large weren't very good at, as we all tended to be a bit light-headed at that time of the day! There were many occasions, when we were supposed to be involved in very serious matters, when we were prone to be giggling. The great John Drainie was almost always in these broadcasts, and another great character of that era whom it's a joy to remember, Tommy Tweed, was always one for working pranks and pulling everybody's leg. There was an occasion when John Drainie was delivering a long narration about some event in Canadian history. The microphone was usually encased in a sort of baffle screen to prevent extraneous noises in the studio from being picked up, and in the case of this rather large Studio G, it prevented such things as echoes. So this one morning John was having to plow through pages and pages of narration and Tommy Tweed crept round the baffle screen and, with his cigarette lighter, set fire to the bottom of John's script! So there was poor Drainie trying to put out the flames consuming his script, and keep talking at the same time, because it was all live!

Another curious thing of those days was that for the most part crowd noises were made by the cast. They didn't often use recorded sound effects, because they weren't supposedly as easily timed or controlled as live actors! So very often we would be called upon to represent angry scenes in the House of Commons, or tribes of Native North American Indians. And we devised among us a way of making a very effective sound effect to represent Indians potentially in revolt. I should explain that there was a popular chain of grocery supermarket stores in Canada at that time, and there still is, called Loblaws. We found that if we all stood around and said "Loblaws" over and over again, we would sound very like troops of Indians revolting. That amused us all a great deal at that time of the day!

The principal radio producer/director of that era was the CBC director of Radio Drama, Andrew Allan. Andrew had collected around him what amounted to a radio repertory company, a team of very skilled and by this time very experienced radio actors, including John Drainie and Tommy Tweed, Bud Knapp, Alan King, Ruth Springford, and many more. Andrew called everybody Mr. This and Miss That—there were no first name dealings, whatever their relationships might be outside the studio. And, of course, this whole group who worked together so frequently were on very friendly terms. But there was a certain kind of barrier, you might say, between the actors and Mr. Allan.

I came from a different kind of background, and I remember when I first did a production for Andrew. There was a large cast of 15 or 20 actors, all of whom knew Andrew and had worked with him often. The director would communicate with the actors through the glass panel which was in front of the control room by speaking through a microphone and a loudspeaker in the studio. Andrew was giving his directions to the actors with regard to character and situation, volume and timing. I, at that time, had not yet come to realize the considerable deference extended to Andrew by all the actors. So after he had talked to me through the microphone about some aspect of my character, I—as I had grown used to doing in all the previous radio plays I had done—said, "Yes, but isn't it possible perhaps at that point that this man is rather more concerned with the welfare of his daughter," or whatever it was, having to do with the plot or the character. I became aware that all around me in the studio my fellow actors were becoming quite frozen with horror because I seemed to be, not necessarily questioning what he had said, but offering another kind of opinion, which I realized afterwards wasn't the custom at that time. However, I must say, Andrew was very good-natured about it and got through it in a very friendly way. One or two of the other actors said to me afterwards, "Boy, you were pushing your luck there, talking back to Andrew. People don't do that, you know." And I said, "Yeah, I began to realize that!"

We went on to do hundreds of shows together, Andrew and I. He became and remained all the rest of his life a great friend of ours. The shows we used to do were partly a very popular series of dramas under the serialized title of *Stage*—at this point it would have been—'*53*. Whatever year it was, it would be called *Stage so-and-so*. It was a one hour live transmission from 9:00 to 10:00 on Sunday nights, the single most popular radio entertainment which CBC put out, and I did many, many of those over the succeeding years, largely with Andrew, but later with other directors.

Recordings were beginning to become more frequent for radio shows. The ground rules for performers were beginning to change. There was the matter of payments and the acceptance by the CBC that uniform payments for actors were not just or acceptable. And then, as television shows began to be more frequent, the whole question of credits began to be more important. I became more and more involved in the activities of ACTRA, our professional association. This was the acronymic title of the Association of Canadian Television and Radio Artists. I served on the executive board of ACTRA for a long time, and on various committees to try and improve the role and the status of actors and artists. Also, of course, I was concerned with my own welfare, rewards, and recognition in the same way.

One of the factors about the earliest days in Canada with regard to radio and television was that there was no gradation of payment to actors related to their skills or their prominence, or the kind of parts that they played. The CBC had a very grand and almost pontifical attitude towards artists, and had conceived the idea that they could buy actors like office supplies, that they just had to make up their mind how many they wanted. You were paid entirely on the basis of the length of time that the show you were in occupied on the air, regardless of whether you were playing King Lear or "My Lord, the carriage awaits." You had to do whatever bargaining or negotiating, or just plain ordinary bluffing in some cases, with various CBC officials, entirely on your own. Some people were better at it than others. Some were instinctively good at it, and some were hopeless. I was about halfway between the two. I had been with Al Parker—my London agent—for about ten years at the time we came to Canada, but when I started to work professionally in 1936, I'd not had an agent. So I did have a bit of an understanding about these sorts of things. I combined that with the knowledge of agenting I had learned from Al to take care of myself, and other actors, too. I was instrumental in making clear to the CBC that payment ought to be based on skill and prominence, and according to the scale of the work that a performer did in any given show, rather than on the flat-rate principle which they had established.

The CBC was imaginative to the extent that they realized new blood would need to be recruited, because there were no people around who had first-hand experience of television—except such people as I, who had done a bit of it in the UK before I came to Canada. So I was invited to take part in a course designed to train directors for this new medium of television. We were allowed to select the material for our final projects. I chose, deliberately, a piece by Thornton Wilder, who wrote extraordinarily imaginative kinds of dramatic work, *Our Town* being the most well known. He had also written a shorter play called *Pullman Car Hiawatha*. It was an imaginary journey of a Pullman car of a train going across the United States, and the various people who are traveling in that train, and why they are on the train, and the relationships that develop while they are on this long journey. In order to illustrate the imaginative potential of television, I selected this play because it had something of the promptings of the imagination which I think all good drama ought to have. I shot the whole thing in a bare studio. No representational attempts at setting at all. Finances were very limited and I thought, "Well, here's an opportunity to challenge and stimulate the imagination of the audience." I opened with a shot of the floor of the studio, and into the frame came a hand bearing a piece of chalk, drawing a line on the floor. We pulled back and saw that the hand is that of someone we should call the Narrator or the Stage Manager, rather like in *Our Town*, where there is an introductory figure who sets up the situation. This guy then addressed the camera and said something to the effect of, "This line I am drawing here is going to represent a train. And a particular part of the train, called Pullman Car Hiawatha. In the course of this journey a number of passengers will reveal why they are on this journey and how they are feeling, and what happens to them by the time they complete their journey." Then, from the four corners of the darkened studio, came the various characters, each of them carrying an ordinary wooden kitchen chair, which they put down within the long rectangle being drawn by the presenter. We faded up the sound track of some rail noises, and were then on the train. The audience now accepts that this setting is on the train, and the play develops.

Our radio series *A Touch of Greasepaint* began in 1954. I have always been deeply interested in theatre history. When I was a student at the Royal Academy we used to have a session every week with a lady who was a professor of theatre history. She would give long—and I'm afraid rather boring—talks about the background of the theatre and its origins. Well, most of my fellow students cut these lectures. But I was quite interested in *why* the theatre was what it was, and how it had developed. So I became an addict of theatrical history. I had collected books even in my earliest times, of theatrical reminiscence and history. When I was among fellow actors, I had fallen into the habit of relating a lot of this stuff, this theatrical memorabilia which I had assembled. There was a dear chap named Alan King who was a prominent actor and writer on CBC radio. I worked very frequently—once or twice a week—with Alan on different shows. He said to me one day, "Look, all this stuff that you know and are interested in about theatre history might very well be turned into a radio series. There are all sorts of dramatic memorabilia which are like a historical gossip column. They could be turned into a good radio series. Then one could do scenes from lesser known plays, or plays associated with famous people in different parts of the world." We hit on it as being a kind of theatrical scrapbook, from all periods of history, and all through the world.

I would assemble the material and the basic outline of the given episode, then I would pass my notes over to Alan and he would put them into proper presentational order, together with a couple of scenes from a given play or extracts from letters or diaries. Every week, each half hour episode of *A Touch of Greasepaint* would feature Alan and me as the only regular actors, with an occasional guest, more often than not female, to play a lead role. The two of us would play all the male parts. We were quite used to doing that. I certainly was used to playing two or three different characters in the same play in radio drama. Virtually from the word "Go" it became immensely popular. This series, initially commissioned for only twelve or thirteen weeks, eventually lasted more than a dozen years.

Some of the elements and ingredients we used in *A Touch of Greasepaint* served later as building blocks for *Merely Players*, my one-man show. For example, we did a number of shows about the great actor Henry Irving and his life and career, in the course of which we did scenes from *The Bells*. One of them, the last scene, became a part of *Merely Players*. In 1955 we did a stage presentation of *A Touch of Greasepaint* to raise money for a theatrical charity. It was an evening in which we played some of these scenes which we had originally presented on radio. The series was a very worthwhile venture. People still remember it to this day.

Later, on television, I wrote and played a series of 10-minute episodes under the title of *Presenting Barry Morse*, which aired in conjunction with a CBC drama program called *Encore*, using various pieces of theatrical history in a personal presentation for television, which would come as a kind of epilogue to whatever the main program had been. All kinds of subjects and characters were involved, including such titles as "How Theatre Came to Canada" and "The Stormy Partnership of Gilbert & Sullivan." There was another one about "The Man Who Killed Lincoln" and his connection with the play that was playing on the night Lincoln was shot. It happened to be called *Our American Cousin* in which John Wilkes Booth— who had been an actor—had played, so he knew what was going to be happening on the stage during the various times of the evening. My theory was that he picked a time for the assassination when he knew that there were going to be only two women on the stage, and that by jumping onto the stage at that point, he could more readily escape. Then there was the whole dramatic career—if you might call it that—of "Charles Dickens: Would-be Actor" and his extraordinary success reading his own works. So I did a whole series, in many cases derived from programs which we had prepared and presented on the radio in *A Touch of Greasepaint*. Sometimes I would have guests who would join me, like Corinne Conley, who played opposite me in a scene from *East Lynne* for a show on melodrama. Toby Robins did a scene with me from *Much Ado About Nothing* and we explained how and why it was that women first acted on stage. *Presenting Barry Morse* ran from July 3 to September 25, 1960.

Then we did a notorious radio show called *The Investigator*, which was an examination of the rascality and lunacy of Joe McCarthy, and the persecution of alleged Communists in the USA. It was a wicked witch-hunt among intellectuals and artists of various kinds, among them many people in our profession. One of the Canadian writers, Reuben Ship, who had been a victim of this purge in Hollywood, wrote this play called *The Investigator*. He had been virtually hounded out of Hollywood on suspicion of having leftist sympathies. This was a tragic contagion which swept across the Excited States—as we always used to call it—until McCarthy was exposed as the fanatic he was. The play was a fantasy which assumed that McCarthy had been killed in a plane crash, and that his spirit was seeking admission to Heaven, and then—having been resoundingly rejected by Saint Peter (played by me) at the gates of Heaven—he was dispatched to Down There, where he fell in with all sorts of other similar persecuting rascals of history. It was a marvelously constructed piece. The performance by John Drainie as McCarthy was so convincing and realistic that when this show was heard in the States a great panic broke out among people who'd heard part of this show and had got the idea that McCarthy had indeed been killed!

For the year 1954 it was decided that, for the first time, the professional associations in our field should present annual awards in different categories. It was rather like the Academy Awards, but on a smaller scale. These were to be presented at a banquet and ball held at the King Edward Hotel in Toronto. There was balloting by all the membership of all the associations, and Sydney and I went along to the ceremony. They were to go to the Best Actor in television, the Best Supporting Actor, and all the rest of the standard categories. There was also to be the CCAA Gold Award, which was the joint award of the two English and French speaking professional associations who jointly were

Here I am as Charles Dickens.

known as the Canadian Council of Authors and Artists. Their award was to go to the overall best—regardless of whether the individual was an author, composer, actor or director—for "Outstanding Artistic Achievement in any Entertainment Field." Well, greatly to my delight, I was given the award as the Best Television Actor. Then there came the moment when the supreme award, the CCAA Gold Award, was to be given. And, to my real astonishment, I was awarded that! It took the form of a small gold card, which was a lifetime membership of the CCAA. That was the first of those Gold Awards: a great event to culminate our now three years or more in Canada. I won the award for the so-called Best Television Actor a number of times, but I never took those sorts of things very seriously. I think awards for the arts are a bit ridiculous. Nobody would think of going into the Louvre or the National Gallery and pinning a rosette on the Best Picture. They'd lock you up as being manifestly insane. But we still go on doing it in our trade. It all has to do with hype, ultimately. I gave the various statuettes I was awarded to Melanie when she got married, and she used to use them as doorstops, which was about the best use I could think of for them.

In Town Tonight was a weekly late night chat show I hosted on television for the CBC in Toronto. It was live, and one evening I arranged that we would do a show about wines. We invited three prominent wine critics and to start the evening off I said, "This evening we are going to discuss the ever delicious subject of wine. You all know that there are wide divisions of judgment about wine, and of course the basic thing that we have to start with is knowing the difference between red and white." I suggested that our guests be blindfolded and that we pass among them a glass of this or that, and ask them to tell us—from their depth of valuable experience and knowledge—their impressions. Two out of the three of them couldn't tell the red from the white! So there we blew up the whole subject of wine snobbery, and we also showed that wine isn't necessarily to be valued by virtue of its label or price.

In 1955 I did a TV production of Shakespeare's *Macbeth*, directed by my good friend David Greene. David's then wife Kate played Lady Macbeth in this production, and Macduff was played by Patrick Macnee. There still were no agents in Canada, and I had to negotiate my own contract. There had recently been an announcement by the CBC management that they were going to establish (having been shaken out of their policy of standard *minimum* payments for performers) a *maximum* fee for anybody, to do anything, on television. They sensed that the cost of performers was going up just as the size of the audience and the entire industry were growing. In typical bureaucratic fashion they dreaded the thought that these lazy layabout bums known as artists were going to start asking for fees which, God forbid, might even be larger than the salaries that *they* were being paid. So they made a public announcement about this maximum fee. No matter the nature or length of what was being done, the maximum fee was going to be established at $1,000.00.

So the time came when I was asked to play *Macbeth*. I had to meet with Sidney Newman, who was called something like the Director of Television Drama of the CBC. He said, "Well, you will have heard of the CBC's announcement with regard to payment for television performances. It has been established that our maximum payment for anybody to do anything on television will henceforth be $1,000.00. Now, we are prepared," he said, "to pay you that." This was going to involve some three weeks of rehearsal, and a live performance occupying about two and a quarter hours. I said, "Oh, well, that's very interesting. Thank you, Sidney. But I would like, just to reinforce the basic fact that *negotiation*, as between artists and the CBC, is still acceptable, I would like you to pay me please, $1,001.00." He reached for his wallet and said, "Oh, well, of course." and attempted to give me a dollar bill! I said, "No, no, no, Sidney, you do not understand. What I want is a contract which specifically states that I am to be paid $1,001.00. Thus preserving, for us the artists, the principle that contracts are subject to negotiation, and not to any dictation from on high, from you guys!" He got very upset and said, "Oh, God, what are you doing? Don't you understand this will have to go all the way to Ottawa? There'll probably be questions asked in the House of Commons, and God knows what kinds of hullabaloo it'll make! Why don't you just take the dollar?" I said, "No. It's not the dollar I'm interested in. It's the principle. And if it has to go to Ottawa, and if it has to be discussed in the House of Commons, well then so be it. But that's what I want to have as the contract for my playing the title role in *Macbeth*."

Well, it did cause a lot of hullabaloo, and it did go to Ottawa, and it was discussed in the House of Commons—how this upstart actor was asking for a dollar above and beyond the announced maximum for television appearances. But—let's hear the trumpets—*I won!* The final irony of this struggle was that the CBC couldn't accept being beaten for a mere dollar by this actor. When my contract arrived, my fee was stated to be "One thousand and *fifty* dollars"!

David was very excited about this show, and so was I, of course. We had worked on the adaptation, and *Macbeth* is among the shorter of Shakespeare's plays, so we were going to do it at full-length and it was going to occupy something like two and a quarter hours. Imagine—a full-length *Macbeth*, done live! It was a most exhausting affair. In those days, on the day of a show, a play would be worked through as many as three and perhaps four times. There would be a rough work-through first thing in the morning to introduce the actors to the set—because until you moved into the studio you didn't work on the actual set, you worked only in the rehearsal studios on a chalked out ground plan. On the day of the show you would work in the set itself. Then there would be a second run-through in which the cameramen would be introduced to what the camera angles would be, and where the various cameras and microphones were going to go. Then there would be a dress rehearsal, where you work through the show in costume and makeup, with the sound and camera and lighting crews, and with the director sitting up there in the box, calling the shots. Then, finally, you would go on the air and do the show live.

Well, I may not have many claims to fame, but I think I probably am the only actor in the history of the whole wide world who's ever done four full-length performances of Shakespeare's *Macbeth* in one day. Naturally, you try and conserve yourself a bit as the day goes through, saving the best of yourself for the live performance.

This particular live performance involved—like all live performances did—certain unexpected happenings which you couldn't always cope with. In this instance there were several very extravagant fights, in the last act. Young Siward was played by a very keen young actor who was involved in the fight which takes place immediately before Macbeth's confrontation with Macduff. David and I were very keen that these fights should be as realistic and exciting as was humanly possible. And, of course, in those days I was a good deal younger and fitter than I am now. Well, we had very carefully rehearsed this fight, to result in Young Siward being disarmed, and losing his sword. Then Macbeth gets *his* sword across Young Siward's throat and by leaning on it, is supposed to cut his head off. We couldn't show that of course on television, but the idea was that as Young Siward is disarmed and Macbeth gets his sword up over his throat and starts to press in—we would go to black, and then fade up on another camera to Macduff.

Well, this was all going marvelously. We only had another five minutes or so to go before the end of the play. I was full of excitement, and we got up to the point where I was about to put my sword up to his neck. But we had fought with such energy that the edge of my sword had become serrated, almost like the edge of a saw. To my horror I realized as I pressed my usually blunt sword against the neck of this young actor, that the serrations were actually cutting his neck, and blood was starting to come! Well, my friend David Greene in the control room was calling the shots, and was supposed to go to black and fade up on the other camera, but he was so excited by the sight of this blood appearing on this poor young man's neck, that I could hear him even through the headsets being worn by the cameramen, saying, "Oh, look, there's blood! Hold it, hold it right there!" And I could see that they weren't going to black! Well, when they finally did, my next move was to rush up the stairs to confront Macduff. I couldn't stop to see how the young actor was. All I could see was that he was sinking towards the floor, with his hand to his throat, covered with blood! As I was addressing Macduff and preparing to fight him, I could see out of the corner of my eye that they were dragging this young actor off to the side of the set and starting to minister to him. Well, mercifully, it all turned out all right, and he didn't suffer anything more than a minor cut more or less across his Adam's apple. It didn't require stitches. Among other evidences of the wear and tear inflicted on us actors that day, poor old Patrick Macnee, by the time we got to the show, had virtually lost his voice! He was scarcely able to get above a croak.

Our production was well praised and highly regarded, and it was something of a triumph to have done a full length, totally live *Macbeth*. The show was broadcast on September 25, 1955, which also celebrated my twenty-year anniversary as an actor. It also resulted in my winning the Best Actor Award from the Canadian Actors Association.

One Toronto journalist christened me "The Test Pattern," because he said that I was on CBC television so often that I *must* be the original model for that head of an Indian chief which, in those days, CBC used for their test pattern and trademark. The talented Canadian actor Gerry Sarracini adapted that nickname to "TV Test Pattern Morse." In 1953, when I was performing on TV virtually every night of the week, except on Saturday, when there were then no drama shows, Gerry told me that he had a dream. In it, he was watching an NHL hockey game on TV. One team was scoring heavily, and, strangely, all the members of the team seemed to look the same. The camera suddenly brought in a close-up, and to his horror, every player bore the face of Barry Morse. Gerry woke up sweating. "My God!" he screamed. "Now he's got a Saturday night show!"

12

"Those Were My Salad Days"

THROUGH THE 1950S AND 1960S I was involved in a number of stage productions for a very adventurous theatre organization in the USA, in Boston, run by a lady called Alison Ridley. Her company, Group 20, produced summer seasons of classics in a beautiful open-air Greek style amphitheatre attached to Wellsley College, one of the foremost women's colleges in the USA. In 1957 Alison invited me to come down because she had seen some of the television productions I had been doing. She suggested that I play the role of John Tanner in a production of George Bernard Shaw's *Man and Superman*, which until that time had never been done at full length in the USA. Also, later in the season I would play the title role in *Cyrano de Bergerac*. Well, what an offer! It was not immensely financially rewarding, but it was marvelously exciting because *Man and Superman* was a play I had always loved, and I'd been a dedicated Shavian for as long as I'd been in our profession. The first production was to be directed by Jerome Kilty, who was at that time becoming very well known as a character actor and director in New York, and he went on to put together an extremely successful two handed play, which I also ended up doing later on, called *Dear Liar*, which is a dramatic editing of the letters which passed between George Bernard Shaw and Mrs. Patrick Campbell, the famous actress.

In *Man and Superman*, the *Don Juan in Hell* sequence had previously only been played in a kind of concert version, by the famous drama quartet of Charles Laughton, Charles Boyer, Cedric Hardwicke, and Agnes Moorehead. But we did the whole full-length play. It was an immense challenge in terms of the length of the piece itself, and the complexity of it. Playing the leading female role was a wonderful American actress called Nancy Wickwire. It was a knockout success. People came in great numbers.

That outdoor Greek auditorium, open to the four winds, was packed to overflowing every night. The Boston press, who are often very severe with prior to Broadway productions, were full of eulogy. The famous Eliot Norton—who had been considerably critical of *My Fair Lady*, when it was originally presented in Boston before it went to New York, was extravagant in praise! While we were playing *Man and Superman* in the evenings, we were rehearsing for *Cyrano de Bergerac* during the day. That season was a tremendous baptism by fire, as it were, for my first appearance onstage in the USA.

In March and April of 1958, I was in a play on Broadway called *Hide and Seek*, which came about through a series of flukes—like so many things in our lives. I was in Toronto and I knew that somewhere in the States they were running in, prior to Broadway, a production of a play which had been jointly written by a Canadian whom I knew quite well called Stanley Mann, and an English author called Roger MacDougal. One fine morning, very early, about six o'clock, I had a call from Stanley Mann in Boston. And he said, "What are you doing today?" and I said, "I'm hoping to get up shortly!" and went on to explain my obligations for the day. He said, "Well, can you get out of them? Because we have a bit of an emergency, and we need you down here." He went on to tell me, "Our leading man is turning out to be unacceptable." The leading man was a sometime sizable movie star called Franchot Tone. They needed to replace him immediately, and Stanley— knowing that I was at least, if nothing else, quick on the uptake—thought of asking me. So I said, "Well, give me a half hour and I'll see if I can call around and extricate myself from these jobs I'm supposed to be doing, and I'll ring you back." He said, "All right. We'll be standing by and we'll get you on the first plane out of there." And so, to make a long story even longer, I called him back later on, having extricated myself from whatever commitments I'd had, and it was arranged that I be on a flight down to Boston. I was picked up and taken to the theatre and there I was introduced to this company. The director was very well known in his day as a director and playwright; his name was Reginald Denham. In the cast was the originally English but by now long established Hollywood character actor, famous as Sherlock Holmes, Basil Rathbone. The leading lady was Geraldine Fitzgerald, an equally well-known film and stage actress. My character was a young doctor and he and his wife had a child, who through some extraordinary genetic miracle had been gifted with almost psychic powers. The need was for me to go on *that night*! So I set about working with my new colleagues, and did appear that night, which was only about a week before we were due to open on Broadway! The whole thing was a considerable panic. One of the partners in the production company was a well-known

New York character named Fred F. Finkelhoff. He'd been involved with various other Broadway ventures before, and was a very knowledgeable and experienced Broadway figure, almost like a *Guys and Dolls* character. He would always wear—no matter the weather—a hat and a heavy overcoat, with a racing newspaper tucked into one of the pockets. He had deep cynicism about the extraordinary vagaries of our trade.

So I played in *Hide and Seek* for the rest of the week, before we opened on Broadway. I could smell from far off that we were *not* about to have a triumphant success. The play was loose and improbable, and the characters were not very well drawn or developed. It bore all the hallmarks of having been put together in a rather slapdash and hasty way. Try as we might, we couldn't repair it very much. So the day came when we were to open on Broadway. We had our first night, appropriately enough on April Fools Day. Sydney wasn't able to make it down to see the show, but it was not one of the world-shaking events of Broadway history. We stayed up to get the notices, and they were not good. They were patronizing about us, the actors, and destructive about the play. We all met at the theatre the next morning to go through all of the notices to see what hope we might have. There obviously wasn't very much. I remember everybody had handfuls of newspapers, looking for possible quotes that might be used in advertising— if somebody had said something reasonably warm or hopeful. One junior member of the company said, "Look here, here's a good quote!" and we all said, "What? What is it?" He replied, "It says here, 'evocative lighting'!" to which we replied, "Well that's not much good. Where is that from?" He answered rather apologetically, "The *Womenswear Daily*."

After we'd sat there in some dejection for half an hour or so, Fred F. Finkelhoff got to his feet, shrugged in his overcoat and said, "You know, when I was a little fella, my mother used to say to me that if three separate and distinct people tell you you're drunk, you'd better go lie down." Of course, you guessed it, we closed on Saturday. So that was my first venture on Broadway, and as always it was an interesting experience, as they say. It didn't do me any harm, and it was hugely enjoyable to work with Basil Rathbone, whom I'd only known as a movie star until that time.

Later that year I encountered *The World of the Wonderful Dark*, which was a remarkable stage play written by my dear old friend Lister Sinclair— who was well known for his long running CBC series, *Ideas*. Lister and I had long been friends. I had played in many plays which he had written, including a wonderful verse play for TV about Leonardo da Vinci. Lister had connections with British Columbia—though he wasn't born there, but had many of his earliest successes there when he was working in Vancouver—and in 1958 there was being launched the Vancouver International Festival. They invited him to write a play incorporating some aspect of the history of British Columbia. Well, Lister was never one to do things by halves, and he decided to write a play about the Kwakiutl Indians, who were the original human inhabitants of that part of Canada. It wasn't quite the part of British Columbian history which the authorities had expected, but it did show how similar power struggles have been all the way through human history. The Kwakiutl were—just as we are—greatly obsessed with property, and the machinations and deviations and rascally doings of their people were largely motivated by a desire for power and property. In other words, it was a reflection on what life in British Columbia is like today. I played the principal role. We performed in an ice hockey arena in Vancouver, which was converted into an amphitheatre type stage. It was directed by the English director Douglas Seale, who had had great success producing the history plays of Shakespeare in the UK. Playing with us in the theatre—which he didn't very often do—was the great radio actor John Drainie, whom I'd worked with scores of times. William Needles played one of the other characters, as did Hugh Webster. It was a huge cast of 50 or 60, including a chorus.

Sydney and Hayward, during this season of 1958, were playing at Stratford, Ontario. So while they were there I was in Vancouver, and then subsequently on tour in other parts of British Columbia, in Lister's *The World of the Wonderful Dark*, playing in high school auditoriums and such other places. We were all attired in the suitably primitive costumes of the Kwakiutl Indians, and had to be very largely covered—since our costumes didn't cover us very much—with a bronze body makeup, which was a wonderfully effective substance. When you rubbed it on your body or your face with a sponge, it would produce an almost metallic bronze surface. It was, however, terribly difficult to get off. So all of us, wherever we lived in hotels or boarding houses, left a trail of this body makeup. We had literally to sit in the bath and scrub each other. I remember Bill Needles and I shared a hotel space in Vancouver, and we would spend ages sitting in the bath, scrubbing each other's backs, to try and get this body paint off. I think, to this day, in various hotels and lodging houses around B.C. you will still find traces of *The World of the Wonderful Dark*.

Now I must go back a bit to another show, *Salad Days*, which came about in 1956 in this way: Toby Robins, a most beautiful young actress and as lovely in person as she was in appearance, was being courted by a young man named Bill Freedman. I came to know Bill because he would come and pick her up after rehearsal or visit her during a show. He was in business with his father, and they ran a couple of drive-in movie theatres, and had a hand in various other movie houses in Canada, both in Toronto and in Ottawa. So they were sort of in our profession, but not on the performing side. Toby and Bill got married, and went for their honeymoon to Europe, principally to London. In the course of their stay there they went to see a little British musical, which was then the talk of London and the most successful show in the West End, called *Salad Days*. The history of *Salad Days* needs to be explained a bit because it was quite remarkable. It was originally presented by the Bristol Old Vic Company, as an end of season romp. They were dedicated to producing classics, and they'd had great success with Shakespeare's *Antony and Cleopatra*. They decided that for their final production they would do a little in-house musical. A lady in the company named Dorothy Reynolds was friends with a young man called Julian Slade, who was a composer of music. So they cooked up this little musical. The title, *Salad Days*, used to be used as a slang term. People would talk about their "salad days," meaning when they were young. The actual phrase is used by Cleopatra in *Antony and Cleopatra*, when she says, "Those were my salad days, when I was green in judgment." So Dorothy and Julian chose this phrase to be the title for their musical, which is a charming small-scale piece, nothing like those big megabuck musicals you see nowadays. It is designed to be played by a small company of very versatile performers. It was played originally by only twelve actors, playing a total of some twenty parts. It is built around the adventures of a young couple graduating from university, whose romance is blossoming, and they don't know quite what to do with their lives.

This little musical proved to be a tumultuous success at Bristol when it was played there just for the last few weeks of their season. The decision was made to try and present it in London because it had, and has still, a great charm and innocence and freshness about it, as well as some tuneful tunes. So Bill and Toby came back to Toronto with a recording of the numbers from the show, and Bill said, "We should go into management, and put this on!" He and I were, by this time, great friends. He said, "You can direct it, and we've got all kinds of marvelous actors of exactly the kind needed for this show. We must do it!" And, having listened to the music, I very much agreed.

Salad Days was presented first in Canada in the summer of 1956 in the Hart House Theatre at the University of Toronto; a charming small scale theatre, on the campus. We got together a marvelous company made up of all sorts of the wonderful actors there were in Toronto by this time, many of whom were not all that busy during the summer because the CBC was not producing as many radio and television shows as they would during the rest of the year. It was a most versatile company. I had never seen the show—which was a good thing, in a way. I was not at all influenced by what the London show had been. It went on running for something like six or seven years in London, but I never saw it. That was partly deliberate, because I wanted to have a fresh look at the way the whole thing was done. In fact, as well as the existing twenty characters that were in the show, I actually *increased* the number of characters by inventing roles to appear in the various musical numbers. That was partly because of the misgivings some people had. They would say, "Isn't it too English for a North American audience?" To which I said, "No, no, not at all. If it's not English, it's nothing. In fact, we must make it even *more* English. It must look like and feel like a tourist commercial for

My amazing costume as the Kwakiutl tribal chief in *The World of the Wonderful Dark*. I'm wearing bronze makeup on my face, neck, hands and (although unseen) my bare legs!

Great Britain." We engaged Alan Lund, who was the foremost Canadian dancer and choreographer of his time, to arrange the dancing. We recruited people like Eric Christmas and Jack Creley and a wonderful company. Our twelve actors played between them twenty-seven different characters, which made the show doubly interesting for the audience.

Salad Days was a triumph. My diary entry notes, "*Salad Days* opening" followed by umpteen exclamation marks, and then, "God, what a night!" It absolutely slew them! I remember a headline for one of the reviews was "Morse Mixes Merry Madness." A great deal of credit was given to my direction of the show, and the general style of it. The place was packed to the doors for every performance. It became the hottest ticket in town. But by late October the University politely pointed out to us that they would like their theatre back. We were paying perfectly good rent for it, but they had other events that needed to be staged there, and we simply

Publicity poster for the New York production of *Salad Days*.

couldn't stay there any longer. So, with great nerve, Bill and I decided that we would transfer our triumphant production from the Hart House Theatre in the University, to the great Royal Alexandra Theatre. And we did, and it ran there successfully in a theatre three times as big. Then we transferred it again up to Montreal, where it played at Her Majesty's Theatre, and was again a triumph. Everybody said to us, "You must take it to New York."

Although we'd made a certain amount of money with it, we were a bit uncertain about taking it to New York, because it's a different ball game which requires altogether different resources. However, we let it rest through the turn of the year, and discussed various plans of what we might do. By this time everybody was looking forward to our doing other productions, and Bill and I decided to do a play called *Visit to a Small Planet*, written by Gore Vidal.

We jointly put this production on, but because we thought it would be more fun on the "bills" than just having our two male names, we thought it would be more glamorous and intriguing if Toby were billed as our producer. So the credit read, "Toby Robins Presents." This was an early play of Vidal's about the visit of a Martian to Earth, and the comic complications which arise from it. It is a charming and imaginative piece. I played the leading character of Kreton, and we had an all-star cast. This was done at the Crest Theatre, which we took over to produce the show, while we were still cogitating the possibilities of taking *Salad Days* to Broadway. We enlisted a marvelous company: everybody who was anybody in the theatre community. John Drainie was in it. He had been forced to work principally in radio by a boyhood accident he'd had, which had left him lame. He walked with a stick, and his walk was quite a bit impeded. I'd come to know him well by this time, and I was responsible for drawing him in to appearing in the theatre for this production. There was a character of a rather blustering, bombastic senior military officer—a very funny character—and I persuaded him to do it, with his limp. We wrote in a little explanation as to how he had acquired this limp, by slipping on some liquid soap when he was in charge of a laundry unit in his earlier military days.

Austin Willis was also in the show, and Robert Goulet played the young man—he was getting to be quite a name in those days. Dear Jane Mallet was in it. So the question arose about billing, and who was going to be top of the bill, and how was it going to be arranged. Bill and I had discussed this privately, and I said, "Well, the only really fair and sensible way is to bill the company alphabetically." It so happened that the earliest name in the alphabet was Jack Creley, and we had a wonderful Siamese cat in the play. I said, "What we'll do is invent a name for the cat. We'll call her—as if she was a French actress—Felice Chat, so that she will have the top of the bill." The bill would read, "*Visit to a Small Planet*, starring Felice Chat, Jack Creley ..." and so on, all the way through the list. But when we had the meeting to discuss all of this, dear old Austin Willis said, "Oh, this always happens to me! We're billing in alphabetical order, and because my name is Willis, I'm at the end!" So I said, "No, no, Austin, I'll tell you what we'll do." I was thinking of how, on posters and advertising, there would often be a number of credits listed, followed by "And So-and-so." I said, "Instead of that, we'll list the credits and then at the end put 'BUT Austin Willis.'" Everybody laughed and thought that was a great gimmick. Everybody agreed, and so it was. And Austin got noticed more than anyone else, because at the end of the list of stars it said, "*But* Austin Willis." It was a very happy and marvelously successful production, directed by yours truly.

Not long after *Visit to a Small Planet* we did another prior-to–New York production of *Salad Days*. We revived the show to play first at the Crest Theatre in Toronto, with almost the same cast as we'd had before. We ran it at the Crest for quite a long while. We were—as far as I know— the only producers at that time to take a play to New York entirely with our own money. We had made enough money out of *Salad Days* and *Visit to a Small Planet*, and some other things that we had done, to take our production to New York, not to a standard Broadway theatre, nor to one of the grubby fringe theatres which existed in those days, but to a perfectly comfortable and centrally situated theatre which was housed in a hotel, in a quite fashionable area, not far from Central Park. We took it there, opened on November 10, 1958, with a wonderful company of extraor-

ABOUT OUR NEXT PLAY...
THE CREST THEATRE FOUNDATION
presents the
BILL FREEDMAN — BARRY MORSE
Production of
THE BROADWAY HIT COMEDY

VISIT TO A SMALL PLANET

by GORE VIDAL
Directed by BARRY MORSE
Starring alphabetically
FELICE CHAT, JACK CRELEY, JOHN DRAINIE, ROBERT GOULET, JANE MALLETT,
BARRY MORSE, TOBY ROBINS: but AUSTIN WILLIS
OPENING TUESDAY, 18th FEBRUARY

The cast of *Visit to a Small Planet* listed alphabetically; note the ingenious billing for Austin Willis.

dinarily gifted actors, but none of them known in New York. We were rely-
ing entirely on the sort of notices we'd had in Canada to launch us for a
run. But, as rotten luck would have it, there was a newspaper strike which
started just a couple of days before we opened. Bill and I were just deci-
mated. With no reviews, and no possibility of newspaper publicity of any
kind, how was our show going to get known? People said, "Well, there've
been newspaper strikes before, and they don't last long. If you can just hang
on for a couple of weeks, it'll all be over and then you can get your reviews,
and you'll have a good chance to have a run." Well, the newspaper strike
was *not* over in one or two weeks. It went on eventually for about seven or
eight weeks. We kept running, trying to keep ourselves afloat, until all of
our financial resources were used up, and we had to close the show—without ever having the notices which had been our only hope of getting audiences. We hung on until the eighteenth of January, 1959.

So there we were—ruined. In fact, we owed $26,000.00. A terrible
burden at that stage! We sold our house, which we had in Toronto on Kil-
barry (appropriately enough) Road, near Upper Canada College, where
Hayward was going to school, and moved back into a duplex apartment,
to try and get our finances together.

The next summer we went back to Group 20 in Boston again. That
season we did a production of *Much Ado About Nothing*, in which we all
four played, which opened on the June 22, 1959. I played Benedick, Hayward played my page, Melanie played one of the maids, and Sydney played
another character. That season, also, we did another production of Shaw's
Man and Superman, in which Sydney played with me. Another lovely
actress, Rosemary Harris, had the female leads in both of those pieces.
There was also a production of J. M. Barrie's *Peter Pan*, in which I didn't
play. Sydney played Mrs. Darling, and Melanie and Hayward played the
children in it. It was quite wonderful in the open air. They had rigged up
flying gear so that Peter Pan was seen flying above the bushes and trees.
Mr. Darling and Captain Hook—the two joint leading male roles—were
both played by the great actor Eric Portman, one of the finest actors of his
era in the world. Then, to wind it all up, I played the title role in *Oedipus
Rex*, one of the greatest parts in dramatic literature. What a season! That
was a marvelous summer. We had always all tried to stay together, but this
was the first time we were all together in a theatre company. We stayed in
a rented house near the theatre. Towards the end of the season in Boston
I had lunch there with John Gielgud. He was playing in Boston, just a little after we had been, in the same play, *Much Ado About Nothing*. Somewhat to my embarrassment—although perhaps he didn't see the reviews—the
reviews of *his* production compared it rather unfavorably to *ours*.

Now we come to *The Caretaker*, written by Harold Pinter. It featured three male characters, had been a considerable success in London and had then opened in New York. The three characters are two younger men—brothers, it turns out—and an older man, a tramp, who is taken on by these two young fellows as a caretaker to look after some more or less derelict property that they've got. It's an interesting character contrast, and I had seen the play when I was in London. It had been transferred to New York with, in the leading title role, Donald Pleasence. Now they wanted to send out a national tour. Harold Pinter was involved in directing it and somehow or other I arranged to go meet him at the theatre to discuss whether I might be suitable to play this part. It is essentially a very English play, and this old geezer needs to have a kind of rough and ready common accent. It's not specified exactly where he comes from. So I got this appointment to meet with Pinter and the New York producer at the theatre where the play was running. I had decided, since I was obviously a bit too young for this part, I should somehow show what I could look like. So I went to a junk shop and got some scruffy beat-up clothes, and made them even more

Me playing Davies (The Derelict) in the U.S. National Tour of *The Caretaker*.

ragged than they were. I didn't shave for a couple of days, put some dirt on my face, and succeeded in persuading a taxi driver to take me to the theatre from wherever it was I was staying. I turned up to see Harold Pinter, got up more or less as this disreputable character, and the result was I got the part.

It was a most interesting tour. We played all sorts of places right across the U.S. of A. *The Caretaker* is a very avant-garde play, full of obscurities and strange developments. I don't think some audiences on the tour entirely understood it. In 1962, we ended up in Los Angeles and all the Hollywood notables came to see it, because it was regarded as a very high quality example of the kind of writing going on among the avant-garde. Everybody was considerably impressed, and while we were playing there producer Quinn Martin saw us. I will talk more about him later.

13

"Immigration Application Supplication Blues"

IN THE EARLY 1950S I BEGAN to get more and more jobs in the USA, working on various television programs. These were shows such as *The Naked City*, *Encounter*, and the *U.S. Steel Hour*. In those days I would have to get an individual permit for each show that I did and, as you can imagine, with all of the bureaucratic barbed wire it was sometimes a bit nerve-wracking as to whether I would get the permit in time to do the show. On one occasion it did happen that I couldn't do a show I was being asked to do. So, I was keen to get a resident alien visa. I wanted to get a Green Card—as it was known even then—and that process looked like it was taking forever. It led me to write the following jingle, "Immigration Application Supplication Blues," which I submitted to the officials:

IMMIGRATION APPLICATION SUPPLICATION BLUES

5:30 A.M.
I've wrestled all night
To get everything right
And the point of this poetic pitch is:
What please can you do
To hustle this through
Rather swiftly, without any hitches.
Now you must get quite sick
Of these pleas to be quick
But I do have a reason—a good one.
(I suppose they all do

But mine really is true—
One wouldn't be kidding now, would one?)
I'm an actor by trade
(Though I've frequently made
Side trips to directing and writing)
And if my Visa comes through
I'll be able to do
A job in the States that's exciting.
Playhouse 90's the show,
Produced with a glow
By Columbia Broadcasting System.
On December the 1st
The play is rehearsed
Now I ask you, how can I resist 'em?

This succeeded in getting me my visa in order to be able to do an episode of *Playhouse 90* entitled "The Second Man." *Playhouse 90* was a very important show to get into in those days, as it was an anthology series of quite uncommon good quality and featured teleplays by some of the best writers in the business.

When I first started to work in California, people would say to me, "Where are you from?" and I would say, "All kinds of different places." Then they would ask, "Are you one of those television actors?" and I would answer, "I'm an *everything* actor." There was almost a sense that there were two armies of people in the dramatic entertainment world, one represented by New York and the theatre, and to some extent the early live television shows that were done out of New York—and I did a good many of those, too—and the other represented by the movie trade, which at first was very resistant to the encroachment of television.

As time progressed, I was commuting fairly regularly both to New York and to Los Angeles for various TV shows. In 1960 I did a TV production of *The Three Musketeers* in New York, which also featured Vincent Price and John Colicos in the cast. This show was put together by the prominent producer David Susskind. I played Athos, and Maximilian Schell played d'Artagnan, the principal role. I was hired because I was able to fight with both hands, and say a few lines at the same time. I used to be quite skillful in swordplay, having taken classes in swordsmanship at the Royal Academy, and I could fight with a rapier in each hand. Indeed, we had a sequence in which I had to fight two guys at the same time.

Some of these shows were live and some were on film. I played roles on numerous series like *Naked City,* and there were other shows such as

Studio One which were a series of original plays written for television. There were many, many television appearances which after so many years seem to either run together in my mind or I can't recall at all—in many cases mercifully, I'm sure. I do remember once playing a cross-eyed character in one of these shows. He was French and he was supposed to be a con man. I played him entirely cross-eyed, on a live television show. It was very difficult to keep it that way because I didn't know when I was on and when I was off!

I also remember working on a show for Alfred Hitchcock called "The Jail," which originally aired as a part of the *Alcoa Premiere* series hosted by Fred Astaire. In this teleplay, the noted writer and dramatist Ray Bradbury developed the idea that at some time in the future most things had been taken over by machinery, computers of various kinds, including the administration of justice. At the time, of course, computers were a relative novelty. In this future time a young man was charged with an offense against the state and marshaled into a huge building crammed with banks and banks of computers. These computers would absorb and assess the evidence, circumstances and facts in his case. All of them were operated by one master button-puncher—played by me.

The wonderful irony of all this was that it seemed to infer that all of this was taking place in the United States at some future time. I thought, *My God, that's a terrifying vision; many steps beyond George Orwell.* In those days there used to be a production meeting at the beginning of the shoot with Hitchcock, the various network people, the sponsors and the advertising representatives. I thought to myself, *Oh, boy, when they hear this script the balloon is going to go up. It's going to be considered an attack on the American way of life. Surely they must see that! Bradbury's suggesting that, if the USA goes on in the direction of automation and mechanization, pretty soon there won't be any humanity in this at all. And machines will run all public affairs and governmental matters. Surely somebody would object to that.* I thought!

But not one word was said by anybody. There was, however, a little episode in the script in which this young man (played by John Gavin) was returning with his new wife from their honeymoon trip to Europe. They were going through their souvenirs and had a little bit of china from Germany, a little something from France, and they had—in the original script— a pewter beer mug they had picked up in England. As it happened at that time the show was sponsored by an aluminum manufacturing company called Alcoa. When we got to this little scene in the script, somebody mentioned the pewter beer mug and a handful of these frightened-face people all leapt to their feet, went into a corner and talked quickly and somebody called Mr. Hitchcock himself. He went outside and all we heard was "Mumble, mumble, mumble." Then they all came back in with their pronouncement—the pewter beer mug must be removed. All because this great corporation couldn't bear even the mention of another metal!

Yet, the whole script was about the decline and demoralization of the entire United States. Nobody had a syllable to say about that. How about that for black comedy? I think Ray Bradbury is among the best of the writers in the science fiction genre. His writing has very serious, philosophic and satiric subtext. It was all quite fascinating. It was the first time I met my dear friend, Noah Keen, who played my kind of second-in-command on the show. He and I took to each other and became great friends.

Starring as Fitzgerald Fortune in *The Twilight Zone* **episode "A Piano in the House." Whenever I can, I wrangle in a beard! (Rittenhouse Archives, Ltd.)**

Another couple of classic shows that I got mixed up in were *The Twilight Zone* and *The Outer Limits*. In *The Twilight Zone* episode "A Piano in the House," I played a fellow called Fitzgerald Fortune who was a particularly acerbic critic and had written savagely un-constructive things about all sorts of people in the music field. Then he gets—or his wife gets—a pianola, or a player piano. This pianola is possessed with magic faculties which torment him with visions of his own insecurities and of his own personal failure. It was a good script, written by Earl Hamner, Jr., who has been quite prominent in television over the years. He created and wrote the long-running series *The Waltons*, among others. "A Piano in the House" was directed by my friend David Greene and the cast featured Joan Hackett, Muriel Landers, and Don Durant. I met Rod Serling, the creator and host, albeit briefly.

The Outer Limits episode "Controlled Experiment" was one which everybody was excited about. It was the first science fiction comedy proposed as a series, and everybody felt it would just sweep the world. The pilot episode, which eventually aired as an episode of *The Outer Limits*, was very good. I played the rather formal, straight-laced, scientifically minded Martian named Phobos, and Carroll O'Connor played the bumbling, remotely incompetent second-in-command, Diemos. Although the teleplay doesn't point out that these are also the names of Mars' two moons, it's a nice inside joke for those up on their astronomy.

Carroll's Diemos runs an "outpost" on Earth, in the form of a pawnshop. He's been here for awhile and likes his job. I, on the other hand (as Phobos, the Martian inspector), have just arrived on Earth to conduct an experiment involving the unusual Earth custom of murder. As my character says, "It happens only here on this weird little planet, nowhere else in the galaxy." After determining that a murder will take place in a nearby hotel in just a few minutes time, we hurry over there and hide behind some potted plants in the lobby. After observing the murder, we use a special Martian machine which enables us to move time backwards, and forwards, and to slow it down, in order to learn more about the act of murder. Carroll was a good pro and we used to play chess to pass the time between takes during the various camera and lighting setups when we weren't required on the set. The show was directed by Leslie Stevens, a very notable director of the day and the guest star was the young blonde actress Grace Lee Whitney, who played Carla Duveen, the woman who shoots her lover while being carefully studied by the two Martians. Grace would go on to appear as Yeoman Rand in the original classic *Star Trek* and in several motion pictures; Carroll O'Connor, of course, went on to do two immensely popular series, *All in the Family* and *In the Heat of the Night*.

Among other shows I had worked on were those for QM Productions. The QM, of course, stood for Quinn Martin. I had worked for Quinn on a number of occasions. He was producer of the famous series about Eliot Ness called *The Untouchables*, with the leading role played by Robert Stack. I played more than once on that series, but I made it a habit at this time not to play typically English parts. I didn't want to get typed, as so often English actors do, under the supposition that they can't play anything else. So I played French champagne smugglers, Romanian drug peddlers, East Side thugs, and all kinds of characters. Quinn realized that I could make any kind of noises that the script required. A great many actors—much better actors than me—can't successfully make any other noises than the ones they get out of bed with in the morning!

And thus began a very successful, and very rewarding, period of my life.

14

"Chasing the Fugitive"

THE FUGITIVE WAS, FOR ME, immensely enjoyable. Not only because of its
great and lasting popularity, but even more because of the splendid group
of people whom it brought together: Quinn Martin, who formulated the
structure of the whole thing; the writers, who contributed so many marvelously diverse scripts; our brilliantly skillful and tireless crew; and of
course our hero, dear David Janssen. The series has become a classic of
its kind. All too many of our colleagues are no longer with us, but every
day I meet enthusiastic young people who are thrilled and moved today by
a drama that we made long before they were born.

Quinn Martin was a man of good sense, good taste, and general
decency, which was by no means universally the case among Hollywood
producers. I had come to know him and to like him a great deal. One fine
day, Quinn rang me up and said, "Look, I'm planning a new series, and
there's a character in it that I'd like you to play—not exactly a running
character, but a recurring character, in that he won't be in every episode
of the series." He continued, "I don't want to tell you anything more about
it, but I'll send you the script to read, then let's have lunch." The script
arrived and it had to do with a man falsely accused of the murder of his
wife, and the subsequent pursuit of this man by a dedicated officer of the
law.

I thought that both of the characters in the pilot for *The Fugitive* were
so "down the middle" in terms of American characterization, that Quinn
couldn't possibly want me to play the man on the run or the law officer, so
I thought the only solution must be that somebody had sent me the wrong
script! So when I met for lunch with Quinn a day or so later, I was all set
to explain this to him when he launched into an enthusiastic description of

the outline of this proposed series, and made it quite clear that he wanted me to play the detective! "Look, Quinn, the character as I see it in the pilot script is a thoroughly conventional rendering of an American detective, just like every movie for the past 20 years," I said. "Well that's the trouble, you see," Quinn replied, "I know that. The character, as presently expressed, is too much 'on the nose.'" And he said, "I know you're always interested in developing slightly offbeat characters, so why don't you think about it and see if you can't develop something that's a bit more unusual?"

Although I had made several television pilots, I had not worked in quite this circumstance before. It was interesting, but somewhat alarming, to be faced with the responsibility of developing one's own character. But I recognized immediately that the skeletal elements of *The Fugitive* were a modern remake of *Les Misérables*. I mentioned this to Quinn, and he said, "Well, yes, that is true, although we're naturally not advertising that. It is loosely derived from *Les Misérables*, but of course it's set in modern times and in the USA." Not many people in those days knew much about *Les Misérables*, as the famous stage production hadn't been yet produced. I've always thought that we in the arts—whichever art we happen to be in—are all "shoplifters." Everybody, from Shakespeare onwards and downwards, who enters any of our activities must acknowledge that we are shoplifters. But once you've acknowledged that, make sure that when you set out on a shoplifting expedition, you go always to Cartier's, and never to Woolworth's!

On that basis and with that idea in mind, I thought that Victor Hugo wasn't a bad role model. So I went back to *Les Misérables*, and especially to the character of Javert, the police officer who becomes obsessed with the pursuit of the hero, Jean Valjean. It's interesting, by the way, that faintly French ring to the name Gerard. There may have been some subconscious echoes of *Les Misérables* in the choice of that name. Gerard—Javert; the names are quite similar.

David Janssen, the star of our show, was not by any means unknown at this time—he was a well-liked and well-respected Hollywood actor who had done a moderately successful television series prior to *The Fugitive* called *Richard Diamond, Private Detective*. I remember talking to David and he said to me, "What do you think of this thing?" And I replied, "I've been around in a lot of circumstances in this crazy trade of ours and everybody tells me it can't possibly succeed, but then, what do I know? What does anybody know? It's a lot like going to the races and trying to pick the horses." David asked me, "Are they paying you decently for this?" I said, "Well, no, I'm nobody in Hollywood. I'm just an ordinary working actor. They're paying me fairly enough, I suppose, but nothing too extravagant."

David confided in me, "You know what? They can't even meet my ordinary going price, but they've offered me a piece of the show." "Well," I replied, "that may not be too bad." David laughed, "Well, you know what ten percent of nothing is!"

Our original pilot script for *The Fugitive*, "Fear in a Desert City," was supposed to be set in the state of Wisconsin. After the series was launched, some citizen— whether within our organization or outside it, I don't know—pointed out that the whole premise of *The Fugitive* would fall to the ground, punctured, if the location was in Wisconsin, because there was no cap-

With David Janssen. He was a real pro and died far too young.

ital punishment in that state! And so, arbitrarily, the locale of the series was shifted to Indiana. We filmed the pilot on location in Tucson, Arizona, and our director was Walter Grauman, connected by family to the man who gives his name to Grauman's Chinese Theater in Hollywood (where all the handprints and footprints of the famous are displayed). He was a very knowledgeable and experienced director; he'd done a great many other shows including episodes of *The Untouchables* series. I later worked with Walter on a number of shows over the years.

The network was very much concerned about the possibility of David Janssen and I being seen in each other's company socially. They really took this sort of thing seriously; it would be as if King Lear was seen taking his daughters out to dinner! However, there was an occasion back in L.A. when David said to me, "Come over to the house and have a meal—I'll have a couple of people there." But he didn't tell me that it was his birthday party! When I got close to the house I realized this must be an enormous "do," because I couldn't park within a couple of blocks of his place. I went up to the house, rang the bell and the door was opened by Jack Benny and he said, "Oh, come in, come in." Then I saw Lucille Ball. The house was swarming with everybody in our trade, and there was David basking in the middle of all this. All these years, people have said David was a bit of a boozer. But anybody who did the day's work that he did could not possibly have survived on alcohol. He was absolutely impeccable in his discipline on the set. He never put a foot wrong in hitting the marks and working with the cameras. He never failed in absolute courtesy towards the crew. David was the absolute, ultimate pro.

Jack Benny and Lucy weren't the only stars I encountered. One day when in Hollywood on a break from *The Fugitive*, I drove to Beverly Hills to see film producer David O. Selznick and his wife, Jennifer Jones, about a possible future project. I wasn't able to immediately find their house, but spotted a woman washing her car, so I pulled up to ask directions. "Hello," I said, "could you tell me where the Selznicks live?" This woman lifted her head up and I saw that it was none other than Katharine Hepburn. She looked at me for a moment, and then said, "Oh, it's *you*—from that television series. But you don't talk like that, do you? Oh, you're not an American." And I replied, "Well, you can't believe everything you see on television."

Up to that point I had played all kinds of different American characters, even for Quinn Martin on *The Untouchables*. I didn't realize it was implicitly something of a compliment that producers and directors never hesitated to hire me to play all sorts of different types of Americans. And I'd have to admit that I'm a little vain about my skill with accents. But *The Fugitive* stood for many years as the only instance where a British actor played an American character in an American television series.

At the beginning, all the experts pronounced that it couldn't possibly succeed, or even get on the air, because it had no successful ending. Of course, these so-called experts had completely ignored the impact of the cinema serials of the 1930s and 1940s, and, to go a little further back, that of the literary serials of the nineteenth century. In both of these cases, the very absence of an ending in the ordinary sense of the word, far from being a disadvantage, actually served as a powerful hook.

When we went over to Tucson for the pilot, I was determined to get away from the conventional cop figures that you saw all the time in movies, the ones with the raincoat and fedora. But once on location, on the set, the wardrobe department fitted me out with that dreadful raincoat and that clichéd fedora. After we completed the pilot, I threw them behind some bushes and they were never seen again. You may have noticed that I never wore any kind of hat or coat ever afterwards, no matter what the weather.

I used to get mail from viewers who noticed that over a period of time, I used both hands to write or to operate things with. I am instinctively left-handed, but I developed a certain degree of ambidexterity, and I thought that might be interesting and intriguing to viewers as being an outward sign of this somewhat divided nature which poor Philip Gerard had. And so, perhaps months apart, if I was involved in writing something, I would in one instance use my left hand, and in another use my right. I also began to use glasses as time went by—my own, because more often than not I had them with me in my pocket. It seemed to me that it would be a hint of the march of time if one started to see Gerard wearing glasses. But

Wearing the fedora and trench coat from *The Fugitive* **pilot. I promptly threw them away behind some bushes.**

then, of course, the interpretation of the character began to emerge in more subtle, less tangible ways. I hope I found ways of illustrating Gerard's sense of dichotomy—his own instinctive responses to situations set against the code which he had drilled himself to observe rigidly—as the series progressed.

There was a huge split of reaction to the two characters, Kimble and Gerard. On the one hand, there was an immense sympathy, and immense warmth towards the character of Richard Kimble. The natural counterpart was the response to Gerard. Somebody at one point dubbed Gerard as "The most hated man in America" and it may not have been far from the truth! Going through the airport, or walking down the street, I would be whacked at by little old ladies with umbrellas who would say things like, "You rotten, mean man! Why don't you leave that nice doctor alone?" The character has had such an impact that even to this day, when sitting in a restaurant, or checking into a hotel in some far-flung city, I may be approached by a person who will exclaim, "I'm so sorry, Lieutenant, but you've just missed Doctor Kimble—he went thataway." Of course, each and every one of them thinks that he's the very first to have made that little joke!

Behind the camera, directing "The Shattered Silence." (Courtesy of Stephen Lodge)

Quinn Martin was very amused by the reaction of the network people, the ad agencies, and sponsors. I remember him saying to me, just before the show went on the air, "Boy, all the people in the commercial world are very worried about you!" And I said, "What do you mean, me?" He replied, "Well, this performance of yours. Because they keep coming to me and saying, 'We've done all this audience testing and they love David. But, boy, oh boy, do they ever hate that guy Morse—you gotta get him out of there!'" Quinn's reply was, "No, no, no! That's the whole point!" In the climate of those days, it was totally unheard of to have in a series a character who you were deliberately meant to dislike. It was very rare for an actor to want to play such a character, but of course, as Quinn patiently would point out to anyone who would listen, the more animosity, the more resistance there was to Gerard, by simple mathematical process, the more sympathy there would be created for Richard Kimble—for David. So that intensity of response was, implicitly, a great testimony to the strength of what we were delivering. Being brought up in a theatrical tradition, I knew very well that if you wanted to play the most rewarding parts, they were often characters like Richard III, carefully designed to be disliked.

We always managed to be absolutely scrupulous and careful in making it clear to anyone who cared to observe that Gerard was functioning with utmost propriety within his duty as an instrument of the law. I suppose that Gerard would say that personal relationships, as between himself and Kimble, are not affected by the accidental happenings which befall them. He would simply say, "Whether or not this man saved my life doesn't affect my duty to deliver him to the legal system which employs me and which has convicted him. Whether he has been wrongly convicted or not is not my business."

Of course, as good as the series was, it wasn't perfect. At three different points in the series, poor Gerard was issued with three totally different wives! Our daughter Melanie discovered another mistake which involved the opening sequence of the show. She came to me and said, "Daddy, I thought you said this was in the States, but that's a French train." So the producers checked it out and it was indeed a clip of a French train with French lettering on the side. Feeling that most viewers wouldn't know the difference, they left the shot in and they were right: Nobody else even noticed.

I directed the fourth season episode "The Shattered Silence," which featured Laurence Naismith and Antoinette Bower. I had done a good deal of directing before in both the UK and Canada, in theatre and television, so this was not new territory for me. By this time, we had gone through nearly four seasons of episodes and our crew had become so beautifully "rubbed down," so beautifully, smoothly operating, that the director's job was made easy. The skill and efficiency of that crew contributed to the polish of the finished product. When I came to direct, I'd only have to lift my head and look toward a particular direction and the crew would realize, even before I said it, that my thought was to have the camera there, then I would indicate where we might have Laurence Naismith sitting, or David standing, or whatever. It was a very easy ride to work as a director on that series.

Quinn Martin explained to me right from the word *go* that this character, Lieutenant Gerard, would not appear in all of the episodes. He would appear in what used to be called the teaser, the opening setup sequence of every show, but wouldn't actually appear in the episode itself more than about one-third of the time. So I had an unusual kind of contract which enabled me to go and do other things. It was perfect for me: I had a substantial role in this immensely popular series and at the same time I was able to play all sorts of other characters for NBC or CBS in New York, go back to Canada for the CBC for television or radio, or back to England for the BBC.

We were all immensely excited by the success of the series and David and I became very good friends. I like to think that David regarded me as a kind of proxy parent, since I was virtually old enough to be his father. David had a succession of ever more youthful wives, which is a very expensive habit in California. I used to say to him, "David, son, if you are going to go on collecting, do, please, if you can, collect something which is relatively inexpensive, like stamps or coins. Don't go on collecting wives, it's a very expensive habit!"

David must have been the hardest-working actor in any series that's ever been. He was in practically every scene of every episode of the show. I know that he was always immensely relieved whenever I turned up in town, because it meant that he was going to get a few days off! But by the time we had reached the fourth season, David was just exhausted, so the decision was taken to end the show. We probably could have run another two or three seasons if not for the terrible burden placed upon David.

Our final episode was a two-parter entitled "The Judgment," which in an ironic twist initially finds our hero, Kimble, back in Tucson, Arizona — right where we began everything four years earlier in the pilot show. David and I cooked up a scenario which we jokingly presented to our producers as a way to wrap up the show. We would establish a shot on a handsome suburban house in Stafford, Indiana. It's a moonlit night, and you can hear a few crickets, and so forth. We're on a high crane and we push in through the upper window. Then, we go tighter onto, say, the left side of a double bed where Richard Kimble is sitting up, alarmed, having obviously just awakened. Then he turns on the light, and shakes the shoulder of his companion in this double bed, which we see, as she turns around and wakes up, is his wife — Mrs. Richard Kimble. And then Kimble would cry out, "Oh! Oh, honey! Oh, thank God. I've just had the most terrible nightmare!"

In the first version of the final scene of *The Fugitive*, our writers had gone a little overboard. They wrote a scene of emetic mawkishness, in which David and I said sentimental things to each other. Gerard said something like, "Well, you know what I feel about all of this.... I hope you won't consider me to have carried any personal animosity toward you. I was just trying to do the job I was hired and paid to do...." To which Kimble replied, "Sure, I understand. After all, a man's gotta do what a man's gotta do." You know, *that* sort of dialogue. I suggested to David that, in order to mock this overly sentimental dialogue on Take One we would play through all this mawkishness as it stood, and we would then throw ourselves into each other's arms and kiss each other firmly on the mouth! So we did just that. Of course, the crew all fell about with laughter, the absurdity was realized and the dialogue was abandoned. Somebody said to me, "Well, what do you think would be the best thing to say?" My reply was, "I think it would be best if we say nothing!" As is often the case on the screen, what you do and what you look is much more eloquent than what you say. The scene was shot in a spare, economical manner with no spoken words between our two characters. Gerard simply nodded, smiled, and exchanged a handshake with Kimble. And thus came the end of arguably one of the best television series of all time and one of the most important events of my career. I'm proud to say that "The Judgment" parts 1 and 2 for many years stood as the highest-rated shows ever aired on network television.

In 1980 I phoned David from New York to let him know I would be coming out to Los Angeles in a few days' time, and we arranged to meet up for dinner. A day or two later I received a phone call from a journalist quite early in the morning, who asked me, "Mr. Morse, have you heard the news? What's your reaction?" I replied, "Well, no, I haven't got up yet," thinking the reporter was seeking my opinion on World War III or whatever was in the news. "Then perhaps you haven't heard," he told me, "David Janssen has died." I was really quite horrified. David was only 48 and that seemed to me to be a tragically young age. It was a great waste, because in my view, David was never properly or fully extended as an actor. I was able to get a hint of what he was capable of and I don't think his capabilities were ever fully made use of.

Despite the gloomy predictions of the so-called experts, *The Fugitive* rapidly became one of the most popular dramas on television all over the world and, even more remarkably, has remained so for the last forty years. In fact, many of today's younger generation of viewers, who weren't even born when we were making the series, prefer it to most of today's offerings. All of which is very gratifying to those of us who had a hand in it, and led the show to be called a "classic," which simply means, in my view, something that succeeding generations have continued to admire and enjoy. Meanwhile, of course, those same "experts" who long since foretold our failure have now joined the ranks of the "hindsighters," crying, "I told you so!" Our old show continues to live on through new films and new TV offerings, but the popularity of the original has never dimmed. To this day I always know when a new country is getting *The Fugitive*, maybe Tanzania or Zimbabwe, because I get this mail written in pidgin English, finding its way around the planet, saying, "What you think, you rotten mean detective person? You do not pursue that nice doctor no more."

And so, the whirligig of time brings its revenges.

15

"How the Other Half Lives"

IN 1963 I WENT OFF TO Mexico City to do a film called *Kings of the Sun*. It started filming on January 8 and was an extraordinary experience. It was one of these multimillion dollar spectacular films which used to be made at that time, allegedly based on the anthropological and historical records concerning those people who were the aboriginal inhabitants of Mexico, known as the Mayans. This film was on a very grand scale, and was directed by J. Lee Thompson, who did a number of other—most of them rather better—movies.

We then filmed around what was then a fishing village called Mazatlan on the Pacific coast. It has grown in the years since then to a huge resort town, but back then it was a relatively small fishing port. It had been selected as the location for the film because the producers were able to engage as extras almost all the local population. Men, women and children were all hired at some revoltingly small fee, like a dollar a day, to appear as extras. It was my first experience with one of these large-scale movie spectaculars. The leading role was played by the late and, by me, not at all respected Yul Brynner. The person whom I had most in common with and got to know quite well was a very fine actor called Richard Basehart. Richard and I spent a lot of time together, generally bemoaning our fate for being mixed up in such rubbish. Also in it were people like George Chakiris, who had recently made a great success in *West Side Story*. I was playing a character called Ah Zok, who was one of a pair of High Priests. The other, being played by Richard Basehart, was called Ah Min. Brynner played his role with great grandiosity and obviously had the highest opinion of himself. He was not at all companionable or friendly. He seemed to regard the whole of the human race as his inferiors. I know I'm speaking

148

My back to the camera as High Priest Ah Zok, about to perform a ritual sacrifice in *Kings of the Sun.*

ill of the dead, but I have to speak as I found. I remember that, as we started to shoot out in the country on location, all of these hundreds of extras were bussed out—or to be more accurate, most of them were brought out in trucks—to this remote part of the jungle. They were not provided with anything in the way of food, so they would bring with them, wrapped in rags or scraps of paper, bits of food which they would then cook over little fires which they would build in the jungle. Of course, we—the pampered Hollywood people—were meanwhile provided with quite adequate and, under the circumstances, elegant food in a proper marquee. Brynner never actually joined us. He always had a table set aside for himself and his minions. On the first day, the extras were all around us in the jungle—many with these little fires over which they were cooking their food—and Brynner said very grandly to one of the assistants who were around, "What's that smell?" and they said, "Oh, that's the extras, Mr. Brynner. They're cooking their food down there." Brynner said, "Well, get them the hell out of here! Get them right over the other side of the hill!" He had them all driven away from where they were trying to prepare their miserable little meals. I remember Basehart and I looking at each other and exchanging a look of "Who made this guy?"

The pitiful amount of money the extras were paid was sufficient to draw them away from their own inherited occupation, which was fishing. So, many of them gave up fishing and would bring out all the members of their families—grandma, granddad, you name it—to come out and work for this pittance. When we were shooting a sequence which involved people landing from the sea and being confronted with a wall of flame which the defenders had built, the Spanish speaking assistant directors announced to all these extras who were lined up that they were going to shoot this sequence which involved running through a wall of flame. They said that anyone who volunteered to do it would be paid some extra pittance, like an extra dollar. Well, as one man, they all stepped forward. They all wanted so much to have this extra dollar. It was a terrible example of the exploitation of this local population. But there was a wonderful, ironic end to all of this. There was a sequence in which we, Ah Min and Ah Zok, were standing on the top of a temple, while the invading forces were trying to break into this walled city. As part of the plot, Brynner had been captured and was tied to a stake just inside the city gate, which the invading army was about to break through. There was this huge setting, we had about eight or ten cameras in different positions ready to shoot, and there had been endless preparation. They finally got everything ready; Brynner was there—tied to the stake just inside the gate—and the hordes of invaders were just outside. They gave the cue to start and Basehart and I were up on the roof of the temple, looking at all this. It had only been going for about a minute or less, when all the assistant directors were shouting through their loudspeakers, "Alto! Alto! Stop! Stop!" Then we heard them shouting in Spanish at the extras, saying, "When you burst through the gate *you must not hit* Mr. Brynner with your spears and your clubs!" All these innocent Mexican people, having been so maltreated by Brynner, thought, "Ah, yes. This is the day when we can hit this man! How nice."

While we were in Mazatlan we were befriended by a young lad whose name was Fidel Ortega, who shared his birthday, April 23, with William Shakespeare. Fidel was one of the extras, who came along with his family, including his mother and father, and I think even his grandmother came at one point. In those days I was a very enthusiastic photographer, and Fidel attached himself to me because he was fascinated by all this camera equipment I had. He used to call me "El Señor Camera"! Sydney and I became very fond of this young man. He was eleven years old at the time. We took him back with us to our hotel one day, to give him some ice cream. He had never set foot in such a place before. When we went into the dining room

Our star, Yul Brynner, menacing the extras.

to get him his ice cream he said, "What a lovely room. This is where you live? You sleep here?" and we said, "No, this is just the eating room." Sydney spoke very good Spanish, and I was beginning to learn a bit of Spanish from Fidel, because he had no English at all. It was charming to be taught my basic Spanish by an eleven-year-old boy. He was forever laughing when I got the words wrong and referred to my arm as my leg or something like that. Anyway, he was absolutely staggered that we actually ate in a different room from that in which we slept. Eventually, after he'd had his ice cream, we took him up to show him our room, and the bathroom attached. He'd never seen a bathroom, and he looked in there and saw the toilet. He said, "What is that?" and we said, "Well, that's where you make pee-pee," using our best Spanish. He said, "Oh, can I make pee-pee there?" He was very excited by this, and we said, "Sure, if you'd like." He was fascinated by this sight of a flushing toilet, which he'd never seen before.

One day his mother asked us if we would go to have Sunday dinner with them, to which we said, "Yes, of course." They arranged that Fidel would meet us and lead us to their home. So we thought, "What can we do to repay this generous gesture?" Sydney said, "Let us get presents for each of the family. We can ask Fidel what they would like. He'll be able to tell us, and then we can go to the Sunday market in Mazatlan and buy these various things." So Fidel took us around the market and we ticked them off, one by one: his grandmother, mother, father, his one brother, and his four sisters. For one of his sisters, I know, we bought a nylon slip, because Fidel had said to us, "She likes shiny things underneath." In the market, while we were paying for one of these various gifts, we noticed that Fidel had moved a little way up the street and was talking to another little boy. We saw, at perhaps no more than ten or fifteen yards distance, that he was giving this boy a coin (amounting to a quarter or so), which we knew was the only money he had. So when he came back to us Sydney said to him, "Fidel, you only had one coin. Why were you giving all your money to that little boy?" Fidel said with great earnestness and innocence, "Oh, he is very poor. He has no mother." When we recovered, we said, "Now off we go to your mom and dad's house. Where's this house?" Little did we know; this family lived (like many other families in Mazatlan at this time), in a shelter made of flattened cardboard grocery cartons laced together over a framework of small branches from trees and bushes. It was quite ingeniously constructed, over a beaten earth floor, along the side of a warehouse. There, the whole of this family lived. Six children, parents and grandmother made nine! They all slept on the ground, except grandmother, who had an arrangement of cardboard and paper which insulated her from the earth. They all had dug out little hollows in the earth, to receive shoulders and hips, so that they could lie more comfortably. That was their home.

We had our meal made from beans cooked on an open fire just outside this shelter, and quite delicious it was, too. It was a revelation of how the "other half" lives which I shall never forget. We learned a good deal more about Fidel and his family. His father was a fisherman, and *his* father had been a fisherman, as was the traditional occupation of the time. But Fidel was an uncommonly intelligent and interesting boy. We gathered that he scarcely ever went to school, because he was out earning money in one way or another, working with his father or running errands, or laboring for other people. We talked to his parents about this, and they were quite seriously concerned. They had observed that he was a very intelligent and industrious minded little boy, but obviously he was not going to get very far if he never went to school. We said, more or less, "How much money do you think he earns?" and we ascertained what it was, and of course it was pitifully little. So Sydney suggested to his mother and father that we send a little amount of money every once in a while to replace what Fidel was making, in order to keep him at school. We succeeded in doing that, and he went on from school to a form of technical school, and eventually after a period of several years he started and ran his own service station garage, because he became skilled at mechanics. I'm afraid we lost touch with him a while back, because he moved away to some other part of Mexico. So, let's hope he now has a family of his own, and is having a full and happy life.

I returned to Boston for another production of Shaw's *Man and Superman* in June of 1964 in a theatre constructed on Boston Common. They built bleachers, like at a football game, around an open-air stage not dissimilar to the open-air amphitheater in Wellesley. This time the leading lady was again the actress with whom I'd first played *Man and Superman*, Nancy Wickwire, a superb actress. Also in the cast, playing a relatively small part as the chauffeur was a man who went on to become a movie star, called Roy Schieder. Sydney played in that production with me, also. It was a notable opening night, and we received extravagantly good reviews. They spoke warmly about the production as a whole, and about me in particular. This was partly because, on our opening night, there was a sudden downpour of rain during the scene in Hell. In this scene, *Don Juan in Hell*, Don Juan is confronted by the Devil. So we were acting away as best we could, and this downpour of rain occurred. I wanted to protect dear Nancy Wickwire, who was dressed in rather off the shoulder period costume, from getting soaking wet. I happened to be wearing a quite voluminous cloak, and draped it around her, improvising a speech to the Devil saying, "*Really*! As well as everything else about your domain, your weather is quite intolerable!" Of course that brought a huge round of applause from the audience, and the critics were very generous in applauding my quick wittedness. But the downpour didn't damage the production at all, the audience didn't move, and the shower of rain didn't last very long. So that was a third production of *Man and Superman*, and I was getting to know it quite well by now.

It was around this time that I got involved with the play *Eh?*, a marvelously primitive kind of piece about a chap who has a rather limited personal life. The character, Valentine Bross, works as an engineer taking care of machinery in some factory and his life is so restricted emotionally that he more or less falls in love with this machine that he works on. The title is English. There's a certain kind of working class accent mostly in the north of England—and I believe this play was set in Sheffield—rather like the characters in *The Full Monty*. The reason why the title was adopted is that those people will say things like, "Well, I was born on the fourteenth of July in 1945 and so I'm just coming up to 21 years old, eh?" They put "eh?" on the end of everything as if to say, "Am I right?"

There's virtually only one character in the play and it had been done in a small London studio theatre in the mid–1960s. The play had been quite successful in some highbrow quarters as being a sensitive and intelligent piece, so somebody proposed to bring it to New York. It came about that it was to be presented in a small theatre located in the basement of a small grubby hotel, an altogether fifth class environment. People thought we were absolutely mad to produce a play which was exclusively British and even within the British framework rather specialized, being set in Sheffield. It was proposed to put on this production and they wanted to find the leading fellow for this piece who finishes up every sentence he speaks with "eh?"

I met up with a young actor who was put forward for the role, but I have to admit that I was a bit skeptical to think that an American lad who, so far as I could gather, had never set foot outside of the United States, would have the skill to reproduce an authentic accent. Indeed, it did turn

Dressed as a "lady of the evening" for one of my nine roles, in a behind the scenes shot on the set of It's Murder, Cherie.

out that he had this extraordinary skill, so this actor—a young man by the name of Dustin Hoffman—was hired to do this play. The play opened to a certain amount of success before transferring to an off–Broadway theatre in 1965, where Dustin went on to win a number of honors, including the *Theatre World* and *Drama Desk* awards. But most importantly, it led to his being seen, and subsequently getting his starring role in his breakthrough film, *The Graduate*. I think I'm right to say that when he first went to see the producers about that film they had only seen him in this play *Eh?* His performance had been so good that they assumed he was an English actor and couldn't possibly qualify for this part in *The Graduate*! They were quite staggered to find that he was a perfectly straightforward young American. And that's how Dustin Hoffman's career was launched. I think I got the directing job because they were just grateful to have somebody who had some English knowledge and English background. But, I thought it was a worthwhile thing. Dustin Hoffman is a most gloriously gifted actor and we got along very well.

A while later I was back in New York to rehearse for a play called *The Man With The Perfect Wife*. It was written by a Canadian woman named Patricia Joudry. It was going to be tried out, prior to appearing on Broadway, in the Royal Poinciana Playhouse in Palm Beach, Florida. The leading part was played by the then very prominent movie star Jennifer Jones, and produced by her husband, David O. Selznick. I was to play her husband in the piece. Poor Jennifer Jones was a very troubled lady, to put it mildly. The first thing that started to occur while we were rehearsing in New York was that she was regularly, and *seriously* late. She would appear sometimes an hour, or even an hour and a half late. Since hers was one of the two leading parts, it meant we couldn't do much in the way of rehearsal, and we would just have to hang about waiting for her to appear. But we continued on with rehearsals, and as we got near to the time we were about to open, the director, who had been trying to deal with this poor woman and the ensuing situation, had a nervous crisis of his own and resigned. It was left to me, as the senior actor in the company, to continue trying to put on this play. It was a foregone disaster, but we played our allotted run at the Poinciana Playhouse, and then went on down to the Coconut Grove Playhouse in Miami. While on that tour in Florida, on the occasion of our twenty-sixth wedding anniversary, Sydney wrote the following to me:

> Remembrance is a form of meeting,
> > Well met.
> Marriage is a form of loving,
> > Best yet.
> 26 years is a form of agreement,
> > Two fold.
> Let's make another—'til death us do part.
> It's the best I can give you, straight from the heart.
> With all my love,
> Sydney

That eased the frenzy of this ghastly mess of a play we were doing. We had continual troubles over this play. I remember there was an incident where Jennifer Jones was supposed to smack my face. At first she couldn't bring herself to do it, and would just wave her hand past my face, about a foot away. She had no idea how to do these things technically, which any properly trained actress knows before they set foot on the stage. I tried to show her how to do this, so that it wouldn't look absolutely ludicrous to an audience. I don't think I ever really succeeded. It was a tiresome time, but we finally got through it.

I went back to Canada to do what became a rather notorious TV show for CBC called *It's Murder, Chérie!* directed by Leo Orenstein. It was an extraordinary idea for a series, in which I should play all sorts of different parts. I played *nine* different characters, two of them women! One was a belly dancer, for which I had an emerald stuck in my navel, and I did an elaborate belly dance. The other female character I played was a prostitute. The taping of it was extraordinarily exhausting, because we had to shoot all these scenes separately so I could change costume and makeup to become all these different characters. There had been a lunatic prospect of turning it into a series, in which I should play various different characters week by week. Perhaps mercifully it never came into being!

16

"A Season to Remember"

WHILE *THE FUGITIVE* WAS STILL in production, I found myself one blustery day toward the end of 1965 sitting in the University Club in Toronto. Across the table from me sat Brian Doherty—beaming with bonhomie and bubbling with news of the Shaw Festival of Canada. Would I like to have a bash with them next year? Of course at this time my life was taken up with the pursuit of Dr. Kimble on television, so I replied that I must confer with my producer and my agents. But the offer was an irresistible one and I was intrigued. Brian, of course, was the Founder and the first President of the Shaw Festival, at Niagara-on-the-Lake, Ontario.

With Sydney's blessing, I went back to California and confronted my amiable boss, Quinn Martin. Full of wild surmise, I told him of what I'd like to do, and he—the good workmate that he was—indulgently agreed (rather in the manner of one dealing with an old friend stricken with some unaccountable malaise) to give me at least the three months that I thought would be necessary to get the season launched. He made this possible by shuffling the shooting schedule of *The Fugitive*, making the best use of the time I would be in California. Then it was back to Toronto and Brian—yes, I would accept their offer to become artistic director of the Shaw Festival of Canada for the 1966 season. The venture had already begun to infect me with a desperado daring and I suggested that we make the season longer than ever before—nine whole weeks!—and that we do three plays, the first of them one of the largest, longest, and most complex in the whole Shaw canon: *Man and Superman* (and at something like full length). Then *Misalliance*, then *The Apple Cart*.

The Shaw Festival is the only theatre in the world that specializes in plays written by George Bernard Shaw and his contemporaries. Therefore,

157

its productions encompass the years 1856 to 1950—the lifetime of Shaw himself. The plays written during this period are now considered classics— but many were cutting-edge modern when they were first performed. These are plays about issues and ideas which are still with us—plays which still have the potential to make us laugh, cry, and marvel. Shaw was not only a great playwright, but also a great prophet of the twentieth century. He valued the way the stage could become a platform for the communication of ideas and through his plays he sought to confront audiences with issues of social and political importance. He aimed to stimulate not only the hearts, but also the minds of theatre-goers. One of the major innovations of Shavian drama was the unusually large role he gave to thought and debate— but thought enlivened with a love of wordplay and paradox.

So our plays were picked and the dates were set. I met a scrubbed, blue-eyed choirboy named Raymond Wickens, who was our business and stage manager, publicity director, and Lord-High-Everything-Else (a role he would reprise during our *Merely Players* Canadian tour two decades later). He took me down to Niagara-on-the-Lake, a place I had never set foot in before. We viewed our theatre—the Court House. Its interior was painted an acidulated public-urinal green and looked bleakly unpromising. There was no time for dismay to settle in—we would have to do something about that situation later. Now was the time to cast our plays.

We began an exciting round of cajolery, blandishment, arm-twisting, foot-licking, exploiting of old friends, inflammation of total strangers, and the outlay of almost everything *except* money. The fever was catching: all manner of theatre workers, some eminent, some novices, were willing to throw in their lots with us under working conditions and for rewards which, in most cases, were infinitely lower than they could reasonably expect in their normal working lives. This was the grandest kind of largesse, the richest subsidies any theatre venture could ever have. Their names are a luscious litany to remember—Zoe Caldwell, Pat Galloway, Betty Leighton, Susan Clark, Tom Kneebone, Leslie Yeo, Hugh Webster, Norman Welsh, and a young man of sonorous voice and twinkling-solemn manner named Paxton Whitehead (who would himself have a fine future with the Shaw Festival)—and many, many more—fine troupers all!

While we were assembling our troupe, we pressed on with two other projects which became known among us as "warming up the town" and "beating the drum." At that time, the citizenry of Niagara-on-the-Lake were not unqualified or unanimous in their enthusiasm for the Shaw Festival. There were those who hoped that we would just quietly go away or, better still, that a righteous providence would visit fire and brimstone upon us and all of our sinful pleasurable works. We encountered bloody-mindedness as well as saintly kindliness, but quite perceptibly the town started to warm up. And we beat the drum in every way we could, short of spending money. A wider world began to hear of the Shaw Festival, and Raymond brought the exciting word to us while we wrestled with rehearsals that we were actually selling large numbers of seats.

Publicity was the most important thing, and the contribution that I was able to make in terms of publicity was the fact that I was now playing—albeit a secondary part—in what was becoming the most popular television series on earth. I knew that was a plus, but we had to get more immediate publicity as best we could. Through a friend at the CBC I got them

Norman Welsh, Hugh Webster, Pat Galloway, and me, as Don Juan, in the "Hell Scene" from *Man and Superman.* **(Courtesy of Robert C. Ragsdale, F.R.P.S.)**

to agree to do a bit of a promotional documentary about this Shaw Festival, and they agreed that they would shoot some of the rehearsals of our first production, *Man and Superman*, while we were rehearsing in Toronto, and they would then come down to Niagara-on-the-Lake, which at that time was scarcely known of, and shoot footage of the locality and the beautiful little town. Then, as the producer said, "We'll wind it all up with an interview with you in your office."

But, of course, I neglected to tell him that I didn't have an office. Whenever I went down to Niagara I shared a room with my young friend Ray Wickens. I had no such thing as an office. So they started to shoot this promotional footage. They went to rehearsals in Toronto and shot flashes of scenes that we were working on there. They went down to Niagara and shot scenes of the lakefront and the Niagara River. And then they said, "Now we'll come to your office and shoot this interview."

I had previously talked with Ray and said, "What I'm going to do is this: if you would get hold of a couple of bent-wood chairs and a folding card table, we'll set them up on this traffic island which stands right in front of the courthouse." The courthouse was our theatre, and the traffic island is still there and has a little clock podium on it. The whole traffic island is the size of a small room with the centre, about the size of a small table, occupied by this clock. And so when they said, "Where can we come to shoot this interview with you?" I said "Come out the front of the theatre, across the road, and you'll find me." The traffic goes both ways around the island, and there we set up these two kitchen chairs and this folding card table.

When the CBC crew arrived at the traffic island I said, "This is where we can do our interview." They were staggered. But the producer was imaginative enough to see this as enormously exciting. Here we were doing the first full-length personal interview with the new artistic director of the Shaw Festival, right in front of the Shaw Festival theatre, with the cars going both ways around us. The chap who was producing was also doing the interview, and he allowed me to burble on about Shaw and all his great achievements at considerable length. Then he realized that this would have immense appeal to all kinds of other stations, besides just the local branches of the CBC. In the event, it was shown clear across North America! We couldn't have bought this much publicity for tens of thousands of dollars. They had this crazy guy—me—sitting there talking about this Shaw Festival, and viewers had just seen me in the rehearsal shots playing the lead in *Man and Superman*. Here I was sitting in my jeans on this traffic island with all this stuff going on around me, telling about the glories of Shaw. It ended up being shown not only clear across Canada, but also all over the USA.

We moved down to Niagara and into the Court House, still public-urinal green. We built the stage and elevated the seating just in time for dress rehearsals—and a preview. We also arranged to have a monstrous rocket fired from the roof of the building by the local military at the moment of the beginning of the first performance. The eleventh hour and close to the starting line. Late at night on the eve of our opening, our stage manager, Larry Wayne, appeared with gallons of paint and dozens of rollers and brushes and we set about the task of painting the auditorium a friendlier shade. All of us! All those pampered show business layabouts were up ladders with babushkas round their heads painting for dear life. We were still putting on the finishing dabs when Raymond appeared, dinner-jacketed, to tell us that our first night audience was at the doors. We scampered to the kitchen, which was serving as our dressing room (the sexes loosely divided by a sagging curtain), to get our slap on. Then the five-minute call. Hundreds of wires have arrived from well-wishers. Pinned to the call-board with a stage nail was a message apparently from Queen Elizabeth I: "By your courage in the field and your conduct in the camp, we shall shortly have a Famous Victory.'

"Overture and Beginners, please," came the call.

Scrambling back from the front of the house, where I had been to ensure that all our first night Worthies were properly ensconced, I bumped into Paxton, palely loitering, ready for Octavius. I remember we hugged each other convulsively and he soundlessly mouthed just one word to me, "Relax!" I tried. Suddenly there was a shuddering thud and decrescendo roar—our rocket on the roof was off, and so were we!

On our second night in the dark of the wings, Leslie Yeo gave me a jubilant thumbs up. We had done it—we were sold out! And so it remained all season long. The critics' notices were very favorable, and now the festival had gained the attention of newspapers across Canada and in many parts of the United States as well. We received our first grant from the Canada Council and in a mood of great optimism, the Festival Board at its annual meeting established a study committee for a new theatre—a new state-of-the-art theatre that would become reality in a few short years.

Paxton Whitehead succeeded me in 1967 and served for twelve seasons as artistic director of the Shaw Festival. During his tenure he was able to push through a plan of building a new purpose-built large theatre to expand considerably the capacity for audiences at Niagara-on-the-Lake. Ten years after my tour of duty, Paxton invited me back to direct a production of *The Admirable Crichton* by J.M. Barrie. It was a great pleasure for me to finally return to the Shaw Festival in the 1976 season, and upon rereading the play I was very much struck by how adventurous Barrie was in writing *The Admirable Crichton*. Although the play was commercially very successful and popular, it was also a tremendous satiric examination of Edwardian English society. It deals with a situation where a noble lord, an earl and his family, set forth on a cruise on their yacht with various of their servants aboard. The yacht becomes wrecked on a desert island and they're all marooned. Inevitably their butler, whose name is Crichton, becomes not only the leader of their group and the savior of their welfare and well being, but the ruler of the whole community. J.M. Barrie was quietly pointing out that leadership in societies is not necessarily something that can be inherited like property or a title, but has to be worked for and deserved by people who know how to do things. I proposed to make that whole satiric point very clear in this production, which isn't always done, but it is a very important ingredient.

In addition to my directing duties in 1976, I also played the role of Sir George Crofts in their production of the Shaw play *Mrs. Warren's Profession*,

From left, me, with Kate Reid, Roberta Maxwell, Peter Mews, Christopher Gaze and Patrick Boxill in *Mrs. Warren's Profession*. (Courtesy of Robert C. Ragsdale, F.R.P.S.)

with the lovely Canadian actress Kate Reid. Sydney joined me in Canada for the season, and besides appearing in my production of *The Admirable Crichton* she would also appear in the production of *Arms and the Man*. I started rehearsals for *The Admirable Crichton*. So I was rehearsing two plays at this point, one of which I was directing and the other of which I was acting in. It was an immensely successful season altogether and we spent the whole of the spring and summer there.

Sydney's role in *The Admirable Crichton* was that of a Lady, one of the typical Edwardian aristocrats of that era at the beginning of the twentieth century. There was a danger, I felt, in the presentation of that character, that she could be rather too much like Lady Bracknell in Oscar Wilde's *The Importance of Being Earnest*. I decided to encourage Sydney to turn her into something quite different, very "horsey" with a brilliant red outdoor kind of face and march about and bark at people. It was quite marvelous to see how well Sydney did it! The performance was very successful, as indeed was the whole production. It was quite elaborate, as the author, J.M. Barrie, suggests in the first act, where there is a party given for the staff of this noble family, that there should be something like eleven servants present. People said, "Oh, wow, you can't run to the expense of having eleven different people coming on as servants, couldn't you boil it down to say five?" I was firm that, no, it must be made very clear that this relatively small family, a gentleman and his three daughters, are waited on by *eleven* perfectly healthy grown up people. That's the whole point of it! So we did that and, indeed, in the scene where they're all waiting to board the yacht there's even a small boy there whose duties are to look after the family dog! It makes quite a statement and it was a very interesting and very successful production of a play that isn't often done successfully because it does make a rather large demand financially due to the size of the cast. Sydney sent me a card on the opening night saying, simply, "I hope I got her 'horsey' enough!"

Sydney and Alexandra Bastedo in a scene from *Arms and the Man*. (Courtesy of Robert C. Ragsdale, F.R.P.S.)

Between 1966 and the present day, the Shaw Festival season has expanded, with productions running from April to November of each year, in three different theatres. You can see up to a dozen plays performed by one of the world's finest acting companies, in a beautiful village just 20 minutes down-river from Niagara Falls and less than two hours from Toronto. I am privileged to have been a part of the beginning of this very worthy endeavor and have been very proud to watch the festival's continuing success and growth.

17

"Just an Old Circus Horse"

A TOTAL SWITCH OF DIRECTION for me came about, as such things so often do, by sheer fluke. During those seasons Sydney and I had spent down near Boston playing with Group 20, there had been a young man in the company called Robert Brustein, who played in such things with me as *Cyrano de Bergerac*. I had come to know and like him. Ten years later he had become a highly respected critic, and had recently been appointed dean of the drama department of Yale University.

He got in touch with me one day by phone and said, "Hi Barry. Would you like to come and be a professor?" I thought he was referring to some production he was mixed up in where he wanted me to *play* a professor, so I said, "What's the play? Where?" And he said, "No, no. You know I'm now the dean of drama at Yale, right?" and I answered, "Yes, yes." He then explained, "I want to bring the course we offer at Yale closer to the professional practical realities of life, and back from the rather misty academic world it has tended to occupy." He said, "I know you're always saying you're just an old circus horse," which is some jokey way I used to describe myself due to the variety of work I had done. He said, "I thought it might be interesting to you to come be a professor at Yale and work with a repertory company I want to set up here which will be rather like Group 20." So I said, "Well, gosh, how long for?" He answered, "Well, as long as you like!" It sounds extraordinary, doesn't it, for me having had virtually no education at all to be offered a job as *a professor at Yale*—and I remember saying to him, "You realize don't you, I can scarcely read and write!" He said, "Oh, rubbish! And that's not the point! You've spent a great deal of time in the real theatrical jungle, and that's what I want our students to be exposed to." I told him I'd get back to him, and I would consider it.

A stage play called *Staircase* came around at this time. It's a two handed play where both characters are male and are homosexual partners. So I went back down to New York and into discussions with my longtime friend and partner, Bill Freedman, regarding this play, which he wanted me to direct on Broadway. It's a very interesting and challenging English play and was quite controversial for its time. Bill Freedman and his partner, Charles Kasher, had the rights for the USA and wanted to do it for Broadway. So that was being considered and thought about, and was due to open in January 1968, so it looked like it might be convenient for me to be just up the road in New Haven, headquarters of Yale University, while the play was running.

Before *Staircase* got going, I prepared and directed a film about Charles Dickens. The leading role of Dickens was played by Michael Redgrave. The young woman he befriends was played by Juliet Mills—John Mills' daughter. Very good and charming she was. Also playing in it was my darling Sydney. It was a fantasy-biographical study of Dickens based on the idea that a young woman interested in his work is wandering about London and actually encounters him. He is, in effect, embodied for her, and then takes her to the parts of London where he lived and worked—in today's world. It was shot on various locations around London and was called *Mr. Dickens of London*. One of our locations was Westminster Abbey. It was very difficult in those days—and I'm sure even more difficult now—to get a permit to shoot in Westminster Abbey. The only time they could give us permission to shoot was in the middle of the night, from midnight to 6:00 a.m. Part of the movie had to do with Dickens thinking back on his life and work almost as a ghost, so a scene was shot in Westminster Abbey so we could see Dickens looking down on his gravestone there. Well, Redgrave had various troubles in his life. I had been in a play before with his wife, Rachel Kempson, so I knew something about her life with Michael, who was given to occasional bouts of drinking. It just so happened that on the very night we were going to shoot in Westminster, and he had a great deal of dialogue to speak, he had—shall we say—*indulged* himself a bit and was obviously not in any shape to shoot. So I had to rearrange all the shooting so as not to require him to speak very much dialogue. In the end it was very successful and was nominated for an Emmy.

We then started to rehearse *Staircase* in New York. I'd been talking for a while with Eli Wallach about his part, having decided quite early on that Eli would be a good choice for one of our leading men. The other role was to be played by a wonderful Irish actor whom I'd worked with before named Milo O'Shea. We started to rehearse on West 47th Street at the Biltmore Theater. This play by Charles Dyer is about a pair of barbers who've

Biltmore Theatre

PLAYBILL

the national magazine for theatregoers

STAIRCASE

The playbill for our groundbreaking Broadway play, *Staircase*, featured this rather eye-catching visual design. (Courtesy of Bill Freedman, Ltd.)

had a long-standing homosexual relationship in Brixton—in those days a rather run-down slummy area of London. It is set in the barbers' shop and is a charming, funny and, in many ways, touching play. It opens with one of the two barbers—the two partners—giving the other a haircut, because it happens to be a Sunday and they're not open for business. It deals with the way their relationship has grown and developed, or in some ways declined.

Milo O'Shea and Eli Wallach share a tender moment in *Staircase*. (Courtesy of Bill Freedman, Ltd.)

The show opened for previews in December 1967 and the official opening was on January 10, 1968. The play was largely very well received. I like to think this was because, taking due credit for myself, it contained very truthful, wildly funny, deeply touching performances from Eli and Milo. I felt it was extremely important their performances should be realistic. We all know that male homosexuals are not necessarily flagrantly gay—in the sense in which they are so often portrayed. Unfortunately there was a film of this play made later on where the parts were played by Richard Burton and Rex Harrison, two very well known actors who should have known better. They parodied and mockingly exaggerated male homosexual characteristics. They camped themselves cross-eyed! That was very damaging to the text of the play, which is written in a highly perceptive and sensitive way. It wasn't meant to be played as if it were some sneeringly exaggerated revue sketch. Both of my actors—Eli and Milo—were very sympathetic to my idea of not pandering for cheap laughs because they happened to be playing homosexuals. That gave the right sort of depth and quality to the play. The result was that while it didn't get wild press, it was dealt with respectfully by all the critics. Some of them were very enthusiastic, and it settled in for a bit of a run. *Staircase* was the first show on the subject of male homosexuality to play in a Broadway house, and certainly one of the first pieces to deal with the subject in a serious manner. I am proud to have been a part of it.

While keeping an eye on *Staircase*, I also went up to Yale, as I had

Posing with Eli Wallach at the *Staircase* after-party in Sardi's.

made an agreement with Bob Brustein to join his faculty as an adjunct professor in the drama department. I went there to start my work on January 28,
1968. Now—what was I going to profess, I asked myself? As I pointed out
to Bob, the average actor doesn't spend all of his working life playing in
Shakespeare or Greek tragedy or classics of Chekhov or Ibsen quality. The
average actor spends most of his life playing in run-of-the-mill rubbish.
The real practiced actor knows if you're halfway serious and dedicated,
and you're playing in the works of Shakespeare, he'll see you through. The
quality of the stuff is so good it's not very easy to muck it up. But if you're
dealing with rubbish it's all too easy for *it* to muck *you* up! We decided I
would attempt to prepare the young actors at Yale with the means to deal
with rubbish. We tried to be quite frank about our subject, so it came to
be listed as Course 119—Rubbish. The course became widely known and
very popular. I simply got hold of all sorts of material which actors in the
course of an ordinary professional career would be expected to work on,
like commercials, soap operas, scenes from *Getting Gertie's Garter*, and
other material of that kind—the standard form of work actors are likely to
come across.

There was never a dull moment. It became very tempting, in a way,

"Barry Morse in *Hadrian VII*"—my name on the marquee in Australia.

when Bob Brustein had the idea of my staying on longer. Of course, I had only committed myself for one semester. Sydney said "No, you mustn't stay on there. Before you know it you'll have a long beard down to your knees, and you'll become completely engrossed in being a professor." I decided not to stay on at Yale. It had been very interesting, and whether my students learned anything or not, I certainly did! It was wonderful to have the experience of exposing students to the facts of life.

In New York, Sydney started rehearsals for the stage production of *Hadrian VII*, an immensely successful play based on the work of an eccentric Edwardian writer named Rolfe. The play had originated in London, and now it was to be presented on Broadway. One of the co-producers was our old friend Bill Freedman. Sydney was offered the not very large, but very colorful and worthwhile part of the landlady. It's an extraordinary fantasy in which a neglected and downtrodden young English writer, through a series of flukes, gets to be made Pope.

Coincidentally, an offer was made to me in February 1969 to play the title role in *Hadrian VII* in Australia. I accepted the job and on March 14 I flew to Australia where we began rehearsals. This was an entirely Australian company, aside from myself, and so I met all sorts of people I'd not known before. I found I was very well known in Australia because they'd been carrying *The Fugitive* all the time it had been on. That's one of the reasons they booked me to do it, I suppose, realizing I would attract a certain amount of attention and sell a few seats. We opened at Her Majesty's Theatre in Melbourne on the twelfth of April. I became friends with one young actor in particular, John Derum, who later became the director of the Australian National Theatre. *Hadrian* was almost reverentially received, and was a kind of play which didn't turn up all that often in Australia in those days. So I was made much of. We played several weeks in Melbourne, and moved on to Sydney where we opened on May 23. We were the last production in a lovely old theatre called the Tivoli before it was destroyed. It was very successful, and the reviews were very enthusiastic. On my fifty-first birthday the company threw me a huge surprise party, and gave me a great floral display. The message on it was "A Happy Birthday to our shepherd—From your sheep." I was on very chummy terms with all the company there.

This was when I first came to spend time with an organization, which still exists, called The Glugs. I more or less christened The Glugs, which

was a small informal club of journalists and other people concerned with the theatre, who would meet once a month to have lunch. At that point they were just known as a "playgoers club." They eventually gave me as a keepsake souvenir, on the last occasion I got together with them before I left Australia, a copy of a minor comic classic of Australian literature called *The Glugs of Gosh*, which I still have. This is a book about an imaginary tribe of people called the Glugs, who live in an imaginary country called Gosh. It was written by C.J. Dennis, and was first published in Australia during the First World War. I said to them "I do hope you'll all keep getting together like this. You know— you really ought to give your-

As Hadrian VII—here I am smoking away! I'm wearing glasses with no glass, and a toupee. (Courtesy of Bill Freedman, Ltd.)

selves a name." I was holding this book in my hand, and I said, "You should call yourself the Glugs." And such it is. They wrote to me asking me to send them a recorded message tape for their thirtieth anniversary gathering! And I did. So I'm still in touch with these nice people. They're always urging me to make another visit to Australia, but who knows when I shall be able to. Inside the book they wrote, "To Barry Morse, a saintly bloke—from a bunch of Sydney sinners. With happy thoughts of some memorable confessionals." and they all signed underneath—July 1969. That was one of many happy times I had in Australia.

The suggestion had been made that I take over the leading role of *Hadrian VII* on Broadway when I returned from Australia, which was what happened in the end. Sydney had then been playing the show in New York for some seven months, and I hadn't seen her in about five months, which I think is the longest we had ever been separated. When I arrived in New York I went into rehearsal for joining their production, replacing the very good actor who had created the leading part, Alec McCowen. The production had become in my view, somewhat frozen. That's one of the big snags about long runs. It's terribly difficult to maintain the freshness and enthusiasm and sheer vitality the play probably had in its first night performance. Of course, I had just had the chance to try out the play in Australia to a variety of audiences, and I had some ideas about how the structure and physical handling of the production of the play might be improved. We did manage, eventually, to make some changes which were not popular in all corners of the New York company, because people get settled into a long run and don't want to be bothered with re-rehearsing. Anyway, it was all done more or less amicably, and I settled in to playing in the Broadway production, still at the Helen Hayes Theatre, with Sydney and all the rest of them. My dear Sydney played nearly a whole year in that play, which is something I've never done. I think the period of about six months that I ended up starring in *Hadrian VII* is the longest I've ever played in a run of a stage play. It is very difficult because you get so bored. It takes a lot of cheering yourself up, especially if it's an emotionally intense thing like *Hadrian* was, to get the same kind of intensity eight times a week for months and months on end.

On Saturdays we used to get quite a few Catholic school parties coming to see our matinees, because *Hadrian VII* was a thoroughly Catholic subject. One matinee day Sydney and I were just making our way to the theatre, which involved crossing over Times Square, and we saw a crocodile (as it used to be called), a little line of schoolgirls being led along by a pair of nuns. They were just coming along Times Square, and when they were up to the opposite side of the street from us, I saw a young fellow dash up alongside one of the nuns and snatch her purse. She was carrying a quite large under-the-arm purse, and he took off down the side street with it. Well, in those days I was thoroughly fit and more than a little athletic— so I took off after him! This attracted a certain amount of crowd attention, being 1:30 or so on a Saturday afternoon, and there were workmen on nearby scaffolding who were shouting (because I was fairly recognizable from *The Fugitive*), "Go get him, Lieutenant!" and, "Atta-boy, Gerard!" I was running and running—and gaining on this young man! I began to think, "What am I going to do if I catch up to him? What if he has a gun or a knife? I'm likely to get killed!" I became a little unsure if I should continue the pursuit when—mercifully—he realized I was gaining on him, and there was a great deal of public attention, and the chances of his being caught were rising by the second. So he threw away the purse and ducked off down an alley! I was able to retrieve the purse, and run back and restore it to the good sister, who was suitably grateful, and all the schoolgirls were jumping up and down with excitement, and I said, "Well, there you are now. Where are you bound?" She said, "We're coming to see *you*!" They were actually coming to see the matinee!

At the same time I was doing *Hadrian VII* I had the opportunity to play in a movie called *Puzzle of a Downfall Child*. It was directed by Jerry Schatzberg, and starred a very popular and beautiful leading actress called Faye Dunaway. I played an older sometime lover of hers. I had several scenes with her, including one in which she'd had rather too much to drink—the character, that is, not Faye Dunaway. She was called on to make rather elaborate overtures to me. It was quite an unusual scene—certainly for me!

On November 15 we closed *Hadrian VII* after what many people felt was an amazingly long run, especially for a play many wouldn't have thought to be very commercially promising. It was altogether a very enjoyable time, especially because Sydney was with me in it, and also because other dear old friends were in the company, including Gillie Fenwick and Bill Needles.

We then embarked on a short tour of *Hadrian VII,* which included both Sydney and myself, and played in Florida. We put together a not so elaborate production which went for a number of weeks to Palm Beach, Fort Lauderdale and Miami. The cast included some different actors than had been with us on the Broadway run. We opened at the Royal Poinciana Playhouse in Palm Beach. *Hadrian VII* is a rather serious play—not immensely tragic, but you might call it a rather intellectual play. I had played once before at this same theatre a few years before in the regrettable production *The Man with the Perfect Wife.* I'd learned then that the audience was about the most vapid you could possibly find, almost entirely made up of overly rich people who hang about such places as Palm Beach, and feel it a social duty to "look in on the theatre," as long as it's not too serious or taxing. Well, as you can imagine, *Hadrian VII* was a bit of an intellectual struggle for this kind of audience!

I recall the theatre manager coming around to me after opening night, very impressed with the quality of the production and the performance, and even more impressed, he said, that "most of the audience stayed right till the end!" I said, "Well, for Heaven's sake—Why wouldn't they?" He replied, "Oh, no. Very often people—once the intermission comes, and they've had a couple of glasses of this or that, and admired each others dresses—they'll go off and not stay for the second half." We went on to play the Parker Playhouse in Fort Lauderdale, another spot considerably favored although not quite so pretentious as Palm Beach. We took it down to the Coconut Grove Playhouse in Miami, and then closed on March 15. We had a good time with it, even though we weren't out all that long, and the play did very well despite its being a bit beyond the intellectual reach of some Florida theatregoers!

18

"Casa Calmada"

I FELT IT WAS TIME THAT perhaps I should start spending some time doing something different. The idea had been lurking in the back of my mind for quite some time. My thinking was I might try and pack up this hurly-burly life and settle down to write, which I had long wanted to do. Through such things as the *Touch of Greasepaint* series, I had a bit of a stab at writing on a sketchy, casual basis. I always thought I'd like to try to settle down and *really* write. All kinds of topics were going around in my head. In those days the cost of living in Spain was considerably lower than it was either in the UK or Canada and the States. We were also encouraged by staying with Sydney's younger brother, Dick, and his wife, Mary, who have lived for many years in the southeast corner of Spain, near a town called Jávea. They had gone there on their honeymoon sometime around 1946, and took with them camping gear. They came upon a marvelous stretch of silvery sand beach, which they decided would be a lovely place to spend a couple of days. They pitched their tent on this beautiful beach, and that area later became one of the major tourist centers of Spain, known as Benidorm, populated all year round by thousands of people. As a result of that first experience on their honeymoon, they always had a soft spot for that part of Spain. A few years later Dick decided to take early retirement and go back to Spain to see if he couldn't "grow a good orange," as he used to put it. They went to Jávea, and found a charming house in a little hamlet called Portichol. In the course of time they did succeed in having an orange grove in which they did grow good oranges.

We, having been to visit them a number of times, had come to enjoy the Spanish way of life. Sydney already spoke Spanish reasonably well because she'd spent some time when she was about 17 or 18 living in Chile in South America. In April of 1970 we set off in a rented car around the coast, with the idea of spying out what parts we liked. We stayed in some of the Paradors, which are a chain of historical and architecturally very beautiful buildings run by the government as hotels. In some cases they were monasteries or grand houses built by ancient families of Spain. While we were on that holiday, Dick and Mary learned there was some land only about half a mile from their house towards the lighthouse called Cabo de la Nao which was likely to be for sale and had lain more or less neglected for many, many years. This land ran all the way down to the sea, and was very beautiful. We had in fact driven by it and commented on it, not knowing it was to become available soon.

While we were away from Spain after this holiday, Dick and Mary continued to research this place for us. Dick and Mary sent us a telegram including the details we wanted, as well as the dimensions of a piece of land *below* the plot we were interested in, which a farmer was using to grow vines. It was apparent it would be advantageous for us to buy both plots of land, running straight down to the sea at this beautiful little bay. On the main piece of land was a building: A ruin, really. It was just a tiny casita, made of stone, which was about 200 years old, and totally neglected. Finally, we were able to negotiate through the extraordinary tangle of the Spanish legal system to purchase both these pieces of land.

We got in touch with the local master builder, a wonderful character called Bartolomé Agrasot. He had been building and rebuilding all sorts of structures in the area for many years. He consulted with us regarding where and how we might start to build our house. Bartolomé, who would have been in his 70s at that time, was a marvelously wise and imaginative master builder. I went to look at the land, and considered where the sun fell in relation to the land, what its geographic location was, which views would be advantageous, and so on. But when Bartolomé came to see the land with me he pointed out that this ruin of a tumble-down casita, the existing cottage, was situated on just about the best point of the property. He said we should consider working with the existing structure. We opened the casita up and had a look, and lo and behold, it was very substantially built. Bartolomé felt there were parts of it which could be used, and he had access to quite a stock of old building stone which he could incorporate into a new house, but in the old style. So I started making numbers of drawings of the sort of house we might build. The building of our new house took several months.

While work continued on our new home in Spain, I was asked to work on several varied productions. The first project, *The Wit and World of G. B. Shaw,* was close to my heart. It was a joint CBC/BBC film directed by Harry Rasky, and was a quite remarkable attempt to line up against some of the actual locations what Shaw had written about the horrors of the First World War. We went over to France, to the town of Arras—which was the closest town at various times to the front lines, and is surrounded by thousands and thousands of graves, and went round looking at graveyards and trenches. It was very moving to be there. As part of this Shavian perspective of the First World War, I was able to stand in one of the trenches which had been ours—the Allies—and throw a rock without too much exertion across what had been no-man's-land, towards the German trenches no more than 35 or 40 yards away. It was horrifying to realize these poor lads would be stuck in these trenches mowing each other down for weeks and months on end. We shot a sequence in which I played the Devil from Shaw's *Don Juan in Hell* from *Man and Superman*. We started on a high crane shot, shooting across acres and acres of these white crosses in the war battlefield graveyards. It looked from the opening of this shot as if the whole surface of the earth was covered with nothing but these crosses. As we zoomed in to a particular group of crosses, I popped up from behind one of them in the character of the Devil and said, "Have you walked up and down upon the Earth lately? I have; and I have examined Man's wonderful inventions..." and I went on to speak that wonderful speech from *Don Juan in Hell* about mankind's destructiveness. It's a flesh creeping speech, and worked so well in the context of this film and Shaw's views on war. We saw while there groups of schoolchildren being taken around the different sites of remembrance. One day, while sitting at a cafe we saw two different groups of children—one of which came from England, the other from Germany—who were almost certainly the grandchildren of some of those lads who were buried in those fields.

Soon after, I appeared in a very interesting film called *Asylum*, which is still quite frequently shown. It is what used to be called a portmanteau film, made up of three or four different stories. It was written by Robert Bloch, who wrote the original novel of Hitchcock's famous film *Psycho*. I played an old Polish tailor. Briefly, the plot was about a chap, just appointed director of a lunatic asylum, who examines the various patients confined there and the circumstances leading to their becoming insane. The cast was a very starry one, including Richard Todd and my old friend Peter Cushing, who played with me as a mysterious customer who went to have a suit made by my character, and the ensuing macabre events. It was a very good film.

Next up was *The Adventurer,* a series produced by Lew Grade (later Lord Grade). He was a great pioneer in all sorts of things. *The Adventurer* was about an international adventurer, but I'm afraid it wasn't very firmly

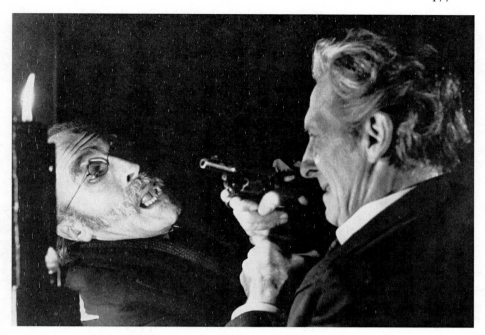

A scene from *Asylum*, with my old friend Peter Cushing.

conceived or very well written. The title character was a fellow apparently of independent means, and therefore with the freedom to wander here, there and everywhere. He dedicates himself to bringing rascals to justice in an unofficial, surreptitious way, and on an international scale. The idea was it would be set in all sorts of elegant places.

The central character was played by Gene Barry. He had originally been a dancer, but then had gone on to win popularity in an American television series called *Burke's Law*. He was the eponymous hero of that series. His friend and ally in *The Adventurer* was a character, mysteriously and perhaps deliberately not given any first name, known simply as Mr. Parminter. The name Parminter suggested a rather fluffy, woolly kind of fellow, so with the aid of a droopy mustache I made him terribly, terribly British—what they would call in England a chinless twit. I would say to Gene (the central character's name was the same as Gene Barry's) in the most preposterously posh English accent, "I say, Gene, do you really seriously think that he's a, you might say, a *spy*? Oh! Oh, *really*? Oh, *dear*!" Parminter was supposed to be attached to the British Foreign Office in some way. It was great fun to have a comic sidekick character to put alongside the upright and eternally righteous Gene figure.

Gene Barry, I'm afraid, was rather tiresome, because—and I must be frank—he seemed to those of us who worked with him, and certainly seemed to me, to be enormously obsessed with his own importance, omnipotence and infallibility. In my view he was not greatly gifted as an actor. I will say he did have a lot to pick at in the way of the quality of the scripts. Many directors found him, shall we say, somewhat difficult to handle. I came to realize that if one treated him in a flattering way, one could get along with him really quite well. We gradually got ourselves into the situation where I was directing quite a lot of the episodes of *The Adventurer*. We started off shooting in Nice, in the south of France, and then went to Paris. We also went to Holland. It was aimed to present all sorts of elegant, exotic, glamorous settings in which Gene could carry on his activities, and his chum Mr. Parminter would turn up and express suitable astonishment and admiration from time to time. I didn't appear in every episode, and not all that much in some, but I did direct quite a lot of them. We shot our studio stuff in Elstree, north of London, and also we filmed in various areas of London itself.

The thing about Gene Barry was, I found if I treated him like one of my infant grandchildren, alternately flattering and cosseting him, I could keep him reasonably good humored and happy. First thing in the morning if I were director, I would say, "Oh Gene, don't you look marvelous! What a lovely suit that is! My word! Beautiful fabric, isn't it? You feeling all right? You look marvelous, I must say! How do you keep your hair so..." and all that stuff. Then I'd say, "Well Gene, I'll tell you what we'd like you to do— Just come in through that door there, and ... well—No, actually—I think I'd get the knob in the other hand, don't you? It'll be easier..." and I'd direct him like that. We got along not too badly.

Following this period of work, Sydney and I returned to Spain to our house, which came to be called Casa Calmada, meaning in rough translation The Tranquil House, because it was meant to be a peaceful and quiet home base. Calmada actually means "becalmed" or "calm after storm." I think it was Sydney who suggested this—her Spanish was always better than mine. She thought it was a suitable name for our house, which we viewed as the home where we expected to live tranquilly, likely for the rest of our lives. Needless to say it didn't work out that way. We actually stayed this time for the best part of a month enjoying Casa Calmada.

I was soon drawn into another series project called *The Zoo Gang*. It was only a miniseries of six one-hour episodes, because most of us who were in it were already committed to other projects and could only provide a limited commitment. It was based on a story by Paul Gallico, the American author who became famous for his lovely book *The Snow Goose*.

The idea was for a series featuring four principal characters who had come from different countries and worked together in France in the Resistance during the war in the 1940s when the Germans were occupying much of France, and who—many years later—come together again to be a general philanthropic group/commando unit helping those who get themselves into difficulties and also suppressing the villains of the world. They decide to call themselves by the code names they adopted during the war, which were different animals. The three other actors involved were all very well known. John Mills—the great English character actor—his character was British and was called the Elephant. Lilli Palmer, the European actress who settled in England and was at one time married to Rex Harrison, played the Leopard. Brian Keith, the American actor who had done a great many outstanding things in film and television, played the Fox. And I played a Canadian, called the Tiger, whose actual name was Alec Marlowe. He had been a wartime lieutenant in the RCAF, and by the time of the series was running an auto repair shop in Vancouver. He was meant to be a mechanical genius who could do just about anything with cars, planes, boats and mechanical devices.

The show was set in various parts of Europe, though most of the shooting was done in the south of France. We all stayed at the Hotel Negresco in Nice, which was very pleasant. We shot up and down the Côte d'Azur, although because the weather was sometimes rather surprisingly chilly I used to call it the *Over*Côte d'Azur. I wore some of my own clothes in this series because I've always liked the idea of characters in films looking as if they actually *owned* their clothes rather than looking as if they'd just been wheeled out of a wardrobe department, carefully pressed. I was playing a rather informal fellow, so this approach to costuming suited my character. We worked hard and pretty well every day, filming all our location work in anticipation of shooting the interior studio material when we got back to England, at Pinewood Studios. *The Zoo Gang* featured very good scripts by and large, and we all enjoyed working on it. We wrapped up filming in June of 1973.

I stayed on in London, doing some work for the BBC down at Ealing Studios, and after that went to Jerusalem. Harry Rasky was making a television documentary called *Next Year in Jerusalem*, to be shot in Israel, about the extraordinary range of religious activities which have occupied that part of the world. I was to play the Emperor Saladin, who was the sultan of the Muslim empire and a great hero in Muslim history. He became leader of the Islamic forces and fought many battles, including the one which led to the capture of Jerusalem in 1187.

My scenes were shot mostly in the open countryside, and in order to

Me in front of the Hotel Negresco during the filming of *The Zoo Gang*.

play Saladin I wore suitably historic and impressive Islamic clothes. The conditions of shooting were a bit primitive because we had only a small film unit; it was a rather modest CBC production. To help with the question of wardrobe, I said I would change in the hotel before we set forth. Well, we stayed in a hotel in Jerusalem called the Holy Land Hotel. I discovered on the first day that the appearance of a chap looking like a twelfth century Muslim emperor in the Holy Land Hotel in Jerusalem in 1973 was calculated to cause a certain amount of alarm. It was continued when my driver arrived to take me out into the countryside, and he said, "I think it might be a good idea if you lie down on the floor in the back of the car until we get outside of the city. Who knows what excitement your appearance might create in passersby who see a Muslim emperor sitting in the back of the car." So I agreed to do that, and proceeded to continue doing that every morning!

Along some of the far-flung roads we traveled on our way to the filming location, I was able to see the remnants of one of the latest wars which have inflicted Israel, and there were armored cars and half destroyed tanks along the roadside. One time, one of our crew, a local chap working with us, spotted (coming over the horizon in the distance) a bunch of mounted Arabs and said, "Oh dear, this doesn't look good." We said, "What's the matter? We can avoid them—we won't be shooting so as to see them." But he said, "No, it's not that. We've had instances recently where people have been hijacked by roving bands who have robbed them of everything they could carry. I think we'd be best advised to put all our camera equipment and microphones and the rest of it back into one of the vans until these guys have gone by. I'll talk to them and tell them it's all right, and they needn't bother us." And he did, and they didn't.

Having survived that, I returned to London and began to hear about a new series called *Space: 1999*.

19

"Drama Is About Chaps"

MY TWO PREVIOUS SERIES, *The Adventurer* and *The Zoo Gang*, had been done under a contract I had with Lew Grade. There was an option in that contract which gave me the choice of doing other things with his organization, and gave him the choice of asking me. And he did. He asked me if I wanted to play Professor Victor Bergman in this new science fiction series *Space: 1999*. I didn't know Gerry or Sylvia Anderson, who were the producers, and I really didn't know very much about them, beyond the fact they had been responsible for a very popular puppet series called *Thunderbirds*.

Martin Landau and Barbara Bain were signed to play the leads. I knew of them, and of their work, in *Mission: Impossible* mostly, and they knew of my work through *The Fugitive* and various other things I'd done in the States. I didn't know at the time, but there was in fact only one completed script for *Space: 1999*, which had to do with Moonbase Alpha being launched into space. The original episode was called "Breakaway," and it contained almost no explanation of the characters. They were just a collection of names. But, because I like doing this sort of thing, I started to expand on what I thought might have been Victor Bergman's background and how he came to be the sort of fellow he is. I don't still have a copy of the biography I wrote—I gave it to Gerry and Sylvia to pass on to their writers as perhaps being some kind of help towards what they might produce in later scripts. I put a good deal of time and thought into it. It never was made use of.

I didn't want Bergman to be a typical anonymous American which was indicated in the initial script. I didn't think he was entirely British, either. I visualized he acquired a kind of orthodox English accent, more or less like my own, by virtue of having spent many of his more mature years as a Professor at one of the older Universities of the UK like Oxford or Cambridge. I thought Victor, who was going to be the senior "Space Uncle" figure, would be a chap with differing backgrounds and of mixed race, ultimately a great deal more eccentric an individual than he eventually became. In the biography I wrote I visualized his having been brought as

With Barbara Bain and Martin Landau in *Space: 1999.*

a child refugee out of Austria before the war because one of his parents was partly Jewish (which I took from his name), and he then studied in various parts of the world, principally, and more recently, in England. I worked out all the chronological details to bring him up to the age he was presumed to be at the time of the shooting of the series.

I tried to invent a character for Victor Bergman based vaguely on Einstein, thinking he would be of that general mentality, a chap who is so much concerned with abstruse scientific matters that he has very little knowledge of or interest in the day to day happenings of the world. I looked on him as being an absent-minded and other-worldly chap who might tend to put on odd socks, wear a cardigan with the elbows out, or go about in tennis shoes without any laces in them, and be generally untidy and careless about his dress and appearance, that he might have a straggly and rather unkempt beard and not pay any attention to having his hair cut, and be, in other words, kind of an absent-minded professor. I didn't succeed, of course.

I had the idea Victor was particularly interested in music, specifically the music of Johann Sebastian Bach because it is the kind of music which would appeal to a guy of scientific mind as it is so marvelously organized. Once in a while when I got the chance I would whistle little bits of one of the Brandenburg Concertos as a little thing to help him along when he was working something out. I hoped I was going to be able to make more use of that but I wasn't able to very often.

I suggested I not wear the same silly uniform we all eventually did wear—but, oh, no, that idea didn't go at all well! Gerry and Sylvia were terribly keen on those dreadful uniforms. At least I felt they were dreadful, and unimaginative. They were designed by Rudi Gernreich, then a top-of-the-pops ladies' fashion designer, of all ridiculous choices. What does a ladies' fashion designer know about what's going to be worn by people going into space 25 years ahead? I suppose they felt it added to the prestige of the thing.

So, immense attention was being paid to these uniforms, and they were—of course—uniform. I can remember an early production meeting, the first time we all sat down with Gerry and Sylvia, and they started to talk about the fact Rudi Gernreich was going to do the costumes. The most important thing was these uniforms. Martin and I looked at each other, and I said in desperation, "Listen, will you give us some idea please—who we are?" They looked quite baffled, and then told us who was going to make the boots! From that moment on I realized we were going up the down staircase.

I felt very strongly, and I think both Martin and Barbara felt—perhaps not quite so strongly—more could be done in the way of individualizing the characters we were. I remember repeatedly saying, at that time rather patiently and I hope good-naturedly to Gerry and Sylvia, and with Martin and Barbara's support, "Couldn't we have a meeting among ourselves—Barbara and Martin, and perhaps a few other principals in the cast, to discuss who we are and how we came to be here?" That's a basic elementary function, I think, of presenting any kind of drama. You don't need to be a genius to realize this—great drama is, always has been and always will be, made out of conflicts and relations between human beings. We never succeeded, that I can recall, in having that discussion.

I mischievously invented a little couplet around this time, because I was being called upon in some script to deliver a long boring speech in front of a map explaining where we were or where we were going to go, or something. The couplet read:

> "Dear Gerry & Sylvia—
> Please remember,
> Geography is about Maps.
> Drama is about Chaps."

That pretty well expressed my feelings about the way the show's style was being developed. I thought it ought to have been embroidered and set above Gerry and Sylvia Anderson's beds! I'm sorry if this is hurtful to Gerry and Sylvia Anderson—I'm sure they are thoroughly worthwhile human beings, are kind to animals, and write regularly to their relatives—but they are not the best producers I've ever come across!

I didn't have any direct input or contact with the writers because by the time *we* started to shoot, they were all toiling away trying to produce scripts coming up. In many instances in my diary I recall meetings between myself, Martin and Barbara, and sometimes whoever the current director was—like Charles Crichton in some instances, to try and get a bit more shape into the scripts we had.

Going into *Space: 1999* I knew very little about science fiction television, which was just as well I suppose. Part of the interesting opportunity *Space: 1999* presented was to feature humans unprepared for their journey and encountering the great unknown. But, of course, how people respond when they are confronted with the unknown depends a great deal on the sort of people they are. I didn't have any very clear idea what kind of creature Victor Bergman, or any of the rest of us, was meant to be.

I suppose there was, up to a point, a conscious effort to design a minimalist look for *Space: 1999*. Keith Wilson, the production designer, did an admirable job constructing a very elaborate and I'm sure very costly set which was an imaginative representation of the way space exploration *might* have developed. Of course, the speed of development hasn't kept up with the predictions of our series. Something we all realize and no doubt was in everybody's minds at that time is that the twentieth century was the most swiftly developing of any century in the whole history of mankind. The pace at which scientific and other kinds of discovery accelerated would have been unthinkable in former centuries. Unfortunately not all of this discovery has been beneficent. All too much of it is directed towards destruction. Your friend and mine, Bernard Shaw, makes the Devil point out in *Man and Superman*—which was written in 1903, remember—that mankind is impelled towards invention, all too often with destructive purposes in mind. The Devil in a notable speech says that mankind, having developed all sorts of other means of destroying people and things, is now within reach of destroying himself. I think those are the sort of thoughts that would go through Victor Bergman's mind. It was, I think, one of the shortcomings of the series, that there was all too much concentration on physical action, and not enough on psychological speculation. But then, I wasn't doing the writing and I wasn't the producer.

I recall *all* of my fellows with great pleasure and happiness: A good team, a good group, and therefore an implied compliment to Gerry and Sylvia, who brought us all together.

Martin and Barbara, first and foremost, of course—my two co-agitators, are both immensely skilled and experienced in our profession. They are *first class pros*! That is a term of great approbation which has rather gone out of usage in more recent times. It simply means people who through sheer hard work have trained themselves to a degree of facility and technical competence to be able to make the best of any material which as performers they are confronted with. I'm sure they would be the first to agree that with *Space: 1999* they had been confronted by something which was not the easiest material they had ever had to deal with. Nonetheless, they addressed themselves to it with admirable skill and with the considerable experience they had gained from working in previous television shows, notably *Mission: Impossible*. They came over to live in London, which must have been quite a challenge for them. They rented a charming house up in an area of London called Little Venice. They must have stayed in London for about 3 years altogether. They were married at that time, and in my observation, both in the workplace and outside of it, were marvelously happy together. They certainly were a joy to work with. No hint of any kind of grandeur, such as sometimes comes with such people. Much better fellows, in the real, true, theatrical sense, than many others I can think of. They have both continued on their different paths to work successfully and happily. Martin has been very busy, mostly in films, including *Ed Wood*, for which he won an Academy Award, having already been nominated twice previously. Barbara is a three-time Emmy Award winning actress, continuing to work in television and film, and is very highly acclaimed for her challenging work on the stage, including Samuel Beckett's *Happy Days*, and Eugene Ionesco's *The Chairs*, among others. They were both a great comfort to everybody else in the unit, not only to the other actors, but the crew as well. The crew was confronting a whole new genre, you might say, but they again had to deal with the sketchy material of our scripts. Martin and Barbara's adaptability, professionalism, and, above all, their kindly and good-natured attitude towards their fellow artists and the members of our crew were quite admirable. They were inventive and patient and tolerant, and all the things a good pro is expected to be.

Then there was Nick Tate, an Australian chap, who continues to work in film, television, and the theatre. He is also now known as "The Voice" due to his great success as a voice-over artist. And dear little Zienia Merton, who's one of the few people in the *Space: 1999* outfit whom I've kept in touch with to the extent of chatting on the phone and occasionally seeing. Sydney and I used to meet up with her quite often because she lived not too far from us here in London. She starred in a short film entitled *Message from Moonbase Alpha*, which was written by Johnny Byrne and premiered at the *Space: 1999* convention in Los Angeles in September 1999. She's a dear, lovely girl. All of them—Nick, Zienia, Prentis, Clifton and Anton—were relatively inexperienced and were being thrown into the deep end with Martin, Barbara and myself. We were all insufficiently prepared, as I shall go on saying till my dying day. They had to hammer their way through it and stay afloat as best they could. And they—to do them all equal credit—dealt with it all with admirable patience and good nature, and good humor. My recollections of those young people at that time was that they were immensely hopeful, naturally. They wanted *Space: 1999* to be a huge success and to be as popular as they hoped it would deserve to be. But conditions weren't always of the easiest for them. I remember them all fondly. They were very gifted and keen, but I only wish their efforts had been used on material that was a bit more worthwhile.

We had a great many excellent guest stars. All sorts of good actors came and went. They were (almost without exception) wonderfully cooperative. There was Joan Collins; she is a very pleasant and very beautiful lady, and was our guest star in the episode called "Mission of the Darians." She went on to become very famous in the soap opera *Dynasty*. And dear old Brian Blessed—bless his heart—joined us for our "Death's Other Dominion" episode. I'd worked with him before on some other television show. Brian is a great giggler (which is one of his wonderful personal characteristics) and loves a good laugh, and we always got along very well. He's been successful and kept busy over the years.

Christopher Lee was a chum of ours. I'd worked with him before. He appeared in our "Earthbound" episode, and more recently appeared in the popular *Lord of the Rings* movies. He's been in something like 200 films over the years. Another guest star was Catherine Schell, and she had played a regular role in that other series I had done for Lew Grade called *The Adventurer*. So I did know her, and had worked with her before.

Peter Cushing came and starred in our "Missing Link" episode, and was one of our oldest friends, no longer with us, alas. It was a joy to see him turn up on our show. He had been one of the Court Players company, which was a group of different companies of repertory theatres in England before the war. And he actually knew my Sydney before I did. They had been in this company at Nottingham in 1938, before I met Sydney on January 3, 1939. So we knew him right from the word go. Helen, his wife, we came to know later. They had met as actor and actress in a theatrical company, and had been married not quite as long as we had, but almost. They lived for a while in London, in Kensington, not far from us. We would have meals or coffees or visits with each other very frequently. On one of these occasions there was an outbreak of a rather virulent strain of influenza. Sydney and I were having dinner with Peter and Helen in their flat and I was feeling a bit feverish. I didn't know, of course, that I was suffering the onset of this flu. During the course of the meal, I didn't feel much like eating but I was enjoying myself and I hung on as long as I could. I began to feel more and more ill and before the end of the evening, just when I was beginning to think it was about time I should start to make my way home, I passed out, completely passed out. Later, I became delirious and the next thing I knew was that very late the next day, nearly twenty-four hours later, I was still in Peter and Helen's flat tucked up in a bed that they made up for me on the sofa of their living room. I always remember that, and their kindness, very vividly.

I can't remember very much about the episodes of *Space: 1999*, what the nature of the stories were, or the plots. It's all blurred into a mercifully hazy mass.

I do remember our third episode, "The Black Sun," directed by Lee H. Katzin, who had been the director of "Breakaway." It asked the question "What's it all about?" Martin and I felt it might be worthwhile to experiment with a certain amount of improvisation, because there was that famous scene between the two of us in which we drank brandy, and talked about what we thought was our impending demise, expressing what we felt about the purpose of life. We improvised a great part of that scene, with only a certain amount of guidance from the script. It had human values and no explosions, just two human beings. It's very gratifying to Martin and me that on any list of the audience's preferences among the different episodes, "The Black Sun" will almost always come out very near, if not on, the top. I like to think it was because of the input we, the actors, had on the script. It was one of the episodes where we did get to grips with some philosophical speculation, and I only wish we had done it more. It drew into question what we believe and how and why we believe it. That seems to have caught the imaginations of our viewers in all the years since, perhaps rather more than any of the other episodes. If only the general production and the writing had had more of that sort of character about it. It certainly remains in my remembrance as one of the very best episodes, where Martin, Barbara and I were able to inject rather more in the way of human interest in the show.

In mid–1974 I went to Saint George's Hospital to have a barium X-ray, and I later went back and had another one. Evidently the X-rays disclosed I had a polyp on my colon. So in the middle of all this shooting I went into hospital on July 17, had the operation on the eighteenth, and left on the nineteenth to resume shooting *Space: 1999*. Only a couple of months later I went into Saint George's Hospital again, for another operation for a polyp on the colon. I don't know if they didn't succeed in getting it the first time, or if there was another one disclosed. I was picked up from the hospital the following morning—Wednesday, September 11, at nine o'clock, and we started a new episode called "Death's Other Dominion," directed by Charles

Crichton (who directed quite a number of our episodes.) I wrote in my diary with a huge exclamation mark— "Blizzard Sequence!" Straight from hospital first thing in the morning I was obliged to spend the day struggling through this studio blizzard. I evidently managed to get through it all right. It was very comical, that snow storm, and gave rise to a great deal of giggles, especially from Brian Blessed. Dear Brian and I had some testing moments playing together because you'd only have to give the slightest twinkle of your eye and Brian would be off giggling. We had a wonderful time. I also remember John Shrapnel playing his char-

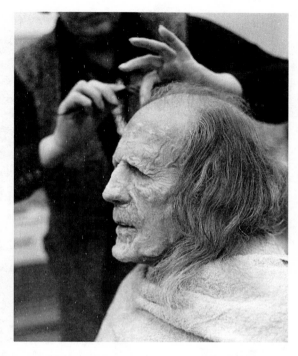

Aging makeup being applied for "The Black Sun."

acter quite like The Fool from *King Lear*. The entire episode had a rather Shakespearean tone to it.

We were all getting a bit stir crazy. I certainly was. It's not very often you spend the greater part of a year shooting a movie or television series without some locations out of doors. Our working day began at 6:30 or 7:00 in the morning, more often than not in darkness. Then when you came out again, after the days shooting, it would be darkness again. It got to be a bit like working down in the mines! We hardly ever saw the light of day. The difficulty about shooting outdoors was the shortage of places which could serve as locations for some other planet. Episode 15, "The Full Circle," was shot out in Black Park, which backs onto Pinewood Studios. So this was looked forward to with great glee among a lot of us, for the opportunity of shooting outside. But, unfortunately, at the time we had a succession of the most appallingly bad weather days England had seen for many months, so the only chance we got to be out of doors was in swamping rain and perishing cold. Some of our colleagues were a bit upset about the prospect of working in this weather. The general feeling was—here we were

Trapped in a glass cage in "Death's Other Dominion."

hoping and praying to get an episode we could film outside, and when we finally get one it's drenching down with rain all the time! I can't say the episode was particularly impressive or successful, or even one of the happiest times we spent filming, but I for one certainly did enjoy the change. It was very funny to me, because I always get a certain amount of amusement from how members of the human race respond in given situations, in or out of favorable conditions. There are considerable differences between shooting in a studio and shooting on location. One obvious thing is when shooting out of doors you don't have the same kind of control over sound as you do in the studio, especially if you are down in Buckinghamshire, where Pinewood is located, because you're not all that far from Heathrow Airport, we had aircraft coming and going and interfering with our soundtrack fairly often.

The "War Games" episode concerned the fears which lead us to destroy each other in wars, and how we can conquer our fears. It's like George Bernard Shaw said: mankind's worst destructiveness comes either through anger or from fear, and in many cases the anger and the fear are without foundation. The human race does get itself into terrible states of anger and fear, and thereby into terrible programs of destruction.

Another episode, "Space Brain," concerned some alien force which flooded the whole of Moonbase Alpha with soap bubbles. It had to be shot with all these bubbles and foam, which had to be pumped into the set. We did the first take and this foam gradually spread onto the set and filled it up. The director cut and said, "All right, now, take two," and everybody looked very blank because no one had thought how to get all these soap suds out of the set! It took hours and hours, the result being that by the time we came to take two, we realized we could not stop for anything. Whatever happened, we had to keep going. Take two began and they started pumping in all the soap suds. Unfortunately, when the young boy who did the clapper board came in front of the camera and said, "Three-eighty-nine. Take two," and did his clapper, he slipped on this foam and fell to the floor! Well, being the good technician he was, he stayed put because he knew if he got up, he would spoil the take. So we went on playing the scene while he was being smothered by the soap suds and foam, scarcely able to breathe. Thankfully he did survive, and we all had a good laugh about it afterwards.

Another episode was called "The Infernal Machine," and our guest was Leo McKern. I admired and liked him so much. Leo was a wonderful actor, one of the greatest actors of our time, and he was always remarkable in everything he did. He won raves on both sides of the Atlantic for his series *Rumpole of the Bailey*. He played so beautifully a character called Companion in this episode, as well as the Infernal Machine itself. I'm proud to say I was partly responsible for suggesting that he should play both the guest roles in this episode. It occurred to me that with this script, if you had an actor of the huge range and versatility which Leo had, you would be doing the script a great favor if you had him playing both the parts.

It's interesting to note almost all of the episodes mentioned here (for me the most memorable) are those which are concerned with ideas, philosophies, and human reflections, and not with explosions and models and special effects. Following completion of the last episode, we returned to shoot extra scenes for some previous episodes, "The Last Enemy" and "Space Brain" among them, and finally we finished shooting the first series on February 28, 1975.

The directors varied in their different ways and were all very good and workmanlike. But at the end of the day, however gifted a director is, he can't very often (I won't say never) do better than the material he is confronted with. I can remember, harking back to my days as a professor at Yale, I used to say in my opening speech to my students, "What we are going to try and do here is create the Taj Mahal out of chicken droppings!" Now I won't go so far as to say that our directors on *Space: 1999* were attempting to make the Taj Mahal out of chicken droppings, but I have to say that the script material was—with great respect to the writers—not of peerless worth.

We never had the kind of contact with the writers which we would have liked. Johnny Byrne and Christopher Penfold did a lot of scripts for *Space: 1999*, and they were under immense pressures of time to keep up with our schedule. There were many instances where trying to polish and improve scripts went on up to and including the time we were shooting. Given Johnny Byrne and Christopher Penfold's undoubted talents I think they would be the first to say they could have done better, more cohesive, detailed and delicate writing if they'd had more time to do it in.

All science fiction—or the best of science fiction—ultimately must have to do with exploring beyond the existing limits of the mind. Beyond the realms of thought. Beyond the realms of current conceptions. That's what science fiction means to me. I think of science fiction as being anything which can't be rationally and logically explained in the way of human behavior or physical activity. It defies the laws of gravity or time. It encourages people to view things from a totally different and, sometimes, completely obverse perspective—for example—to visualize a world in which the law of gravity is reversed so that when I drop a piece of paper it goes upward instead of downward. That sort of thing is very valuable for reexamining things we often take for granted. So many simple prejudices are built up. So much human division is built up. We accept points of view we inherited somewhere or other without examining *why*.

There again, my friend Shaw comes to mind. One of the many wise things that Shaw said occurred when people asked him why he had a beard. In his younger days, beards were far from commonplace. People would go on forever saying, "Why do you grow a beard?" He used to answer, if it was a man asking the question, "No, no, no, no. You must explain to me why *you* shave. That is a much more extraordinary piece of behavior." And it's true, isn't it? If we imagine a society in which all the males scrape over half their heads with a sharp knife every morning, we'd say, "Oh, poor savages! We must try and send them some gin and some Bibles, and then we'll be able to save them!" But that's what we all do! Shaw remembered when he was a tiny boy he went into the bathroom one day and saw his father shaving. He said to his father, "Father, why are you doing that?" His father looked at himself in the mirror for a couple of minutes then shook his head. He gathered up all the various paraphernalia, went across to the window, opened the window, and threw it all out. It suddenly occurred to him he didn't have the least idea *why*, except that everybody did it.

The stimulation science fiction can provide is very valuable. A prod. A nudge. To examine and reexamine *why* things are. One can learn very often from inverting things, a bit more wisdom about the things that *are*, once we've considered things as they *might be*. Sometimes we can be grateful for things as they are! Of course, science fiction very often has, and I think should have, a philosophical moral purpose.

The best of science fiction is not the kind which simply puts people into comic costumes or uniforms or fancy flight machines, but which deals with extensions or elaborations of thought. Of ideas. Of dreams. I always think about the Duchess in *Alice in Wonderland*, who said that she always set herself to believe two impossible things before breakfast every day. Those were her intellectual precepts. I think it's terribly important to maintain that openness which allows for impossible things to happen, which pushes back the horizons to the point where the impossible becomes conceivable.

That's where the importance, ultimately, of science fiction lies. It is, or should be, an attempt to push back the frontiers of thought in the same way as in the ancient days of exploration people pushed back the known frontiers of the world. We all know the world has been pretty well researched and examined and explored and plotted and that's that. There it is. What we haven't learned, unfortunately, in parallel to the technological advances, are comparable advances in wisdom, so as to be able to know how to treat this planet we've now so thoroughly researched, with some degree of understanding and respect.

Any worthwhile art, whether painting, music, poetry, drama or whatever, should try and reach a fuller understanding of our species, or other species, or the nature of our planet. Mind you, the best does not need to be preachy or sermonizing. The most wonderful thing in the works of Shakespeare is that you're absorbing aspiring thoughts at the same time as you are being highly entertained. That's the great power of Shakespeare. He's a staggering entertainer.

Now, back to *Space: 1999*, which dealt much too much in hardware and special effects, and not enough with ideas, thoughts, philosophies and feelings. As to the characters being one-dimensional and wooden, it is my firm opinion that they were. Martin and Barbara have to be congratulated, just as much as I should be, that we managed to squeeze out something approaching an individual character for ourselves, because we had very little to go on in the way of writing.

I have heard Martin and Barbara feel this was not the case, that the characters were multidimensional and subtly played. Well, I'm sure they were subtly played, but that's thanks to Barbara and Martin! They are too modest to suggest that a great deal of that subtlety was down to them. Of course, the characters were being constantly refined. Changing and developing relationships grew among the characters within the length of time I worked on the series—around a year and a half; within that time relationships and characteristics were developed which were able to be made use of. As time goes on you develop a kind of almost instinctive faculty for enriching the character you're playing, in the face of what any individual script calls upon you to do. I do remember I let my hair grow rather long to indicate Victor had other things on his mind than getting his hair cut or taking care of his appearance.

Can I explain my departure from the show? Yes, I can. Thankfully I don't harbor any sense of grievance or objection. In Gerry Anderson's biography it is said he felt a great loss to the show with "actor Barry Morse being dropped from the second series." Well, I'm glad to hear he felt that. The phrase "being dropped" is a bit of a misnomer, though, because it was virtually by mutual consent I dropped out of—*dropped out of* is the more accurate description—*Space: 1999*. From my point of view I had spent well over a year—16 months—virtually imprisoned in the studio, with no opportunity, or very little opportunity, to do anything else. I felt I hadn't created a particularly vivid character for Victor Bergman. It had boiled down to me—as Barry Morse—drifting through and saying whatever was set down for me.

Gerry and Sylvia had separated by this time, and she was no longer a part of the *Space: 1999* production. Changes were to be made. There was going to be a new producer introduced into the series, a chap called Fred Freiberger, who had been a producer of *Star Trek*. I think he was not particularly interested in maintaining the character of Victor Bergman. However, whether Gerry Anderson himself thought he didn't really need me, I don't know. Whether they thought Freddie might be able to improve the quality of the series is not for me to judge. He was supposed to be representing American tastes insofar as the reception of *Space: 1999* was concerned. He obviously felt improvements could and should be made in various ways. There were endless discussions—mostly not involving myself, but my agent—about whether or not I should return for a second series.

One of the things my agent was very resistant about—naturally—was that they proposed for the second series I should be paid rather *less* than I had been paid for the first series! I hope I've not ever been greedy about money. I certainly don't always measure the worthwhileness of jobs in relation to the amount of money they provide, but I wasn't interested in taking a pay decrease.

The outcome eventually was, virtually by mutual agreement, I didn't go into the second series. I finally went to Gerry and wickedly said, "Look, my dear, I've had a lovely time. I do wish you every kind of luck, but I shall be glad to go away and play with the grown-ups for a while."

For better or for worse, that's the way it all happened. I have been delighted to learn that Martin fought "like a tiger" for me to come back to the show. I wasn't aware of that at the time, but I can imagine it was the kind of friendly thing he would have done, and I'm very grateful to hear it. It's always amused me that I disappeared without any trace. People used to ask me, and still do sometimes, "Whatever happened to Victor Bergman? Why did he suddenly disappear?" And I say, "Well, I guess he fell off the back of the Moon!"

I do know that Martin Landau, Barbara Bain and myself—having formed a very close and loving professional association during the shooting of the first series—were all rather regretful I was not going to be with them for the second series. And while the show wasn't the most vivid or enjoyable experience I've ever had, the *doing* of it, on a purely working level, was enjoyable—thanks to Martin, Barbara, and all the other admirable and very likeable people who worked on it.

Recently, I was approached by a small company called Powys Media to write the introduction to a new *Space: 1999* novel called *Survival*, which was focused around my character, Victor Bergman. The author, Brian Ball, invented an alien woman character who becomes romantically involved with the old professor. The story also examines the fate of Victor, attempting to explain his disappearance. The woman was given the name of Yendys—which is the name of my dear Sydney spelled backwards. I was very touched by that. As well, I recorded for them the very first audio novel for *Space: 1999*, a story called *Resurrection*, a continuation of the "End of Eternity" episode which featured Peter Bowles as the malevolent alien Balor.

Space: 1999 has many fans around the world, and I think with younger people—people who in some instances weren't even born when we were actually doing the series—it has a strong impact because it reminds them of where we've been and where we may be going as we enter another millennium. It'll only take the wrong hand on the wrong button at the wrong time for the human species to be completely wiped out. It's a sobering thought, an alarming thought, but a very realistic thought. I think that is what has impressed so many people. Those ingredients I think are part of the serious subtext of *Space: 1999*. Those are the sort of speculative soul-searching questionings which could and should have played a larger part in the dramatization, but at least we touched on them some of the time.

It's all too easy with hindsight—which is always infallible—to put your finger on where things went wrong. Well, ultimately, we can't say that it did go wrong. The series has maintained a very loyal cult following ever since those days thirty years ago when it all began. The support the series has maintained has been in many ways, to me, quite amazing.

Over the years since *Space: 1999*, I have been to many conventions celebrating the series. Sydney and I often said to each other how very touching it is that these groups of young people are so kind and devoted to each other. They've become very much involved with each other and regard themselves as virtually members of the same family. I regard those young people as my honorary grandchildren. It is an extraordinary thing to me that just one more television show should have impelled such a nice group of people to have remembered it for such a long time. The conventions are very gentle and peaceful and loving occasions for a whole lot of people of different kinds, statuses and backgrounds not only being brought and held together by a common interest but also by a sense of concern and affection for each other. It shows how different kinds of the human race can come together and wish nothing but good to each other and to the rest of the world. I'm terribly pleased and touched by that.

There are many conglomerations of people who come together for much less honorable purposes.

20

"Don't Leave Home Without It!"

ONE OF MY FIRST TV PROJECTS after the end of *Space: 1999* was a film for television called *Truman at Potsdam*, about President Harry Truman and the famed Potsdam Conference at the end of the Second World War trying to set up peace in Europe. A number of notable people appeared in this film, including Jose Ferrer and Ed Flanders, which was produced by the eminent American producer David Susskind and directed by George Schaeffer. The film was shot mostly in Hamburg, with a few scenes in London. We were not actually allowed to go into Potsdam itself, as it was in what was in those days called East Germany.

It was an enjoyable time and I remember one of the sights there was to go to the fish market early in the morning. So I went with Jose Ferrer and Ed Flanders to see this great event at six o'clock in the morning! Jose and I would sit about the set and scribble jokes, making up brief biographical rhymes, things like:

> "Truman ain't human
> and Winnie's a ninny,
> but Stalin's a darlin'!"

We also made up a cast for a rather skittish, lascivious drama. The play was to be presented in Latin, taking place in the sleepy town of Coitus in the foothills of Mons Venerius. The cast consists of:

> CAST
> Spewton   (a Flemish outcast)

Scrotum	(a wrinkled retainer)
Gonorrhea	(a Greek runner)
Testes	(two hangers on)
Umbilicus	(a naval attaché)
Pregnant	(a lady in waiting)
and	
Flatulence	(a big blowhard)

Oh, my! The way that bored actors pass their time on the set waiting around to be called for the next shot.

Also at this time, and for several years, I was hired to appear in all of the advertising spots for American Express Traveler's Cheques, where I became associated with their famous motto, "Don't leave home without it!" It was an extensive media campaign involving television, print advertising, and radio spots. It was all a very enjoyable experience and involved shooting in various exotic travel destinations around the world. These commercials were aimed principally at Canada, and a very nice job it was, too. It paid well and wasn't too demanding in terms of time. Inevitably if you become reasonably visible by virtue of having played in popular series, there are various propositions that come along for commercial endorsements. For a long time there was a great deal of snobbishness in general in our trade among the senior actors. For my part, I wasn't snobbish about the whole thing but I certainly didn't want to do commercials for projects or products which I took to be sort of tacky. However, I had used and was still using the American Express Traveler's Cheques. So I could quite genuinely present myself as a satisfied customer. They didn't have to talk me into it—they bought me into it! The campaign, which ended up running more than five years, was conducted concurrently with a similar series in the USA featuring Karl Malden.

I was invited to host a show for the CBC celebrating their twenty-fifth anniversary of television broadcasting in Canada which aired on October 2, 1977. I suggested to the producers that we collect clips from all of the old shows that we'd done years before and make it a kind of anthology. But when they went to look in the archives they found that almost all of the old shows that we'd done in the earliest days of television had been destroyed! The bureaucrats had come along and said, "What's all that stuff there, all those old tins?" And they were told, "Oh, that's the kinescopes and films of all the old shows."

"Get them outta here," the bureaucrats responded, "we've gotta make room for the paperwork." So in came the file boxes and out went a great number of the earliest shows that we had done—the history of Canadian television. Rightly or wrongly, mercifully or not, they had been disposed of. I was very angry at the time.

In the New Year Sydney and I planned a trip back to Spain to look at some of the other beautiful parts of the country which we didn't know. One of the cities we visited during our journeys was Seville, where we stayed in the Barrio de Santa Cruz. In this district there was a maze of narrow passageways that you couldn't drive through, because they were pedestrian alleys. In ancient times these were used by horseback riders.

Having walked back and forth through these alleyways of Santa Cruz, we came to the end of the alley that faced the main church on the plaza. As we got to that corner, two youths swung toward us on a small moto, a motor bike. I stepped aside and at once the rider snatched Sydney's bag right from her shoulder, breaking the shoulder strap fastening, then rode off down the alley. After a breath's pause (I thought at first they were just sloppy riders), I realized what had happened and sprinted off after them. I yelled in my best and loudest Spanish, "Robbers! Stop them!" When the two young men turned left at the end of the alley, I was only about 25 meters behind them because they'd had to weave back and forth to avoid various other pedestrians in the alley, which was no more than 6 or 8 feet wide. On the next section, there was a group of three or four tourists who stood back when they heard the moto coming rather fast, and during the next stretch of about 100 meters, which was pretty well clear of pedestrians, the moto gained even further. So by the time I got into the next plaza, they turned right onto the main road. I realized at this point that I'd lost them and, moreover, we'd lost Sydney's bag.

Because we had not yet checked into our hotel, Sydney's shoulder bag contained a good deal of our valuables. I had my own passport and paperwork in my jacket pocket, but Sydney had hers in this shoulder bag and we had not yet given the valuables to the hotel management to put into their safe. So the bag, as well as containing all the valuable papers, contained various pieces of jewelry consisting of earrings and rings, a string of quite good pearls, and a cameo brooch, coming to a value (a substantial value for those days) of about £1,300 worth of jewelry. Of course, it was worth much more in sentimental terms because one of the rings was Sydney's mother's engagement ring and another of them was my mother's engagement ring; they were the kind of things that, naturally, Sydney treasured immensely. There were also other items, including Sydney's British and Canadian passports, her resident Visa for the US of A, her international driving license and a Canadian one, travelers' cheques, cash in Spanish money, bank machine and bank cheque cards, cheque book for our Spanish bank account, and more. As you can see, it was quite a blow.

Failing to catch these youths on the moto, I then turned back seeking Sydney and found about five minutes later that she had fallen in attempting to run after me, injuring her shoulder and bruising up considerably. She had been helped by a quartet of French tourists and also by a neighborhood Spanish woman who lived in one of the houses alongside the alley who said, somewhat to my astonishment and alarm, that "This sort of thing happens everyday." So we got to the nearest street where there were vehicles and took a taxi to the nearest police station. After hours of waiting, the plainclothes jefé (chief) we spoke with was very bored and seemed quite anxious to escape, although he was kind enough to mention that he recognized me from television. Eventually completing our report form—which required, of course, our mother's and father's surnames and our passport numbers (which we couldn't possibly give them since Sydney's passports had been stolen!)—Sydney signed it and we finally left the station and caught a taxi to take us back to the hotel.

Upon hearing of our troubles our driver confided that "Seville had become a violent and lawless city." He showed us the club he kept beside his seat to ward off attacks. He said, "There are all sorts of people unemployed and some hungry among the young people in Seville." In the midst of all of this a woman at the hotel said a very wise thing to Sydney, who was considerably distressed and not only by the injuries that she'd suffered. She said, "Nothing goes backwards, Senõra, what's done is done and what's gone is gone. Let it go and don't distress yourself." Well, I thought that really very wise. We heard numerous stories of robberies and attacks that were occurring all over the city on a daily basis. Needless to say, we were not in much of a holiday mood at this point in either mind or body. An article appeared in the local newspaper the next day reporting on our robbery, with the news story reporting that "El

One of Sydney's last professional portraits, and one of the loveliest. Taken in Toronto around 1980.

Tienté (The Lieutenant) from the famous *Fugitive* show had actually been robbed himself," and so on. Presumably someone at the police headquarters sold the story to the press—more than likely the chief. Unfortunately, we weren't able to recover Sydney's bag or any of our valuables. We decided that it was time for us to leave and thus cut our vacation short.

I had, in the meantime, received an offer to play in the H.G. Wells film *The Shape of Things to Come*, which was also going to be shot in Canada, and a second project for television, the miniseries *The Martian Chronicles* based on the book by Ray Bradbury. *The Martian Chronicles* was to be shot in Malta. They were using some of the rather rugged kind of landscape that exists in Malta as if it were the surface of Mars. I had never been to Malta before, but it was very enjoyable. The island was formed from an old volcanic eruption and was quite a curious kind of almost lunar landscape. The film was an anthology of several different stories and I played the part of Peter Hatheway and Nyree Dawn Porter played my wife, Alice. I had several scenes with the star Rock Hudson, who just a few years later died quite tragically of AIDS. Another actor who was in it was Roddy McDowall, who had become well known first as a boy actor; he was English by birth, but gained great success in Hollywood. In general, the quality of science fiction can vary a great deal and some of it is really quite mindless. People with bits of bent wire on their heads pretending to be Martians and all kinds of stuff—but that was not so of *The Martian Chronicles*. Ray Bradbury gave it a serious, philosophic, and satiric subtext and I think it was overall quite a good piece.

Once I was finished shooting my scenes for *The Martian Chronicles*, Sydney and I were off to Toronto where I began work on the film *The Shape of Things to Come*, directed by a Canadian, George McCowan. Unfortunately, this movie turned out to be a bad remake of that lovely old story by H.G. Wells. A quite excellent movie version had been shot years before, but this version was all done, as often happens, on a peanuts budget. And, as the man once said, "If you pay peanuts, you get monkeys." After that was finished, I was off to Vancouver to film *The Changeling* with George C. Scott. It was directed by Peter Medak and I played the part of a rather crazy Hungarian parapsychologist. This, on the other hand, was quite a good film, in the suspense genre. Also in it were Melvyn Douglas, John Colicos, Jean Marsh, and Trish Van Devere. *Variety*, the trade magazine, called it "a superior haunted house thriller."

Then I was immediately off to Dawson City, via Whitehorse, in the Yukon, to play in *Cannibal Joe*, the film about Robert Service. This was a great adventure and I played this old character named Cannibal Joe, who, upon falling into terrible privation in a remote part of the Yukon, was supposed to have eaten his companion after the man died. It was so paralyz-ingly cold outdoors that we could only shoot for a few minutes at a time because the camera itself would freeze up. The *oil* would freeze—never mind *us*! So we had to keep dodging back and forth in and out of the var-ious cabins and huts that we shot in and around. The Yukon is really a very fascinating part of the world. Residents talk about it as a world of their own. If you are leaving Dawson City they say, "Oh, you're going outside, are you?" as if you are going to another planet. It's quite remarkable, but it must be awfully tough living there.

Following *Cannibal Joe* I had to go to Los Angeles to do the looping, or the post-synching, of *The Martian Chronicles* at the MGM Studios in Culver City. I was only in L.A. for a couple days before coming back to Chicago to do a radio series there for an organization called the National Radio Theater of America. This was run by an immensely gifted fellow, who became a great friend of ours, called Yuri Rasovsky. He had realized that radio in the U.S. had been totally trivialized and that there was hardly any good, quality radio left. Most of the radio stations were occupied by dismal, silly chat shows or disk jockey shows. Once his organization was set up, he also began to quickly realize that there were hardly any actors in the U.S. who were in any way skillful or experienced in radio perform-ing, because radio drama had been virtually out of existence in the States for such a long time. So he happened to consult my agent in New York, Milton Goldman, who didn't hesitate to say, "Well, if you want a really experienced and versatile radio actor, look no further than up into Canada where my client, Mr. Barry Morse, has been playing in radio dramas—hun-dreds of them—of every conceivable kind, for many, many years."

So Yuri invited me to come to Chicago to work on a serialization of an English language version of *The Odyssey of Homer*, where I played the title role of Odysseus. Nothing like starting out in a large way! Never before or since has such an ambitious undertaking been attempted in Amer-ican public radio. It was accomplished—not by a major network—but by Yuri Rasovsky, a small nonprofit independent producer in Chicago. This production won numerous honors, including the prestigious George Fos-ter Peabody Award, the "Pulitzer Prize" of broadcasting. The critics praised the show, calling it such things as "a feast for the ears" and "a magnificent blend of scholarship and showmanship."

As they say, one thing led to—much more. Other quality productions with Yuri included *The Tempest*, in which I played the wonderful role of Prospero, and then another production called *Death*, written by Woody Allen. This was one-third of a trilogy written by Allen and performed by an international cast. The first act, *God*, was recorded in Chicago with Allen himself playing the title role of God and directed by Yuri Rasovsky. The second piece, *Sex*, was performed in Australia and the final act, *Death,* was recorded in London with me. All three acts were then combined into one program and aired in England, Australia, and the U.S. to great success.

It was then onward to Quesnel, British Columbia for another film called *Klondike Fever*, produced by Harry Alan Towers and directed by Peter Carter, who was an English director who had lived and worked in Canada quite a lot. Other cast members included Rod Steiger, Lorne Greene, and Angie Dickinson. We shot part of it

Performing Odysseus in *The Odyssey of Homer*.
(Courtesy of Yuri Rasovsky)

in Quesnel, then moved to Wells, before going up to the Klondike. I played a Klondike dog handler and I had to learn how to drive a team of sled-drawing dogs. I managed to do it, albeit with a certain amount of falling off, I have to admit!

Right on the heels of that film came *Cries in the Night*, which was released in the U.S. under the title of *Funeral Home*. It was shot on location around Toronto and produced and directed by William Fruet. As you might guess from the title, it was a horror film. Some time later, following completion of the film, I was being interviewed by a journalist from the USA. As I had been pulling faces and making noises at that time for some 50 years, even then the shows had a tendency to become a kind of a blur. The interviewer said to me, "There's a movie you're in showing here now." I said, "Really? Good! What is it?" And he replied, "It's called *Funeral Home*." I thought he was joking and said, "Oh yes, I know that movie. That's the one they're all dying to get into." He exclaimed, "No, really! It really is called *Funeral Home*." Of course it turned out to be *Cries in the Night.*

At this time a change was pending in our lives. Although we had loved

Another shot of me performing Odysseus in *The Odyssey of Homer*. (Courtesy of Yuri Rasovsky)

and enjoyed our time spent in the house in Spain a great deal, we were increasingly aware that we wouldn't be able to be there most of the time, much less all of the time! The robbery in Seville also weighed on our minds, and my thinking had begun to change a bit in that I decided I wasn't going to try and settle down in one place and give up acting to try to write. So we began to entertain offers for the house in Spain and indeed, shortly afterwards, we did accept one of the offers that came, and very good offers they were, because it was a most attractive house in a wonderful location looking directly over the Mediterranean.

And so came the end of our Spanish adventure.

21

"One for Everybody and Two for Mr. Mitchum!"

I STARTED WORK IN EUROPE on a film version of Charles Dickens' *A Tale of Two Cities*. The lead was played by a young American actor, Chris Sarandon, and there were a number of other distinguished actors in it as well, including Kenneth More, Nigel Hawthorne, Dame Flora Robson, Alice Krige, and Billie Whitelaw. I played the Marquis de St. Evremonde, who gets his coachman to drive on although they've hit and run down a poor young girl. Virtually single-handedly, this rascal started the French revolution! I remember one scene where he arrived hopelessly drunk back at his manor and was helped into the house by his various servants, principal among whom was a young lad who was then just beginning his distinguished career—David Suchet. He's become famous playing the Belgian detective Hercule Poirot in films and on television. He was a very nice lad and I could tell that he was going to go a long way. We went over to Paris for quite a while to shoot and then back to London. Also appearing in the film was my old friend Peter Cushing, although we ended up not having any scenes together.

Not long after that I flew to Zagreb, in what in those days was called Yugoslavia, to begin shooting what stands as one of the largest and best miniseries ever produced—*The Winds of War*. This series more or less traced the history of World War II. The leading character was played by Robert Mitchum, and I played a German character, Wolf Stoller, who was a diplomat attempting to weasel his way on behalf of the Nazis into good offices with the Americans. It was a very good part, an interesting role, and I had a lovely long scene with Mitchum. I got along with him very well and greatly admired his personal manner and views on life. He had a skeptical view of our trade and how fluky it was. Our director was a fearsome character called Dan Curtis, who was a draconian, obsessively active and noisy kind of figure. He spoke all the time he was on the set through a bullhorn, one of those miniature loudspeaker things. It didn't matter if he was talking to someone only six feet away! We had a number of funny adventures with him, one of them involving a large-scale scene in which my character was giving a diplomatic reception in a grand embassy-type house. In order to introduce some informality into the proceeding, Curtis arranged that the guests should enter down the grand staircase—not coming down the steps, but by a kind of fairground slide which had been put down over the staircase. Of course, it was very difficult to shoot and rather time consuming because, between each take, everybody who'd come down on this slide had to climb back up again to the top and be given new mats to sit on and have their wardrobe and makeup rechecked. Dan Curtis became very impatient with this and was yelling through his bullhorn more than usual. He eventually realized that what was consuming so much time was getting everyone back up to the top of the staircase. As assertive people so often are toward certain people, he tended to be quite subservient as far as Mitchum was concerned. I remember him shouting through his bullhorn, "Get everybody back up to the top of the God-damned staircase, quick-quick-quick, and get the mats up there, too! Get enough mats up there, one for everybody and *two* for Mr. Mitchum!" Well, Bob Mitchum looked back at him and said, smiling, "What the hell do I need two mats for—I've only got one ass!" Mitchum was delightful to be with and I worked with him again later on in another film called *Reunion at Fairborough*, which was shot in England, as well as the sequel miniseries to *The Winds of War*, entitled *War and Remembrance*. So I got to know him quite well.

The Winds of War was filled with numbers of actors from the USA, England, and Europe, including such names as Ali MacGraw, Jan-Michael Vincent, Polly Bergen, Elke Summer, Peter Graves, Topol, Ralph Bellamy, and others. Also working on the picture was a delightful fellow who became a good friend—and still is, I'm glad to say—Jeremy Kemp. We had some delightful dinners in Zagreb during the filming.

There was another sequence being shot for the film out in the countryside about the Holocaust. I wasn't in this, but I went out there because I had become quite chummy with Mitchum and I wanted to see how they would shoot this very complicated and horrific scene. There was to be a re-creation of a mass grave in which various victims of the Holocaust were being buried, some of them still alive! For the filming the majority of the bodies in this re-created grave sequence were dummies, of course, but they wanted to have a few live people on the top who would be moving so that one could see that indeed they were about to be buried when they were still alive, many of them dressed in the conventional striped kind of semi-uniforms that the victims of the Holocaust were forced to wear in these concentration camps. There had been a lot of publicity about the shooting of the film and indeed some of the people working as extras in these terrible scenes had actually been victims of the Holocaust in these various camps and were prepared to give chapter and verse evidence as to what the conditions were like, which was very valuable to the production. We were shooting at night and it was a bitterly cold January, and many of these extras were obviously suffering from the cold quite a lot. Our crew was a very decent bunch of guys trying to keep these people warm by having blankets on hand to put over them when they were between shots and giving them swigs of brandy and so forth. The Yugoslav brandy was marvelously effective and I became rather fond of it myself! On this particular night our director, Dan Curtis, was even more loudly impatient than he usually was, because it was all taking much too long, he felt. I should note that he was quite courteous to me, partly because I think he recognized that—whether or not I was good—I could be quick. Mitchum was also marvelously professional and skillful and he and I had a long dialogue scene together which we managed to get through in just one take, endearing us to Dan Curtis. But at the mass grave it was bitterly cold, and Dan Curtis was up on a high camera crane with his bullhorn, shouting more loudly than ever because he was quite a distance away from the actual pit. After a number of takes, one of these characters, who was dressed in these ragged and rough prison type clothes, was obviously in some distress because of the cold. One of our assistants decided to take him off and get him some medical attention. So he and another crew member were carrying this old man out of the pit and off the set when they were observed by Dan Curtis, who yelled through his bullhorn, "What are you doing down there, Goddammit! Stop movin' people around, whata ya think you're doing...." The assistant politely called up, "Uh, sorry Mr. Curtis, but this gentleman is not well and we're just going to see if we can get him warm and get some medical attention for him." Curtis replied, bullhorn at full volume, "Alright, well ... get him the hell outta there then." The crew members started to carry the man off when Curtis came back on his bullhorn and said, "No! Wait a minute! Hold on there—is that our wardrobe?!" He was more concerned with a couple scraps of wardrobe than he was with a human being.

After this experience I was back again in Canada to rehearse a stage production of *Sleuth* with our son, Hayward Morse, a very fine actor in his own right. *Sleuth* uses only two actors and is skillfully constructed. The younger man plays, in effect, three different characters. This was to be done in a dinner theatre setting and most dinner theatres are without a proscenium arch, which made the production of a play like *Sleuth* a bit tricky. One has to design a set which is not in the usual theatrical style, but has the audience virtually on three sides of it. However, with the help of the designer we did succeed in producing what was a very effective, and successful, production of the play. We opened *Sleuth* at the Variety Dinner Theatre in Toronto on May 5, 1981, and had a triumphant success and marvelous notices—the sort of notices only Sydney could have written! We were packed to the doors every night. I, as well as playing the principal part, directed it and Hayward was very supportive. Sometimes it's not that easy or successful when parent and child work together in the theatre. But in this instance it worked wonderfully well. I still have a couple of stills of Hayward and me up on my fireplace mantle that were taken during that production.

Around this time I met with a chap named John Reardon, who was going to direct a new mini-series called *Whoops Apocalypse*. I enthusiastically agreed to join this production and enjoyed it very much indeed. It was made in England and was produced by Independent Television (ITV) at London Weekend Television, filmed in front of a live audience. It went very well and was a wildly farcical and satirically very funny examination of the world somewhere in the future—unspecified—in which the United States has virtually taken over the whole of what remains of civilization. They have as their

In the stage play *Sleuth*, with Hayward.

As U.S. president Johnny Cyclops in *Whoops Apocalypse* **with Lou Hirsch.**

president a Texan, an ex–*Tarzan* movie actor called Johnny Cyclops, whom I played. He was really kind of dumb and I played him with a broad Texas accent. It was very funny but wasn't shown in the States very much, partly because it savagely satirizes the institutions and policies of the United States. *Whoops Apocalypse* was written by David Renwick and Andrew Marshall. Among the other actors involved, Rik Mayall was in the show; he's gone on to become very well known in British television. My character, President Cyclops, was trying to run his reelection campaign while also dealing with the Russians, a deposed Shah in need of asylum, and a new weapon called a Quark bomb. One of the Quark bombs was stolen by an infamous terrorist called Lacrobat, played by John Cleese. It all builds in a viciously funny way to doomsday.

In October 1982 my brother Len had a heart attack and stroke. In midlife, Len had taken up the sport of marathon running and he ultimately became one of a small number of Centurions: men who had taken part in hundred mile races, both running and walking. What happened initially to poor Len was that in the course of a cross-country race, in the winter, he

In the Oval Office of the White House with Lou Hirsch and John Barron.

slipped and fell, running across a primitive plank bridge, and damaged his hip. That injury went on to become so serious he had to undergo a series of *three* hip replacement operations over the next several years. In the first two cases, the surgery turned out not to be successful. In one case the cement fastening the hip deteriorated and the hip joint came loose. He went through the tortures of the damned.

Sydney and I were off to Canada once again, this time to raise funds for Theatre London in London, Ontario. I played Scrooge in *A Christmas Carol*, and Sydney played several roles, including Mrs. Cratchit and Mrs. Dilber. She was immensely good and the run turned out to be enormously successful. Having been originally scheduled to run up to Christmas Eve, the show was so successful that we ran it almost up to the end of February! This organization, Theatre London, a very worthwhile theatre project, was in deep financial trouble at this particular time. I was delighted to stay on and play *A Christmas Carol* much longer because it was going to raise just that much more money for the theatre. The editorial cartoonist from

Here I am, standing with my bicycle, proudly watching my brother Len run a marathon.

the *New Brunswick Telegraph-Journal*, Josh Beutel, even sketched a picture of me as Scrooge, saying (in a take-off from my American Express commercials), "Keep the spirit of Christmas in your heart.... Don't leave home without it!" But then I suggested as an extra means of cashing in on this popularity that I should do a performance of my one-man show, *Merely Players*, which I had been performing on an occasional basis. So we did it on one Sunday evening—the last Sunday I was there at the end of the run of *A Christmas Carol*—as a special fundraising performance, and a sort of farewell to London, Ontario.

I was then asked to play Menachim Begin, the former Israeli prime minister, in a very good and highly acclaimed miniseries simply called *Sadat*. Anwar el Sadat, of course, was the president of Egypt and Nobel Peace Prize winner who had a lot of diplomatic dealings with Begin and Israel when they were trying to make peace between the two states. I felt that I should tell the producers that I am not Jewish, and when they said that didn't matter I added (with my fondness for poor jokes), "Well, I just hope there

Editorial cartoon of me in character as Scrooge, printed in the *New Brunswick Telegraph-Journal*, referencing my American Express affiliation. Photograph by John Beutel, © the Bentel Collection, Provincial Archives of New Brunswick.

are no nude scenes, because then it'll be a matter of 'where ignorance is bris'"—bris being the Hebrew word for circumcision. I contacted a friend of mine at the BBC to dig up some recordings of Begin from the archives so I could assess his accent, which had changed quite substantially during the latter part of his life. He initially learned English through listening to the BBC overseas radio. As the years went by, his fluency in English became considerably better but it also became more and more influenced by an American kind of accent. He was meeting with and having discussions with numbers of U.S. diplomats. It was very interesting to listen to these recordings from different periods of his life. I flew then to Mexico City to shoot *Sadat*. It was produced by an American outfit and directed by Richard Michaels. The reason we were filming in Mexico was that diplomatic relations between Israel and Egypt were such that they couldn't get permission for us to shoot in either of those countries. So it was decided by the producers that the most convenient place to shoot would be in Mexico because landscapes there could be made to look like Egypt or Israel. The cast included Louis Gossett, Jr., as Sadat, and also featured John Rhys-Davies, Madolyn Smith, and my old friend Jeremy Kemp.

In preparation for the year 1984, I started on a project which was a biographical radio series on George Orwell in honor of his book *1984*. I was to play Orwell and the author and director of the series was Steve Wadhams. The series was recorded in Toronto and would air on CBC radio. It was of uncommonly good quality.

Next up was *Reunion at Fairborough*, another film with Robert Mitchum, and quite well received. I had quite a good part in it and also in it were Deborah Kerr, Red Buttons and Shane Rimmer. It was directed by Herbert Wise and shot at Shepperton Studios. Various parts of the movie were shot on location, and I particularly remember filming in the American Services Cemetery in Cambridge for several days. Mitchum and I continued our warm friendship.

Throughout this time my brother, Len, had remained in Orsett Hospital and his condition had worsened, becoming very serious. His doctors were proposing that his leg be amputated and I remember traveling up to the hospital on several occasions to meet with doctors to discuss this with them. Eventually, the amputation did take place.

Len was moved out of Orsett Hospital to St. Andrews' Hospital at Billericay. He was very gravely ill. Sydney and I went to see him in the hospital and things were looking so serious that we stayed there until 2:15 a.m. on January 2, 1984, eventually getting home at about 5:00 a.m. Later in the day on January 2 we went down again and we were joined by Len's wife, Maisie. We stayed on through the rest of the day and the night; Len died at 2:45 p.m. on January 3 and it was a merciful release, really. His death was a great blow to all of us, but especially to Maisie, who had been his wife for 44 years. They had never been able to have children, which was a great sorrow and deprivation for them.

Len's funeral was to be held in the City of London Cemetery where he was given a plot because of his last work as Court Usher at the Old Bailey. I wrote the obituaries for Len, one for the *Hackney Gazette* and one for the *Metropolitan Police Magazine* called "The Job." The police always refer to themselves as being "in the job," as if it were the only one. Of course, Len was an immensely respected, and in some ways famous, member of the Metropolitan Police. He served longer than any other police constable in the whole history of the Metropolitan Police, which goes back to the early nineteenth century. His funeral and cremation were on January 12. There was a great turnout. The commissioner of the Metropolitan Police was there and most of the senior officers, and I made an address in honor of Len. It was a very, very moving occasion.

But the death of Len, unfortunately, wouldn't be the last of our family tragedies.

22

"The Golden Journey"

Sᴅᴅɴᴇʏ ᴀɴᴅ I ʜᴀᴅ ᴀᴛᴛᴇɴᴅᴇᴅ our local church, St. James's Piccadilly, quite regularly whenever we were in London. Located within easy walking distance of our flat through St. James's Square, the main principles of the church were things that Sydney and I agreed with strongly. They were inclusive and welcoming of both human experience and human diversity. We were proud of the fact that the church is widely representative of both married and single people, heterosexual and homosexual, those who have a natural faith and those who struggle with belief.

We became involved in the planning of a celebration to honor the three hundredth anniversary of St. James's. We cooked up a kind of St. James's Festival, which would include a series of various events to celebrate this momentous anniversary. The festival itself opened on July 13, 1984, and the Queen Mother, Queen Elizabeth, attended the 11:00 a.m. service. She was born in our parish and had attended St. James's as a child. I arranged to be in a suitable period costume, with a beautiful wig, as Christopher Wren, hosting the whole thing and welcoming everybody. The Queen Mother was very gracious and kindly agreed to have a drink with us after the service, which was very enjoyable. The festival continued through July 28 with many varied talks, exhibitions, and shows, and coverage was given on the BBC. I went to participate in various ways virtually every day.

But before this, we thought that it would be a good kind of publicity stunt for the church if we arranged for a marathon reading of the Bible—the whole of it—from start to finish nonstop. Almost inevitably, I became the general producer of this project, which we decided to call the "Bible-thon." We ended up with all kinds of sports figures, arts figures and political figures, and the difficult thing, of course, was arranging the timing of

215

the whole thing. I was able to work out, from samples that I took from different sections of the Bible, roughly how long a given section would take. I was very proud of the fact that in the event, when we finally completed it all, my timing was only eight minutes out! This was after four days and three nights of straight, nonstop reading.

Prior to the event, preparations were underway at a breakneck speed. We had to make arrangements for the church to be open 24 hours a day for four days on end, and for the ushering and superintending of people coming in and going out during all that time. I was going to the rectory every day to press on with the arrangements, because in addition to our scheduled readers we had to establish a system of understudies. Inevitably there are going to be people who don't arrive at the time when they're supposed to, because their cat's had kittens or they've lost track of the date they wrote down, or so on! The Biblethon finally began on May 28, 1984, at 1:00 p.m. The first passage in Genesis, chapter 1, verse 1, begins, "In the beginning...." It continued on through the next four days and three nights and ended at noon on Saturday, June 1, with the Archbishop of Canterbury reading the final passage from the book of Revelations. Our total schedule ran 96 hours and we had marvelous adventures with people dropping in. The church was fully lit up and a big screen had been erected outside on Piccadilly showing what was going on inside the Church. All kinds of people wandered in—people who were homeless, people who were hopeless, tourists from around the world, and people from throughout London. It was a marvelous, marvelous event.

For several years I had been deeply involved with activities at our church of St. James's, but I see now it was almost entirely for the love of Sydney. I was not ever a truly "convinced" Christian, although I'd been brought up in a kind of Christian way, sent to Sunday school, and sung in the choir of St. Columba's. I followed Christian practices more or less for most of my life and Sydney, of course, was brought up at a boarding school run by Anglican nuns and was a very good Christian. But, throughout it all, I had always had my doubts about the virtues of Christianity, or indeed any other religion. I had increasingly been troubled by the fact that so much dissension and destruction and mayhem and murder are wrought in the human community in the name of so-called religions. The last time I looked, there were no less than 36 wars being waged on this planet, almost all of them in the name of so-called religion. I can't believe—I simply *cannot believe* that if there is some almighty power he has confined himself entirely to This, That, or The Other selection of followers. If there were such a creature I wouldn't want to know him!

One fine Sunday, as we were leaving St. James's after the 11:00 service, walking back down through St. James's Square, Sydney suddenly said to me, sighing, "I'm not sure I believe in all this." I responded, "Believe in all what?" She replied, looking backwards, "All that stuff, you know, the Christian...." Stunned, I interrupted her in mid-sentence. "Now you tell me! After all these years bashing my brains out, turning up religiously to do all these things for love of you, and now you're not sure you believe in it all!" We both thought about it a lot, and talked about it some more, realizing that we both had come to have rather serious doubts about our Christian convictions.

Nevertheless, even though I had long harbored doubts about Christianity, I have always had the "itch," or the desire, to be "up to something" which might be making things better. It was partly due to those feelings that I became involved with a charitable group called the Samaritans. It was started by an Anglican priest named Chad Varah, vicar at St. Stephen Walbrook in the City of London in 1953. He began with the realization that there were many people who needed help in dealing with the stresses of their everyday working lives and that the need for counseling was quite sizeable. He also began to understand that he couldn't possibly cope with all the various people who were seeking guidance and comfort by himself, so he started to recruit people who thought themselves able to counsel and support people who were in emotional turmoil. It began as a telephone service and later began to offer personal counseling as well. The Samaritans grew very rapidly because it was emerging more and more that in our high paced and high pressured modern world there were all sorts of people who were on the verge of, or thought themselves on the verge of, suicide.

Having come myself to this period of uncertainty—I hesitate to call it a spiritual crossroad—about what I might want to do, I decided to investigate what it might be possible for me to do at the Samaritans. Upon completion of a course of instruction, I was officially accepted. There would be three or four of us on the phones at a time, handling a fairly steady stream of phone calls. The callers would be in varying degrees of anxiety or distress, or uncertainty. One of the most terrifying things from the earliest days happened while I was working on the night shift and I had a call from a young woman who was in very considerable distress and in declining consciousness because she had taken an overdose of some pills. She had intended to commit suicide but after she had taken the pills she had regrets and second thoughts. During the call she was intermittently sinking into semiconsciousness. Somehow, I had to keep her on the phone long enough to find out where she physically was so that we could get on another phone line and alert emergency services to dispatch paramedics and an ambulance to her. It was touch and go, but eventually we got the information and she was saved.

I became quite interested in people who were less than fully educated. We would attract numbers of calls from "street people" who were not particularly articulate and could only express themselves in four-letter words. All too often when one of these rough characters would appear at the office, perhaps not so sober and "F-ing" and blinding all over the place, the Samaritan in charge would say, "This is one of Barry's!" I would talk to them and find out what was on their mind. Because of my background growing up in the slums of the East End of London, I had a good knowledge of what you might call gutter language and quickly found myself as the "specialist in rough trade." I did my best to listen to all sorts of conditions and colors of people. I stayed working with the Samaritans in this capacity for more than five years.

In 1989, Sydney and I celebrated our golden wedding anniversary— 50 years together. We started to plan what would become known as our "golden journey," during which we would revisit all sorts of places we'd been in when we first met and in the early years of our marriage. We set forth on February 25 to Falmouth, in Cornwall, to visit our dear old friends Don and Jo Manning Wilson. They had moved to their new home in Cornwall the previous year, where they hoped to enjoy their retirement years. Their home would be the first stop in our golden journey celebration. The next stop on the journey was in Filkins in the Cotswold's to visit one of our other dear old friends Doreen Oscar, who (along with Don Manning Wilson) had also been one of my fellow students at the Royal Academy of Dramatic Art. We spent Sydney's birthday there before going on to the very handsome town of Buxton, in Derbyshire, where we stayed in a lovely bed and breakfast house to get as near as we could to where we spent our honeymoon. We set off, while we were there, to see if we could find the farm cottage where we actually spent our honeymoon. We eventually found what we thought must be the farm, although we couldn't remember clearly enough as so many of the cottages in that district look so similar.

Then we went up to Bradford in Yorkshire, where both Sydney and I had been separately in the theatre repertory company before we met in Peterborough in 1939. The city of Bradford had immensely changed and its population at this time was a high percentage Indian. We stayed just outside the main city and drove around in our rented car to look at all the sights of the district. The theatre in which we had separately played—and then later together with Carl Bernard in 1940—was unfortunately destroyed a number of years ago, but was replaced by the Film and Television Museum, which is on the site of the famous old Prince's Theatre. The Alhambra, the old music hall in Bradford, has been very handsomely restored, so we went to visit it. We also went to visit other towns nearby where we played, and the various places we had stayed in digs, and of course we went to Harrogate, where we played in 1941 in the repertory company there.

On March 14 we went to Peterborough. Of course, that theatre which was known as the Theatre Royal and Empire has also been destroyed. We went to look at the site of what had been "our" theatre, where we actually first met on the morning of the third of January 1939. We also went to look at the site—the building no longer exists—where Sydney's digs had

Sydney and I shared our lives for more than 60 years.

been. We continued our journey right on through March 19, revisiting the places of our youth on what had become a sentimental journey for the two of us. We returned to London, and the day of our actual golden wedding anniversary arrived, March 26, 1989. Dozens, if not scores of phone calls, cards, and letters came in from friends, family, fans, and well-wishers from all over the world.

It was a most memorable time for us, indeed.

23

"Battling On Bravely"

ON TUESDAY, THE NINETEENTH OF February 1985 at the Middlesex Hospital in London, my dear wife Sydney was diagnosed as having Parkinson's disease. This was a great blow because we knew enough about it to know that it was an incurable disease. At this point Sydney was just coming up to her seventieth birthday and we knew that she would get progressively worse.

Our daughter, Melanie, at Christmas 1984, was the first to observe those characteristics in her mother—my dear Sydney—that led us to believe that Sydney might be experiencing the onset of Parkinson's disease. Sydney, who had always been quite athletic, had developed a very slight shuffle in her walk and seemed to move a little bit slower than usual. Melanie also noticed that from time to time she would have trouble getting up from a chair, or getting a thought fully articulated. She just didn't seem to be the same Mum that Melanie knew so well and had seen just months earlier. Melanie, seeing her mother perhaps only two or three times in a year, was quick to notice that something was amiss, whereas I was with Sydney on more or less a daily basis: it was much more difficult for me to notice those subtle changes in her physicality.

Sure enough, Melanie was right. When we returned to England from Toronto we went to see our family doctor—and he said afterwards, "When I first saw Sydney walking down the hallway towards my consulting room I guessed that she had Parkinson's disease." His diagnosis turned out to be all too correct. Sydney was able to live at home with very little change in her routine for the next several years. Even when her condition worsened somewhat, I was able to take care of her at home with the assistance of visiting nurses who would come to the flat. But right from the word go, Sydney was very brave and positive about all of this.

Of course, Sydney and I wanted to find out as much as possible about her condition. We discovered that Parkinson's disease is a deterioration of a group of neurons, or brain cells, that produce a chemical called dopamine—a neurotransmitter. Parkinson's is a progressive or chronic condition which can, and sometime does, result in death. The lack of dopamine specifically will result in the weakness or death of the brain cells,

A beautiful portrait with my dear daughter, Melanie. (Courtesy of Melody Thamar Saunders)

causing slowness of movement, tremors, general weakness, and stiffness. Parkinson's disease affects between one and two people in every thousand across the whole of this planet, and for every patient there are another two or three caregivers involved. The disease doesn't just affect the elderly; people in their twenties and thirties are being diagnosed. We also learned that, strangely, men are more likely to be affected than women. A number of notable people are and have been Parkinson's sufferers, among them Mohammed Ali, Janet Reno, Johnny Cash, the Reverend Billy Graham, and actor Michael J. Fox.

When Sydney was diagnosed with Parkinson's disease I was forced with some alarm to consider what the future might bring. As the rate of progression of Parkinson's disease is extremely variable I was considerably worried—to put it at its slightest—by the thought of what the rate of progression of Sydney's Parkinson's might be. I see retrospectively that we were rather lucky that Sydney didn't have swift suffering from Parkinson's. Indeed, for the first five to six years it scarcely affected her at all.

I continued to work as much as possible during this time and was offered a role in the *War and Remembrance* miniseries, a follow-up to the very successful miniseries *The Winds of War. War and Remembrance* covered the latter part of the Second World War and I played General Halder, who was one of the leading spirits among the conspiracy to assassinate Adolph Hitler in 1944; the other conspirators were also drawn mostly from the military command who realized that Hitler was leading them into nothing but disaster. They decided the only thing they could do was to assassinate him. As bad luck would have it, Hitler was only slightly injured, but all the people mixed up in it were executed in the most awful way. The mini-series was shot in the former Yugoslavia, in and around Zagreb, then in Vienna, Austria.

In late 1986 and early 1987 Sydney and I traveled to Toronto to spread an idea about doing a tour of *Merely Players* in order to raise funds for the PAL organization—the Performing Arts Lodges of Canada. I had agreed to serve on the board of directors and I felt that I must really try and do something more than just have my name on their letterhead. In the back of my mind I had the idea to tour *Merely Players* in order to raise funds, but also, perhaps more importantly, awareness, interest, and enthusiasm for the need of a retirement home for seniors in the performing arts. I had a meeting with Raymond Wickens, who had been my stage manager when we were starting the Shaw Festival in 1966 and had proven himself to be extraordinarily devoted, enthusiastic, and efficient in all kinds of theatrical ways. So I drew him into this scheme. We spent the Christmas holidays in Toronto with our family and also promoting the idea of the tour. I shot a film in Toronto during this time called *Fight for Life*, directed by Elliot Silverstein, an American director with whom I'd worked before. I played, opposite Jerry Lewis and Patty Duke, a medical specialist who was advising and helping these two parents (played by Lewis and Duke) who have a six-year old daughter with epilepsy. They fight to get the Food and Drug Administration to approve a drug for use in the USA that at the time was only available in England. My character, Dr. Whalley, was something of a cynic in the piece and I remember the director saying to me before filming, "Here's a switch; you've got Jerry Lewis working as your straight man!" I think Jerry did well in the part and he was very pleasant to work with.

Raymond Wickens threw in his lot with me, (and it *was* a lot) to be my business manager, publicity director, and pretty well Lord High Everything Else in order to rig up this tour of *Merely Players*. It took about six months, in all, to set up the tour, arrange the dates, and the like. As you can imagine, organizing a tour to travel clear across Canada with a small group of people took some effort. We decided right from the word go that the best way of doing it was to travel by road in some form or another, because our whole company would consist of Raymond Wickens, our business manager and publicity manager; Daniel Beck-Burke, our stage manager (responsible for all the practicalities of sound, lighting, setting up the stage); myself; and, of course, dear Sydney. She insisted right from day one that she wanted to come with us. And she did! It was an amazing adventure.

We were determined that, unlike so many other charitable events, we shouldn't be wasting a lot of our revenues on administrative costs. Very often, these very well meaning fundraising events for different charities will swallow up more than 50 percent of their potential revenues in the costs of bringing the event about. Raymond very generously allowed us to use his kitchen as our office! I used to go there everyday at nine o'clock in the morning and Raymond would be there dealing with the mail, ready to deal with the telephone calls, all in order to set up 107 different performances of this one-man show, *Merely Players*, going clear across Canada from the far east coast to the Pacific coast. To be moving from one town to the next, and playing in spaces as varied as we did, from a huge high school auditorium with 1,500 seats to a small village hall with something like 75 seats, involved a great deal of adjustment in terms of the actual staging. And in particular, of course, we needed to know what sort of equipment would be needed in terms of sound and lighting, what the seat prices should be— keeping prices as low as we could, while still making sure that we stood a chance of escaping with a profit. All of these things were being looked into day by day. A tour of this scale had never been planned before in Canada.

The idea of building a retirement home for senior performers had been only recently launched and almost nothing was known about it in Canada. There had been, of course, for many years such retirement homes in other countries of the world. One of the biggest obstacles that we had to face was the public perception, which still persists in many quarters, that everybody involved in show business is rolling rich. It is a plain, simple fact that when I first joined our trade—nearly 80 years ago—if you were what was known as a real pro (that's to say moderately gifted, moderately well-trained, moderately healthy, and moderately lucky) you would not have any difficulty in supporting yourself at some kind of tolerable, minimal level. Whether or not you became rich and famous was anybody's guess. Nobody could predict that.

I remember on one of my visits to the USA, I was invited to speak to the students in the drama department at a high school in the small town of Junction City, Oregon. All of these young people were seated in the school theatre and were told they were going to meet this "famous" actor. So there they all were, looking as reasonably chipper and cheerful as they could at that hour in the morning. I hadn't yet made up my mind what I was going to talk to them about, whether I was going to tell a few jokes and reminisce a bit or what. So I thought, well I'll find out what kind of lives these young people live. So I said, "How many of you got to watch some television last night?" Ninety-five percent of the hands went up. Then I said, "How many of you watch some television pretty well every night?" That same ninety-five percent of the hands went up. Then I said, "Well, that's interesting, shows that you're interested in show business—that's for sure. How many of you would like to be in show business?" To my amazement about 70 percent of the hands went up, wildly! I noticed some kid in the front row who'd been almost jumping out of his seat with enthusiasm, confirming that he'd very much like to be in show business. So I said to him, "Now you, sir, you seem to be very enthusiastic about the prospect of being in show business—why is that?" He looked at me and laughed, pityingly, as at one who's lost his marbles. And most of the other kids laughed, too. He said, "Well, it's obvious isn't it—all that money!" The whole audience applauded wildly. I replied, "Right, now I know what I can talk to you about for the rest of our session." With that, I started to fill them in on some of the facts of life about our profession. The young man in the front row, unfortunately, became so enraged at hearing the facts that he leapt up out of his chair and stalked out of the auditorium. And I say unfortunately because he was the one person there who probably most needed to hear the "facts of life."

Based on solid statistical information from the U.S., Canadian and British governments, we were able to establish that *more than 70 percent* of those people seeking to work in the performing arts field—actors, singers, dancers, performers and the like—have earnings *below* the poverty line. In other words, cannot support life unless they undertake some auxiliary activity like waiting on tables or scrubbing floors! Those are the actual statistical facts and those of us who work within the profession know it firsthand. This was the biggest obstacle that we had. I can't even tell you the number of times I've had to pump out those facts, even to people who are more or less *within* the profession, those people in small town local radio stations who would invite me to go and do an interview or talk and would be incredulous that I was embarking on this nationwide tour to raise funds to build a retirement home for people in the performing arts. Well, perhaps that may account for what in the event happened.

Our stage manager, Daniel Beck-Burke, would also be our driver and navigator—getting us from, say, Upper Rubber Boot, Alberta to Rusty Truss, Saskatchewan, or wherever we were going. We began our rehearsals for the tour on September 14, 1987. We knew that we were going to have to travel with not only sound equipment, but also a certain amount of equipment to bolster up the lighting in some places. Daniel was more than equal to all of this and wonderfully enthusiastic. On Friday, October 2, 1987, we held the first preview of *Merely Players*, which we did in the Ryerson University's theatre itself. A second preview was held the following evening and on Sunday there was a launch gala. We were off and running!

We headed off down the road to St. Catherine's to our first ordinary ticket selling performance. Then we flew off to the east of Canada to Charlottetown, Prince Edward Island, where we wanted to spend a day or two on advance publicity because we knew that we had to beat the drum as much as we could because we had very limited funds for paid advertising. So we wanted to put as much time and effort as we could into advance publicity in the form of newspaper interviews and radio and television. We went on to Halifax, Nova Scotia, and did the same sort of PR things there. Now we launched the tour properly. We had organized the tour geographically from east to west and, for sentimental reasons, I decided that we would do our first full tour performance in Sydney, Nova Scotia, a small mining town that is coupled with another town close to it called Glace Bay. Raymond, Sydney and I had flown out in advance and Daniel drove a white van that we had purchased and which turned out to be ideal for our purposes. Daniel, who earned his nickname "Dan the Van" on this tour, had all the tour equipment with him. The van was large enough to seat the four of us and hold our personal luggage and in the back all of our stage lighting and sound effect gear. We settled fairly soon into a good pattern of travel and Daniel, as our driver and guide, was marvelous. He was traveling in places where in many cases none of us had ever been before, and in some cases never even heard of except for finding them on the map!

There we were—publicizing with our posters and in the media that we were undertaking this tour to raise funds and raise awareness of the need for the Performing Art Lodges. Performers in Canada were not entitled to unemployment benefits, so if an actor had a bad spell they would be desperately up against it. Other countries had retirement homes and in some cases nursing homes, primarily directed to performers. In Canada there was no such thing. There was a depth and a breadth of—not just ignorance—but total lunatic fallacy about the facts of life of our trade. We played "down East" as they say in Canada, towns and cities all across the Eastern Seaboard through the end of November.

The beginnings of the realization that we were up against considerable difficulties in selling tickets for what was virtually a one-night stand tour started to become evident fairly soon. We weren't able to benefit from the glowing notices that we got, because of course they would be read by people in the local newspaper after we'd left their community! But in cities like Montreal and Toronto we had longer runs. When we reached Toronto on the seventh of December, we opened *Merely Players* at the Young People's Theatre. We were scheduled to play the show there for two weeks. Opening night we were packed to the doors and the frenzy of applause that greeted us was quite wonderful. However, matters were such that we were forced to close our Toronto run after playing just one week. It was with great regret that in December we had to call a press conference there in

Planet Productions Ltd. for P.A.L. Presents

An Evening with
Barry Morse

"ENGROSSING AND RICHLY REWARDING... A CONSUMMATE ACTOR"
Boston Globe

"HELD HIS LISTENERS SPELLBOUND... A GREAT RACONTEUR"
Victoria, B.C. Times

"DELICIOUS... DELIGHTFULLY INFORMAL... A WONDERFULLY GENEROUS PERFORMANCE."
London, Ont. Free Press

"Merely Players"

A BENEFIT
FOR
PERFORMING ARTS
LODGES OF CANADA

WEDNESDAY AUGUST 4TH, 1993
8:30PM
IN THE COURTYARD
OF THE PERFORMING ARTS LODGE
110 THE ESPLANADE

Toronto to announce the closing of our tour after fulfilling dates in 23 places. But I also announced the fact that at each and every performance we gave— no matter what the size of the audience—the show was greeted with a standing ovation. I don't mean just a polite bravo, but the sort of receptions that reminded one of the final games of the Stanley Cup ice hockey final! They really were wildly enthusiastic audiences, no matter what their sizes. And too often, unfortunately, their size was very meager in relation to the size of our costs—which were not great, of course. We had done everything humanly possible to keep our costs to an absolute minimum and Raymond and Daniel had done work far above and beyond what would normally be expected. We were forever struggling against the fact that, because we were on tour traveling considerable distances some days, we never had enough time in advance of our arrival to beat the drum in a publicity sense to sell tickets. In the end, I had lost $75,000.00 of my own money and couldn't, with any responsibility for my family, go on incurring such losses and possibly even further debts which would impoverish us for months and years to come.

In the longer term, I'm grateful to say, our efforts were richly rewarded, because the public at large, and various government departments in particular, came to be aware that there really was a need—a real need—for such a facility as we were trying to raise money for. Within the next few years we got the thing done! And the Performing Arts Lodge today stands in Toronto. The facility opened in early 1993 and it's the only building I've ever seen where the residents routinely hug each other in the hallways each morning. There is a real spirit of camaraderie there at PAL. The building is set up so that a certain number of the apartments are rented to younger performers at their full market value. This helps to subsidize the majority of the units in the building that house the senior performers. Upon its opening, I was invited to give a special celebratory performance of *Merely Players* in the Courtyard of PAL. What an evening that was! Daniel Beck-Burke came to run our sound and lights, and his wife, Cindy, ran the follow spotlight which was used extensively. Our granddaughters, Megan Louise and Vanessa, helped, as did Hayward, Melanie, her husband, Pug, and so many other people. The Courtyard was packed full and we even had residents sitting on their apartment balconies, which overlook the Courtyard, watching the show. The evening was a great success and was a wonderful kick-off event for the new PAL building. That building holds a collection of marvelous people from every walk of our trade.

Opposite: **The program cover for the *Merely Players* celebratory performance at PAL.**

With Barbara Bain, in *Love Letters,* our first performance together in 25 years. (Courtesy of Robert E. Wood)

As time went on, it became evident that Sydney wouldn't be safe on her own any longer, so we set up a system of daily nursing care and for a year or more we had a succession of marvelously skilled and devoted nurses who would come on a daily basis. They would arrive around 9:00 in the morning and stay virtually the whole day, so that I could continue to do jobs. That went on until Sydney had a stroke in 1995. This intensified her need for treatment much further, necessitating her staying in a succession of hospitals and nursing homes. From then on she was never at home again.

Nevertheless, Sydney kept battling on bravely. She had a stock response to people who would sympathize with her. She'd say, "Oh, it's not so bad, really; after all," she'd say while giggling and pointing at me, "if you've lived with that one for sixty years, you're ready for anything!"

I would visit Sydney every day in the nursing home, generally in the afternoons. During my visits, when the weather permitted, I would—with the help of one or other of the nurses—get her into her coat, with a sweater on under it, to take her out in her wheelchair into Kensington Gardens. She would respond to this quite well and obviously enjoyed it a great deal. I would wheel her around the gardens past the front of the palace and there were always lovely things to see. Aside from the gardens themselves, there would be children playing and dogs being exercised. On the round pond there are numbers of ducks, geese and swans and Sydney would find all of this highly enjoyable. Quite often, once there I would get her to stand up several times out of her wheelchair. I would anchor the wheelchair against one of the benches and then take her hands, get her feet on the ground, and encourage her to pull herself up. She would be able to do this a number of times. Thus, she was beginning to get her balance—which was the biggest struggle in the effort to get her back towards mobility. The biggest obstacles to getting her mobile once again were the need to strengthen her legs and also to restore her sense of balance when she was standing. I knew that it would take a lot of time to get both her balance and her confidence back.

Sydney had been going to the neurology department at Middlesex Hospital for over 14 years, since her original diagnosis of Parkinson's disease in 1985. In that time, she saw no less than 11 different neurologists—some of them more than once—but more often than not she would see a new face each time we would go, and we would go about once every three months. However, we ran across a chap whom we'd not seen before, a very likeable, interesting and *interested* young neurologist named Dr. O'Sullivan, who was from Brisbane, Australia. He was very interested in learning about Sydney's symptoms over the past several weeks. I would keep a rough log of things that I observed in her. Parkinson's disease is a disease which has almost as many variations as patients. Individual observations are often quite useful. In response to my notes and his examination, he suggested some slight modifications in Sydney's medications which were worth trying and turned out to be beneficial.

For many years I've participated in various fundraisers in the USA and Canada to raise awareness and needed funds for the Parkinson's cause. In 1995 I joined actress June Lockhart for a production of the very good Broadway play *Love Letters* in Portland, Oregon, to raise funds for the Parkinson's Center of Oregon at the Oregon Health Sciences University there. They have one of the most renowned treatment centers on the West Coast, headed up by the wonderful Dr. Jay Nutt. I was invited back again in 1997 and I performed my one-man show, *Merely Players*, at theatres in both Portland and Eugene, Oregon, for the same cause. As well, the Center has invited me on two separate occasions to speak at their Annual Fall Symposium.

Throughout the 14 years after her diagnosis Sydney experienced a great many ups and downs and many changes in symptoms, which is the pattern for Parkinson's disease. By and large Sydney remained quite cheery, but it was always a bit uncertain as to what one would find on a given day. Most days she would be quite cheery and communicative, but occasionally she would be very down and drowsy, almost unable to communicate. I worried quite a bit about Sydney as we got into 1999. She would be "out of it" more and more, and a habit began to develop which I asked the nursing staff to keep on eye on. She would tend to sit in a very deeply drowsy state, not entirely asleep, but in a noncommunicative state with her head sunk right down on her chest. During my visits I would try almost incessantly to get her to lift her head and look up. But she wasn't always able to and it was worrisome. Even when her tea came I would have great difficulty in getting her to drink it because her head was sunk down so much. We soon discovered that she had developed dysphagia, a difficulty in chewing and swallowing. At this point her food was being rendered to the consistency of mashed potatoes in order to assist with her chewing and swallowing.

In September 1999 I left Sydney for a few days to travel to the USA and return to the role of Andrew Makepeace Ladd III in *Love Letters*—but this time I was paired with the delightful Barbara Bain as Melissa Gardner. She was very good indeed in the piece and it was the first time we had worked together in 25 years. I'm happy to report that the hundreds of fans who gathered there to see the play and attend the associated *Space: 1999* convention helped us to raise more than $10,000.00 for Parkinson's disease treatment and research! I then flew up to Portland, Oregon to the studios of MetroEast Community Media to tape my one-man show, *Merely Players*, for television.

My dear Sydney passed away just days after my return to London, on September 30, 1999. It was as if she were waiting for me to return. On this day, as I was about to leave, I asked her as I usually did, "Are you all right?" She would usually just give a little nod or smile, but on this day she actually spoke. Very simply, she said, "Great." So far as we know, that was her last word. Not long after I left to return home, she simply closed her eyes as if to take a nap and never again woke up. Sydney had been ill for so long and there was no real prospect of her becoming well again. Her health had been more down than up and her dysphagia had become even more pronounced. I was with her on the afternoon of her passing and it was— from her perspective as I can see now—merciful. The two of us had decided that neither of us would have a religious ceremony or a funeral; so Melanie, Hayward, and I decided that it would be fitting to sprinkle Sydney's ashes in the gardens in St. James's Square. It's just around the corner from our London flat and a place where we both had spent many blissful hours walking in the gardens over the years. It was, in effect, our back garden. We

Sitting on Sydney's bench, in St. James's Square, Pall Mall, London. (Courtesy of Robert E. Wood)

also contrived to set up a memorial bench in her honor. It has been placed there in St. James's Square and the inscription in the backrest of the bench reads:

Mrs. BARRY MORSE (SYDNEY STURGESS) 1915–1999

It's a lovely tribute to the lady whom I called for so many years, and still refer to as "The Management."

24

"Better Than Myself"

IT'S AN EXTRAORDINARY PROCESS, looking back. Baffling and sometimes maddening. It is very sad to reflect on things that didn't happen, or things that went wrong, or courses you took or decisions you made which turned out not to have been the best ones. On the other hand there is the encouragement of stumbling onto something which turned out quite well, and proved to be the right thing to have done.

There has been a huge gap in my life since I lost my Sydney. But I am back now to being more or less as I've ever been, because I feel that that's what she would have wanted me to do.

On Saturdays I go around noon to Gerry's, a wine store on Old Compton Street in Soho where I have been dealing for many years and have a group of extraordinarily varied and quite wonderful friends. We meet there every Saturday to order our supplies for the coming week. I don't need very much nowadays because I'm on my own, but I do enjoy a glass of wine with my dinner, and I like to keep a bottle or two on hand for when somebody comes to visit. We assemble at Gerry's, and stand about in the shop, have a glass of wine and gossip to each other while all the ordinary customers come in. In the process of spending an hour or so there we order our wine for the upcoming week, which one of the young men who work there will deliver. The half dozen of us includes very often the local bobby, a chap we call John-the-Fuzz.

This is a process which has grown up over the years and has developed such a warm group of friendships that I started thinking about and making some notes towards a possible television series, rather like *Cheers* in a sense, about these habitués of *The Grog Shop*—as I think I should call it—and the extraordinary staff that work there, young men from all over the planet, held together by the diplomatic genius of the chap who is part owner and manager of the grog shop, Michael Kyprianou. Gerry's has probably the widest range of exotic drinkables in all of London, so it attracts an extraordinary variety and number of people, locals ranging from the priests of the nearby Saint Anne's Church to the people of the vice trade who sell pornography and the prostitutes who are attached to them. The variety and complexity of people who gather there makes a very promising foundation for a series.

Over the past few years some people began to believe that I was either unable or unwilling to continue to do jobs because I had to turn so many down as they would have tied me up for too long, or taken me too far away from Sydney, plus the fact that a lot of people think, "Well, he's getting on in years, and perhaps he's not entirely up for it." I like to think of myself, as I always have, as one of the rank and file. I believe the best qualifications for an actor are the perception of a child, the faith of a martyr, and the constitution of an ox. I've always aimed to be as many-faceted an actor as Edmund Kean, who dominated the stage 120 years ago. In one evening's performance, Kean began by singing a few comic songs; played all the roles in *King Lear*; played a short farce; and wound up by doing an acrobatic turn, *Jocko, the Chimpanzee*. Now, there was a *real* actor. My ambition has always been to be an actor's actor. Whenever anybody asks me what my favorite part is I always say, "the next one." I've been what you might call "famous" several times in my life. It comes and goes, like some sort of rash. I'm not going to be particularly grand or choosy about whether I play king size parts, or leading parts. But having been pulling faces, making noises, and pretending to be other people for eight decades, I don't want to stop.

One of my more recent films, *The Taxman*, was filmed in Quebec. Our director was Alain Zaloun and the leading role was played by Billy Zane, a delightful fellow, wonderfully good-looking, and very accomplished as an actor. He became well known for his participation in the *Titanic* film. I played the ghost of his great-great-great-grandfather, who was the founder of the small town where Billy's character now lives. The work itself was interesting, and most of my stuff was played with Billy Zane. Our schedule was a bit taxing because they had agreed that I would not be needed to shoot for more than four days. I didn't know until we were well into filming that they had also given Billy Zane a stop date on his shooting. It turned out that they had not really worked out their schedule very carefully with regard to either of us. They simply had not allowed enough time to shoot the material they needed. The result was that we worked longer days than most of us had ever done in the whole of our lives. Indeed, my final day—

when they more or less had to get rid of me—I worked twenty-one hours on end. The previous day I had worked seventeen hours. I suspect that even in my fairly hectic professional career those are the two longest successive working days that I have ever had and ever hope to have.

Around that time I learned the *Space: 1999* series was being rerun on BBC in the UK. When I inquired about whether or not I was entitled to any residuals there was a lot of hemming and hawing. The company which owned *Space: 1999* at that time said that no, they didn't think I was entitled to any residuals. So I said to my agent here in London, "Well, that's all very well, but I don't think we should necessarily take their word for it. Perhaps they should produce the original contract which makes it clear that I'm not entitled to any residuals." Well, the young agent went back to them and said, "Mr. Morse doesn't doubt your word, but he would like to see documentary evidence of this original contract." They went and dove into their archives and came out considerably red-faced and said, "Well, sorry, but in fact Mr. Morse *is* entitled to residual payments on the rerunning of *Space: 1999*." So there you are—the world is full of rascals, and if we'd been prepared to take their word for it, I wouldn't have gotten anything.

I'm also ashamed to admit that there's a company run by two brothers called "Nu Ventures" that I got myself entangled with a few years ago. They approached me and asked me to do filmed introductions for episodes of *The Fugitive* series that they were proposing to release on video. After the financial failure (but critical success) of our *Merely Players* tour, I seized upon this as an opportunity to try and make some cash for the Performing Arts Lodges of Canada. I told them, "I'll tell you what I'll do. I'll organize and film introductions to all of the videos you want to put out—on the condition that an agreed percentage of the revenues be paid to the PAL organization." They said, "Fine. It's done." I wrote, directed, and organized 26 of these introductions. Nu Ventures made one partial payment of just $100 and were never heard from again. I had even traveled to Las Vegas to a huge merchandizing convention to promote the video line for those bastards. Of course, I tried to follow up but the legal advice I received was not encouraging. To pursue the rascals and make them pay up would have cost me considerably more than we could ever hope to get in return. If a lawsuit were filed, they could simply declare bankruptcy, head on down the road, and open up a new company under a different name. We wouldn't end up with anything except a huge legal bill. It just shows the extent of piracy that goes on in our trade.

Another terrible thing about our trade is that friendships and affections are forever being upset because you always have to go off somewhere to do some other job, and suddenly the close friendships of last year are cut off and you find yourself with a whole new group. Take, for example, our *Space: 1999* outfit. I am friends with Zienia Merton, who is an enormously gifted actress and a very worthwhile human being. I also still maintain contact with Barbara Bain and Martin Landau. I've been very lucky in that way. I've not very often had experiences where I've been at odds with somebody I was working with.

I continue to perform my one-man show, *Merely Players*, on an occasional basis in the United States, Canada, and England. It's great fun and I very much enjoy it. Whether I should be enjoying it if I were doing it every night for a series of months is another thing. What encourages me to enjoy it is that, because it is made up of such good material, it really is a very good show which the customers obviously like. We have a lot of good people on our team — Chekhov, Shakespeare, Dickens, you name it. One of the pieces in *Merely Players* is an adaptation I have made of Chekhov's *Swan Song*. The original is all right, but it features two old geezers sentimentalizing alongside each other and that doesn't work as well as one old geezer being encouraged by a young boy, which is what I have done in my version. The contrast is so much more effective. I'm lunatic to pretend that it's better than the original, but I genuinely think it is. It's a lovely piece, and the more I play it the more proud I am of it.

There was a rather charming encounter I had one day in London when I was coming out of my flat and going along Pall Mall. A young lady came by and I thought, *Wait a minute, is that somebody I know?* I was half inclined to speak to her, but then I thought to myself, *No, no, I don't know her personally.* By that time I had got past her when she then stopped, turned, and said "Hello. You're Barry Morse, aren't you?" I said, "Yes, but do forgive me — I thought perhaps I knew you, but I now realize that probably I don't." She said, "Well, I'm in the same business as you. My name is Meryl Streep." I said, "Oh, well, then I do know you indeed!" We stopped and chatted there on the street for a few minutes. She said she was just over on some short visit and I asked if I could help her in any way. That was the only time I ever encountered her, but she was very friendly and is a very gifted actress.

People nowadays very often will say to me, "You're well in your eighties now. Aren't you thinking about retiring?" My response is that retirement is for people who don't really like their jobs. When I think that I'm well into my eighties I'm reminded that neither of my dear parents lived anything like this long, and my brother, who was the healthiest fellow I've ever known — a lifelong athlete — didn't either. My brother's downfall was as a result of his accident, while for my parents living this long was much less common in their time. If I'm anything like Shaw I've got another ten years, but I want to stay around for much longer than that because I want to see how it all turns out.

A project I am deeply involved with is called the London Shakespeare Workout, organized by a delightful chap named Bruce Wall, who has worked both in the UK and in the States as an opera director. He's directed a couple of things for the Metropolitan in New York. He's a very imaginative, gifted guy. He started this project, the Shakespeare Workout, as a means of acquainting younger and less experienced actors with the idea of playing Shakespeare. It is with great enjoyment that I've done these things with the Shakespeare Workout, about Shakespeare, his work and his time, and his fellows and his world. The people who attend these gatherings are most enthusiastic, and that is always very gratifying and stimulating. What one has to get across to young people if one hopes to interest them in Shakespeare is that Shakespeare and his work do not consist of words on paper apprehended through the eye, but words spoken and apprehended through the ear, and coming straight to the heart. The first thing we do when we get these sessions going is to remind people that 95 percent of the audience who went to see Shakespeare's plays in his own day were illiterate—couldn't read or write—and could be approached only by words through the ear. Once you establish that then you really start to make progress.

To read the words "To be or not to be" on paper, they may not mean very much to you. But when you hear them spoken by this guy on the stage experiencing these tortures and travails, "To be or not to be" starts to have a totally different impact. That's what so many people—academics in particular—can't understand, and partly can't bear. The perception of Shakespeare during his own time was very dismissive. He didn't go to Oxford or Cambridge. He had no university education. He came from this small town called Stratford-on-What? Who is he? He's a common actor. A player. People of our profession in those days were indeed known as rogues and vagabonds. They were the next step to brothel keepers or pickpockets. Who are they to be actually writing plays? The worst thing that the fashionably educated authors of his day could find to say about Shakespeare was that he was a best seller. You look at the box-office receipts of the Globe Theatre and you will see that when they were doing some trashy pseudo comedy of the time, and they were not doing very well, they might have decided to revive *Twelfth Night*. The takings went up immensely. That's because those illiterate audiences knew, "Shakespeare. Oh, that's good. He'll give us a laugh, and a bit of a cry. We'll go." That's the great thing about Shakespeare. It's just wonderful to watch when young people are themselves staggered to find that Shakespeare is just such marvelous fun.

The Shakespeare Workout expanded to include what is called the Prison

Project. The prison service is terribly badly served in terms of occupation and activity. The harsh truth of the prison service is that the most severe aspect of punishment that especially younger prisoners suffer is paralyzing boredom, and a feeling that they have no life. When Bruce decided to start this Prison Project, he got in touch with me and asked if I would like to join with them. When you tell people about it they find it almost inconceivable that one should attempt to do such a thing. Indeed, when I first heard about it I wondered whether it was something that was really going to wash. Naturally, there's also a great barrier of apprehension in prisoners at the idea of having a thing about Shakespeare. But if there's an old geezer like me aboard whom they might have seen on television, then they think it might be interesting or fun to see what this old guy's like.

It's quite a revelation to see the effect this program has on the prisoners. It's quite astonishing the things they turn out once they realize that they're just as capable of writing feeling poetry as William Shakespeare was. Most of them who have had conventional educations have been brought up to believe that Shakespeare is very highbrow and you have to read it on paper, and of course Shakespeare is no such thing. Shakespeare is simply human feelings expressed with human words. One hopes, of course, this program might change the prisoner's general perspective about the world at large, and their own part in it. Many of the young people we find in the prisons have come to think of themselves as worthless, and have finished up in prison mostly because nobody ever gave them any encouragement to think that they were worthwhile human beings.

In June of 2002 we presented a play, a dramatic anthology called *Voices*, at the Royal Opera House in Covent Garden, London. I played, in fact, two or three minor speaking parts in it, one of which was a police officer. *Voices* was written by a combination of four prisoners—three men and one woman. It is clear evidence of the wonderful effects our efforts have. It's their perception of how this Prison Project has impacted and benefited them. These young prisoners were all carried away by the extraordinary power of emotional expression through voices. We had previously done two other performances, one at Oxford and one at Cambridge, in an attempt to recruit new members for the Prison Project gig. And in early 2003, I performed in Shakespeare's *Henry VI, Part III*, alongside prisoners and fellow actors alike.

One of my trips with the Prison Project took me up to Nottingham, which was the first place that Sydney and I went to work in a repertory company right after we were married, when we opened a season on Easter Monday of 1939. This trip had great sentimental repercussions. I didn't get any time to look at the city or the theatre, as we were going on to this prison just outside Nottingham itself. But it is amazing how an echo of that kind, a remembrance of that time and place, even after such a long time as 63 years, can shake you up for the rest of the day. It wasn't the first time I had been back there, but it was the first time in many, many years. More and more things get sentimental values as the years go by, quite regardless of the actual place or the actual time.

I have the great honor nowadays to be the president of the Shaw Society. I've been a member for almost as long as the society has existed, but was elected president in 1998. I have also been involved with a number of plays with the Shaw Society. Among them was *Mollykins*, which was an examination of the charming, almost romantic, friendship which grew between Shaw and a young American would-be actress called Molly Tompkins, whom he called Mollykins. One of our leading and most loyal members of the Shaw Society is the very beautiful actress, Toni Kanal. She and I did this performance, which plays just about an hour and is a lovely aspect of Shaw, acting more or less as an honorary grandparent to this young woman and her equally young husband and their little boy. Shaw, in fact, partly underwrote the cost of educating the little boy. This was just one of his extraordinary befriendings. Another performance I did was a rehearsed reading of a play—this time at the British Theatre Museum—about Shaw, simply called *The Private Life of George Bernard Shaw*, by Elizabeth Sharland. It examined his relationships with many of the ladies in his life. I played Shaw at all ages from 29 to 94, and the women in Shaw's life were played by eight different actresses.

I was also involved in a BBC radio program called *The Master and the Man or the Playwright and the Prizefighter*, based on the correspondence between Gene Tunney and George Bernard Shaw. Tunney's son, Jay Tunney, played his father and I played G.B.S. One of Shaw's greatest friends in his old age was the great undefeated heavyweight champion of the world, Gene Tunney, who was a highly intellectual young man. He wrote to Shaw when he was approached with an offer to make a film of Shaw's *The Admirable Bashville*, all about a young fellow who's a boxer. The correspondence developed to the point where they became great buddies and in Shaw's later years he and Charlotte, his wife, went on a succession of holidays with Gene Tunney and his wife, to various places in France and Italy. Jay Tunney read his father's letters most expressively. I played G.B.S. over a period of about thirty-three years and I was able to vocally hint at that age development. I know Shaw's voice very well because I have all sorts of recordings from various periods of his life.

One of my recent projects has been my involvement in the play *Bernard and Bosie: A Most Unlikely Friendship* by Anthony Wynn. It is a marvelously well-put-together piece about the quite improbable friendship between George Bernard Shaw and Lord Alfred "Bosie" Douglas, the intimate friend of Oscar Wilde. It's really quite extraordinary the range of friendships Shaw was able to establish and maintain throughout his life. I directed and played the role of Bernard Shaw for both the London debut, and for the American premiere of the play in Sarasota, Florida. Rodney Archer, a Canadian/English actor, played the role of Bosie with me in London to wonderful effect. But in Florida, it was my dear son, Hayward, who played opposite me as Bosie Douglas. He is a marvelous actor and was most sensitive and imaginative in the part. The audience reception to the piece in the U.S. was quite extraordinary.

On another evening for the Shaw Society I performed a play based on the letters of Bernard Shaw and Ellen Terry, which is one of the most beautiful correspondences in the English language. It was all conducted over a period of time when, except for one freak occasion, they never met. They were writing letters to each other almost every day despite the fact she was living in London only about a mile and a half from where he was living. I always remember that he writes in the preface to the published edition of this correspondence, "Let those who may complain that it was all on paper remember that only on paper has humanity yet achieved truth, beauty, and abiding love."

There is an interesting fact which I, as an actor, am naturally very proud of. That *all* the best drama in the whole history of mankind, in every language on Earth, has been written either by actors—see William Shakespeare, see Molière—or people of strongly marked histrionic instinct. It's the difference between drama and non-drama, which not too many people in today's world know. Keats tried to write plays, Shelley, Tennyson and Browning tried to write plays—not worth much, any one of them! Because they weren't actors; their plays weren't written by people of histrionic instinct. Henry James is a perfect example. Hugely respected, but he could not write drama. He didn't possess the histrionic instinct. It's a very rare instinct, and a highly developed gift in many cases. Your friend and mine, George Bernard Shaw, is an extraordinary example. The interesting thing about this histrionic instinct which goes to make up great drama, in Bernard Shaw's case, is that he cultivated it himself.

As a young man Shaw was mortally shy. He was not by any means the transcendentally theatrical figure which he eventually became. When he first came to London as a young man he records how he had been invited to the home of some neighbors and friends of his family in Dublin. He was at this point twenty years old. He went down to this house and walked up and down in the rain for three quarters of an hour before he could summon

With Hayward, performing the USA premiere of *Bernard and Bosie: A Most Unlikely Friendship*. (Courtesy of Michael Lindow)

up enough courage to ring the bell to visit these old friends. That's how shy he was.

He then proceeded to write five novels. If you have read them you are a brave soul. They're pretty dull—fascinating, because they are written by him, but dull all the same. What he was doing at the same time was teaching himself to stand up and speak in front of batches of people. Having gone to a meeting of a debating society one night, he was so enflamed with ideas on the subject under discussion that he leapt to his feet and attempted to speak. But, having got out about three syllables, he was overcome by his mortal shyness and sat down, ashamed at not having been able to contribute.

Can you imagine George Bernard Shaw not being able to contribute to a debate? Well, it was true. He then wrote in his reminiscence of these times that he went home so ashamed at this shyness that he resolved—like a soldier who suspects himself of cowardice—to put himself under fire on every available occasion. He started to go to every possible speaking event to talk to whomever was there about his political and social ideas. He spoke on an average of three times a week for the next twelve years! You can see, in the quality of his writing, that the muscles were coming on him, like an Olympic athlete under training. Slowly but surely he started to be able to produce dramatic material, until finally he produced some of the greatest dramatic material since William Shakespeare.

George Bernard Shaw became not only my hero but also one of the great heroes of English language literature by virtue of developing within himself the histrionic instinct. His development is a great example of what human character and the human spirit can achieve once the will is there. If you can focus yourself, as Shaw urges us to do, you can achieve what may seem at the outset to be impossible. My personal creed consists of some lines of Shaw's where he says, "As long as I can conceive something better than myself, I cannot be easy unless I am striving to bring it into existence, or clearing the way for it. That is the law of my life."

If you can make that the law of your life, you can do anything.

Index